The Collective Dilemma:
Negotiations in Education

The Collective Dilemma: Negotiations in Education

edited by

Patrick W. Carlton
New York University

and

Harold I. Goodwin
West Virginia University

Charles A. Jones Publishing Company
Worthington, Ohio

1 2 3 4 5 6 7 8 9 10 / 74 73 72 71 70

L. C. Cat. Card No. 75-84013

Printed in the United States of America

Preface

Collective negotiations is basically a set of interactions among groups or their representatives, the intent of which is to foster an unequal power relationship designed to reap the greatest possible benefits for the groups' constituencies. This book is based upon the idea that an adequate understanding of collective negotiations in education, one that will allow the reader to proceed from theory to appropriate forms of action, begins with a study of the subject from the points of view of several relevant groups. Accordingly, we have assembled in this book a collection of the writings of well-known participants and analysts. This group includes classroom teachers, school administrators, school board members, teacher organization representatives, and university scholars.

Part I sets forth the historical development of militancy and the conflict between special interest groups in education. Part II discusses practical problems and issues in militancy as viewed by those actually engaged in the process of negotiations. Part III, more academic and analytical in tone, places teacher militancy and private sector bargaining in perspective, utilizing the university scholar's conceptual frame of reference as its point of departure.

The application of the tactics of collective militancy by teachers, and increasingly by principals, to obtain those things not attainable in traditional ways, is influencing education profoundly. At the initial level of concern, one finds salaries, working conditions, and policy process involvement as the foci of discussion. This level emphasizes the strategies and tactics of conflict and its resolution which, while obviously important in an immediate sense, are perhaps less significant from a more global viewpoint.

What is not so obvious, yet, in the broader sense, of far greater consequence, is the real essence of teacher militancy and collective action—the issue of the source and nature of the legitimation of school board and school administrator authority, and the redistribution of that authority. The issue turns on two basically contradictory concepts—authority by consent of the governed (the teachers) and authority by tradition and higher organizational office (the board and administrators). Teacher militancy holds within itself the potential for alteration of authority relationships among teachers, school administrators, and school boards and, by extrapolation, of control over the shape and condition of American education.

It is felt that the diverseness of the contributions to this book will prove useful to a variety of readers. University scholars will find the articles valuable in their task of developing a more adequate theory of personnel administration. Teacher militancy and collective action are new variables for which they must account. University scholars will also find, for teaching purposes, the breadth of material necessary to present to students both a practical and conceptual understanding of problems and issues in teacher militancy and collective negotiations. A careful study of the book will aid those who are now teachers, administrators, and school board members, since the contributions by a wide variety of participants in the collective negotiations process will broaden their perspective on current issues as viewed by those on "both sides of the table."

Our purpose, then, is to present a comprehensive understanding of the issues, the problems, and the significance of teacher militancy and collective negotiations to those who will actively engage in or pursue the study of this revolutionary development in education.

PWC
HIG

Contents

Introduction

Only seven short years ago the United Federation of Teachers was elected bargaining agent to represent New York City's 50,000 public school teachers. Most observers mark this date as the beginning of the collective negotiations movement in education. Since that time, enormous changes have taken place in educational employment relations including the enactment of thirteen state statutes requiring boards of education to negotiate with teacher organizations. Approximately 2,000 boards of education have signed written collective negotiation agreements which include terms and conditions of employment for their teaching staffs. In addition, the number and length of teacher strikes reached an all time high in 1967 and 1968 exceeding comparable statistics for all other groups of public employees. Given these enormous changes and the growing sophistication of school boards and teacher organizations toward negotiations, this volume makes an important contribution to the burgeoning literature in this field.

Other persons have edited books of readings on educational employment relations, including the author of this introduction* but few of these volumes are as current or cover such a broad scope of topics. Almost all of the articles included in *The Collective Dilemma: Negotiations in Education* first appeared in 1968 which demonstrates the editors' familiarity with the current literature in this field. In addition, the editors include a group of articles on higher

Stanley Elam, Myron Lieberman, and Michael H. Moskow, *Readings on Collective Negotiations in Public Education* (Chicago: Rand McNally and Company) 1967.

education an area which undoubtedly will be of great concern in future years.

As with most neutral discussions of employment relations, the editors have included articles written by officers and staff members of the "contending" national organizations. The task of analyzing the claims and counter claims is thus left to the reader.

The volume also includes separate sections by practitioners and scholars which represent an interesting dichotomy developing in the literature of educational employment relations. One group of articles and books is aimed at and produced by practitioners, while the other is oriented to academicians. This combination of approaches frequently is attempted at institutes and seminars with the hope that the "thinkers" and "doers" will learn something from each other. Presumably the practitioner is too close to his immediate situation to see the broad picture and the full implications of his actions, while the academician can never achieve the same closeness and understanding of an individual situation. Hopefully, the readers of this volume will benefit in similar ways from the combination of orientations.

Michael H. Moskow
December, 1968

Part One

The Organized Teacher

Traditionally a relatively docile, non-activist group, teachers in many parts of the country have rapidly developed an aggressiveness and social commitment unheard of only ten years ago. This commitment to action is characterized by an increased willingness on the part of ever-increasing numbers of teachers to engage in direct social protest, to "stand up" for themselves in group fashion. The key to their success lies in organization. Individually, teachers have little bargaining power; they are often viewed as relatively interchangeable parts of a massive educational machine. Collectively, however, through controlling the labor supply, they have the wherewithal to change their conditions of work, to come out of the bondage of unilateral managerial control and to assume a larger role in educational decision-making.

Part I is designed to provide the reader a general overview of the collective negotiations movement as it has developed since 1962. Nolte and Linn, in the first article, describe mandatory and permissive collective negotiations laws and analyze the negotiations process within a legal framework. They include a brief discussion of mediation, fact-finding and arbitration as applicable in an educational context. Carlton reviews the historical and social correlates of teacher militancy and describes the evolution of participant attitudes during the negotiations process.

Muir treats the sweeping alterations of policy and action which the National Education Association, operating under the pressure of the American Federation of Teachers, is undergoing. He indicates that NEA and AFT are moving ever closer together in ideology and in actions. Lieberman's article is a logical extension of Muir's line of reasoning, describing the "coming NEA–AFT merger." The uniting of these two major forces for educational change seems to Lieberman to be inevitable.

Collective Bargaining Legislation in Education

John Philip Linn and M. Chester Nolte

That governmental workers should have the right to bargain is not now convincingly denied. The next issue is that of what method shall be utilized in each state to implement this right. Seventeen of the fifty states have enacted legislation either permitting or mandating the right to meet and confer or the right to bargain collectively between teachers and boards of education.

The seventeen are: Alaska, California, Connecticut, Florida, Maryland, Massachusetts, Michigan, Minnesota, Nebraska, New Hampshire, New Jersey, New York, Oregon, Rhode Island, Texas, Washington and Wisconsin. Earliest legislation on this subject was enacted in Wisconsin in 1959 and amended in 1961.

A few other states permit teachers to organize: Illinois, by court decision; Indiana, by law; and Kentucky, by opinion of the attorney general. However, these hardly go further than the right to organize. A few states, such as Missouri and Vermont, actually deny teachers the right to organize or to bargain with their local boards of education.

Of the seventeen states formally recognizing governmental employees' right to bargain, ten limit application of the statute to certificated personnel only, to the exclusion of other occupational groups. The other seven states cover all governmental employees, with some minor exceptions, such as policemen, firemen, elected officials, and executives of government.

Basic Questions Faced by Legislators

The first question is whether a state needs a statute either permitting or mandating some form of recognition for governmental employees. There is a trend toward support of the idea. Considerable

This article originally appeared, in somewhat different form, in the August, 1968, edition of *Compact,* published by the Education Commission of the States. Reprinted by permission. Professors Linn and Nolte teach law at the University of Denver.

negotiation is currently being carried on even in those states which have no negotiations laws, but it is generally held that legislatures have the right to promulgate such laws if they desire. In the absence of law, it is not well established whether boards of education and other state sub-divisions have such a power. Hence, one question which would be settled if a statute of this nature were passed is to *legalize* a practice which is now only *de facto* at best.

The Problem

Today the legislatures of most of the states either have under consideration or will soon be called upon to consider appropriate legislation providing collective bargaining rights to governmental employees. In considering such legislation, the legislators will face, among others, the following four basic questions:

1) Who shall be covered?
2) What is negotiable?
3) How shall impasses between the parties be solved?
4) What organizational structure is necessary to administer the law?

Who Shall Be Covered?

The problem of coverage is not as simple as it may first appear. The choice is between a single statute covering only certificated public school employees and one encompassing all governmental employees of the state, including teachers.

Separate Legislation for Teachers?

Whether separate legislation should be enacted covering certificated personnel only in contrast with statutes covering all governmental employees in the state has not been widely discussed. There now exist ten states having separate legislation for teachers, and seven in which the statutes cover all government employees, including teachers.

Characteristics of Separate Statutes. Where coverage is limited to certificated personnel, the chief school officer is usually exempted in each district. Educational or *ad hoc* agencies or committees are used for unit determination, election procedures, and impasse breaking. These laws also stipulate or imply that the subject matter of bargaining shall include such non-work conditions as curriculum revision, textbook selection, in-service training rules, and student teacher control.

Characteristics of General Coverage Statutes. Teachers are covered along with other groups of public employees. The statute utilizes state labor boards to determine bargaining units, establish election procedures, and initiate procedures for resolving impasses. There is likely to be a statement of unfair labor practices contained in the act, and penalties may be listed for violations of the terms of the statute.

Possible Conflict with Existing Civil Service Legislation. If the choice of the legislature is for a single statute covering only certificated personnel, perhaps no great accommodation need be made to the state's civil service set-up. But when the statute covers all governmental employees, who may be under an existing civil service system, the problem of accommodation may be complex and frustrating indeed. Michigan got around this by exempting all state employees already covered under the civil service system from the provisions of the negotiations law.

Present legislation of a comprehensive nature, other than in Michigan, does not mention how accommodation shall be made. There is, therefore, some "living with" these statutes to iron out their meaning and to put them into practice which must be done before the most equitable way can be devised.

Permissive v. Mandatory Coverage? Existing statutes covering teachers and other governmental employees tend to be about evenly divided between those which are permissive and those which are mandatory in their coverage. The union-type laws tend to be mandatory, while those applying only to certificated personnel tend to be permissive. Logic seems to be on the side of a mandatory law requiring the governmental body to meet and confer with employees and to attempt to reach agreement. There is little substance to the notion that the governmental unit should have the option of negotiating since it is only at the discretion of the members of the boards that negotiations can actually take place.

There seems to be little gain to teachers and other governmental employees to "have the right to bargain without the power to bargain." A permissive law gives the right, but its exercise is only at the discretion of the board. In order to be truly equal, teachers must have the right to force the board to bargain, or else the statute will lack its most important ingredient.

Representation. Questions of representation include whether the representative organization shall have formal or exclusive recognition, whether the state labor mediation board or some other body shall determine conditions of representation, who shall hold elections, and what bargainable items are permitted under the union security clause concept.

Formal representation means that the board of education recognizes the organization but that the organization can speak only for its own members—not for all the employees in the district. On the other hand, exclusive representation means that the organization which has been certified by the board is recognized as representing all the employees in the district, whether they belong to the organization or not. In the seventeen states having legislation on this subject, fourteen either permit or mandate exclusive representation; one state (California) has proportional representation, based upon the numbers belonging to each organization, one state does not specify how representation is to be formalized. Oregon has a "teacher council" form of representation, composed of members elected at-large and not representing any organization.

The method of determining the representative unit varies widely. In seven states, the county or local board of education makes the determination, while in another six this is done by the state labor relations board. Three states do not specify how unit determination is to be made.

One question which causes some problems is what is an appropriate bargaining unit? The trend is toward having separate units for administrators and teachers, although in some state laws this is not clear. Some of the laws specifically exclude the superintendent and any representatives of the board in the bargaining process, but a wide diversity exists and no one plan predominates. The union view, of course, is that the same union should not represent both the workers and management (administrators) at the same time.

What Is Negotiable?

The second problem faced by legislators relates to the scope of bargaining: what items are negotiable and what items are not? Today the scope of bargaining has been considerably broadened to encompass practically every problem in the solution of which teachers feel they ought to be included. While some present agreements are in use in states without collective negotiations laws, in those states having legislation on the subject the scope of bargaining has not been appreciably limited by the statute itself. If anything, the scope of bargaining has been broadened and the procedure clarified by the laws governing negotiations.

In essence, it can be said that negotiations between boards and teachers are conducted currently in two broad, general areas: 1) wages, hours, and conditions of work, and 2) the making of educational policy. In this respect, teachers have been able to go far beyond the usual limitations placed upon the making of company policy by the earlier laws governing bargaining in the private sector of the economy. Even those laws which cover all state government employees, and which are patterned after the so-called "labor" legislation, tend very little to restrict the scope of bargaining between teachers and their boards of education.

It should be remembered that *de facto* negotiations are going on even in those states having no legislation on the subject. These states vary widely in the extent to which local boards have given permission to teachers' groups to negotiate. Even in those states which have legislation governing negotiations between teachers and boards of education, practices vary considerably within each state.

No comprehensive studies have been undertaken which would clarify the picture and answer the question, "What is negotiable?" In essence, there is a tendency to bargain on a broad base of items, including in addition to wages, hours, and conditions of work the right of teachers to enter into the making of policy insofar as boards may legally go in permitting teachers to participate in the making of school policy. No doubt this trend will continue, especially in those states which enact a single law which covers only certificated personnel in the public schools of the state.

Impasse Procedures

The concept of impasse has application at two distinct points in the bargaining process: 1) when negotiating new terms of agreement (bargaining impasse), and 2) when interpreting and applying the provisions of an existing agreement (generally referred to as a grievance dispute rather than an impasse). At either time, the parties may employ self-help or the services of impartial third parties to overcome deadlocked positions.

The Strike. The right to strike has been recognized as an important employee prerogative in the free collective bargaining process of the private sector.

In the public sector the strike has been found to be unlawful conduct because it prevents government from discharging its obligations to provide public services without interruption and deprives the public of protection and their right to essential services. Legislatures have enunciated the no-strike principle in public employment and have often established severe penalties for violation of that law, while, in some instances, they have specifically granted the right to strike to private employees. No-strike legislation may constitute a deterrent, but it has not effectively prevented strikes by public employees. There has been increasing strike activity among public employees, clearly evidencing a substantial dissatisfaction with governmental treatment of employment problems.

Accelerated public employee unionism may also significantly contribute to increased strike activity. Union membership in the governmental sector rose from approximately 900,000 in 1955 to over 1.5 million in 1967. Militant public employee organizations not only support the need of public employees to strike but amass large strike funds in anticipation of the strikes they feel are imminent.

The 1.9 million teachers in this country are exceptionally well organized. The National Education Association has a reported membership of approximately one million; the American Federation of Teachers has a reported membership of 165,000. Teachers in both groups are militant, are engaging in strikes, and are presently amassing large strike funds. The AFT, an AFL-CIO affiliate, espouses the right of public employees to strike. The NEA deleted its no-strike policy at its 1966 convention and adopted a strike-support policy at its 1967 convention by providing funds, legal advice and staffs to assist its striking affiliates. Its recommended procedures to be used when teacher representatives reach an impasse with agencies controlling schools include mediation, fact-finding, arbitration, political action and sanctions. The NEA recommends that every effort be made to avoid the strike as a procedure for the resolution of impasse, but it "recognizes that under conditions of severe stress causing deterioration of the educational program and when good faith attempts at resolution have been rejected, strikes have occurred and may occur in the future. In such instances, the NEA will offer all of the services at its command to the affiliate concerned to help resolve the impasse."

In an examination of the teacher strikes in 1966, the Bureau of Labor Statistics noted that the strikes were of relatively short duration and frequently were intended as a "protest" to the public or the legislature rather than to enforce an immediate employee demand. Their study suggests that it may be shortsighted to focus on strikes exclusively as disruptive stoppages and ignore the significant process of development of the right to representation and collective bargaining.

Where a statutory prohibition against public employee strikes is enacted, it is important to carefully define the word "strike" to avoid a later court ruling that the statute is unenforceable because of vagueness. Legislatures may also feel it important to establish specific penalties for violation of any no-strike law against the employee organization involved as well as against the individual public employees participating in the strike. The penalty imposed on the employee organization may be in the form of a fine or suspension for an indefinite or a specified time period or revocation of the organization's right to representation together with such accompanying rights as dues check-off.

Striking employees may be made subject to fines, suspension, demotion or discharge, depending upon the kind and extent of misconduct. A flexible system of non-mandatory penalties may be preferable to an inflexible system. Similarly, the officer responsible for instituting appropriate court action may be given discretion concerning the time for commencement of that action to effect penalties against the striking employees and their representative organization. The mere fact that a strike occurs may be held quite insufficient cause for the court's issuance of an injunction. The acts of the public employer may be as important to a court in the exercise of its discretion in ordering injunctive relief as the acts of the employees or their representative organization. Thus the relative culpability of the parties might be used to determine whether a strike should be enjoined as well as the appropriate penalties for striking.

The Alternatives to Strikes

Growing unions of government workers have criticized both non-strike legislation and imposition of those penalties arguably intended to destroy unions. They contend that no distinction in fact

TABLE I
Negotiations Legislation in Education

State (Year of enactment)	Alaska (1962)	California (1965)	Connecticut (1965 and 1967)	Florida (1965)
Coverage	All state employees	All certified public school employees and all public employees	Certificated professional employees of local boards below superintendent rank	Certificated personnel representing all work levels as defined in school code
Bargaining Unit Determined by			Secretary, State Board of Education	County Board of Education
Type of Representation		Proportional	Exclusive	Exclusive permitted
Representation Determined by	No enforcement by courts unless union registered with department of labor and complied with all regulations	Examination of membership list	Majority referendum	County Board of Education may appoint or recognize existing committees
Administrative Agency for Unit Determination & Elections			Ad hoc impartial board of arbitration	County Board of Education
Contains Specific Unfair Labor Practices	No	Yes	Yes	No

	Grievances, terms or conditions of employment, or other mutual aid or protection	Employment conditions and employer-employee relations, not limited to wages, hours, etc.	Salaries, and other conditions of work	To resolve problems or reach agreements affecting certificated personnel
Specific Bargainable Issues				
Agreement in Writing	Permitted but not mandated	Not mentioned	If requested by either party	Not prohibited
Impasse Broken by	No specific procedure provided	No provision specified	Mediation by State Board secretary, arbitration by 3-person board	No specific provision
Method of Selecting Impasse Breaker		No Provision	Each party to dispute selects one arbitrator, who in turn selects third	
Strikes	Not mentioned	Not mentioned	Prohibited	Not mentioned

TABLE I (Continued)

State (Year of enactment)	Maryland (1968)	Massachusetts (1965)	Michigan (1965)	Minnesota (1967)
Coverage	Certificated school personnel (superintendent & negotiators for board excluded)	All city and county employees except police, elected officials and executives of government	All public employees except civil service employees of the State of Michigan	All certificated personnel except the superintendent
Bargaining Unit Determined by	Local Board of Education	Local Board of Education	Michigan Labor Mediation Board	Local Board of Education
Type of Representation	Exclusive (2 yr. basis)	Exclusive	Exclusive	Exclusive where only one organization represented
Representation Determined by	Examination of membership list or secret ballot election	Majority election by secret ballot or other suitable means	Majority election	When more than one organization, council of 5 teachers on proportionate basis
Administrative Agency for Unit Determination & Elections	State Board of Education	Massachusetts Labor Relations Commission	Michigan Labor Mediation Board	Local Board of Education
Contains Specific Unfair Labor Practices	No	Yes	Yes	Yes

Specific Bargainable Issues	Salaries, wages, hours, and other working conditions	Wages, hours, and other conditions of employment	Rates of pay, wages, hours of employment, and other conditions of employment	Conditions of service, education and professional policies, relationships, grievance procedures, and other matters
Agreement in Writing	Yes	Yes	Yes, if requested by either party	Yes, in form of resolution or by direction to any administrative officer as appropriate
Impasse Broken By	Mediation by State Board of Education, fact-finding by 3-person board	Fact-finding	Ad hoc advisory arbitration	Adjustment panel of 3 members
Method of Selecting Impasse Breaker	Request by both parties for State Board of Education. Each party selects one fact-finder, who in turn selects the third	Mutual selection from fact-finders proposed by Board of Conciliation and Arbitration	Each party chooses 1 member; these 2 choose third; if fail to agree, MLMB selects third	Each party chooses 1 person; these 2 choose third. If unable to agree, district court appoints third
Strikes	Prohibited	Prohibited	Prohibited (strike is defined)	Not mentioned

TABLE 1 (Continued)

State (Year of enactment)	Nebraska (1967)	New Hampshire (1966)	New Jersey (1968)	New York (1967)
Coverage	All certificated personnel in Class III, IV and V school districts	New Hampshire Statutes: "Towns . . . may recognize unions of employees and make and enter into collective bargaining contracts with such unions and may make any contracts which may be necessary and convenient for the transaction of the public business of the town."	All public employees superintendent and supervisors excluded	All public employees except organized militia
Bargaining Unit Determined by	Majority of local board must so resolve		New Jersey Public Employee Relations Commission	Public Employment Relations Board
Type of Representation	Exclusive permitted		Exclusive	Exclusive permitted
Representation Determined by	Membership list of majority of certificated personnel		Secret ballot election	PERB determination that organization represents group of public employees and rejects right to strike
Administrative Agency for Unit Determination & Elections	Local Board of Education		New Jersey Public Employee Relations Commission	Public Employment Relations Board
Contains Specific Unfair Labor Practices	Good faith required		No	Yes

Specific Bargainable Issues	All matters of employment relations	Grievances and terms and conditions of employment	Terms and conditions of employment, and administration of grievances arising under terms of employment
Agreement in Writing	Yes	Yes	Yes
Impasse Broken by	Fact-finding	1) Mediation and fact-finding by Division of Public Employee Relations 2) Advisory arbitration by 3-man panel	1) Mediation; 2) Fact-finding by board appointed by PERB; 3) Findings submitted to legislative body
Method of Selecting Impasse Breaker	Each party chooses 1 person; these 2 choose third. If parties fail to agree, State Dept. provides list	1) Request by either party 2) Each party selects one member who in turn selects third	On request of either party, or on motion of PERB
Strikes	Strikers' certificates may be suspended one year	Not mentioned	Prohibited; penalties assessed in case of strike

TABLE 1 (Continued)

State (Year of enactment)	Oregon (1965)	Rhode Island (1966)	Texas (1967)	Washington (1965)	Wisconsin (1959 and 1961)
Coverage	Certificated school personnel below the rank of superintendent	Certified public school teachers (superintendents, assistant superintendents, principals and assistant principals excluded).	All teachers	All certified public school employees except superintendent	All public school teachers and municipal employees except law enforcement
Bargaining Unit Determined by	Local School Board	State Labor Relations Board	Local Board but may not recognize labor organizations		Wisconsin Employment Relations Board
Type of Representation	Exclusive	Exclusive	Exclusive	Exclusive	Exclusive
Representation Determined by	Majority election	Majority election by secret ballot	No representation by organization which claims right to strike	Majority election by secret ballot	Majority election
Administrative Agency for Unit Determination & Elections	Local School Board	Unit determined by statute. Election conducted by State Labor Relations Board	Local Board		Wisconsin Employment Relations Board
Contains Specific Unfair Labor Practices	No	Yes, must meet and confer	No collective bargaining agreements	No	Yes

Specific Bargainable Issues	Matter of salaries and related economic policies affecting professional services	Hours, salaries, working conditions and other terms of professional employment	Board may consult with teachers on matters of educational policy and conditions of employment	Proposed school policies relating but not limited to listed issues	Wages, hours and conditions of employment
Agreement in Writing		Yes	Not prohibited		Yes, mandated
Impasse Broken by	Advisory arbitration	Arbitration binding on all matters not involving expenditure of money		Advisory arbitration	Fact-finding
Method of Selecting Impasse Breaker	Board may request consultants; Board chooses 1; employees 1; these 2 choose third	Each party selects 1 member; these 2 select third. If parties fail, American Arbitration Association may appoint third member		District Board selects one member; teachers, one; these two select third	Appointed by WERB from list or three-member panel when jointly requested
Strikes	Not mentioned	Prohibited	Prohibited	Not mentioned	Prohibited

exists between private industries engaged in services which deeply affect the public health, safety and welfare and the activities of public employees to justify the differences in no-strike philosophies. They defend strikes and mass resignation of public employees as necessary to genuine, free collective bargaining. Other observers, impartial practitioners and students of the collective bargaining process also urge the need for limited strike rights among public employees. Still another view is that public employees ought not be denied the right to strike; rather, means should be devised to make strikes unnecessary.

In an effort to afford public employees a viable alternative to the strike, there has developed broad scale experimentation with mediation, fact-finding and arbitration. Generally, such third party procedures have been accepted only after assurances that strike activity will not be engaged in. The law may leave the public agency and the employee representative to work out dispute-solving techniques, or it may establish machinery for resolving disputes that will operate automatically on a given timetable. Wherever such third party participation is a part of the established system of bargaining, the negotiating may be geared for such outside intervention to the detriment of the bargaining process unless the parties constantly keep in mind that the primary responsibility for arriving at agreement always remains with them.

Mediation. Mediation has been found to be an especially valuable method for dealing with important and difficult issues that remain unresolved after earnest efforts by the parties to reach agreement. The function of the mediator is to assist both parties by helping them to see logic in the other's demands and by making new suggestions for the parties' consideration. The mediator does not take sides. He should not make a public statement or report concerning the negotiation issues, the relative merits of the positions of the parties, or the state of the resolution of an impasse. Mediation cannot be effective when conducted in public.

The requirement that mediation be initiated only on the joint request of both parties is usually premised on the belief that it is necessary to assure that mediation is not invoked prematurely or on inconsequential matters. Such a requirement may, however, effectively preclude mediation. There can be no mediation unless the parties jointly agree on the selection of the mediator, the scope of his authority and reporting requirements, and the sharing of his expenses.

For that reason, it may be desirable to authorize the agency administering the law to initiate mediation on its own motion.

Where the state has an existing mediation agency staffed with skilled mediators, considerations of economy, efficiency and sound administrative practice might dictate the use of the expertise of that agency supplemented by *ad hoc* specialists in matters of mediation.

Fact-Finding. Another technique for dealing with impasses is fact-finding. It is not a substitute for mediation but may be employed when, even with the help of mediation, the parties are unable to resolve their differences. Recourse to fact-finding may be at the initiative of either or both of the parties. But, as with mediation, the regulatory agency in the state, which should be continuously informed of the progress of negotiations, must also have power to initiate fact-finding after the time for mediation has expired.

The neutral agency may have sole discretion to appoint the fact-finder or allow the parties to participate in that appointment. The advisory recommendations of the fact-finder are a part of the bargaining process and must be found acceptable to the parties if they are voluntarily to settle their dispute following fact-finding. Hence it seems most desirable for the parties to participate in the fact-finder's appointment. Proper timing of fact-finding is of the utmost importance.

Fact-finding is an orderly informal hearing procedure, before an individual or a panel, wherein the parties adduce evidence and argument going to the issues in dispute and negotiations. The fact-finder should be given power to schedule and adjourn hearings; to place witnesses under oath; and to issue subpoenas for witnesses, books, documents or other evidence. Some states place the subpoena power in the appointing agency rather than the fact-finder, but this appears unnecessary and may create inconvenience and costly delay during a hearing. Following the hearing and within such time limits as will meet the budget-making activities of the public employer, the fact-finder should render to the parties a full written report containing findings, conclusions and recommendations. In addition he may attempt a final mediatory effort with the parties. The parties should be required to respond to the individual recommendations before the fact-finder makes his report public. In this way, the public is fully apprised of the state of negotiations and the positions of the parties in light of the fact-finder's report and recommendations. The people then can bring to bear upon the private decision-making process the impact of an enlightened public opinion. In Wisconsin, for example, such fact-finding has been successful in resolving about 90 per cent of bargaining impasses.

The cost of fact-finding is usually shared by the parties, on the premise that the process may be abused if the cost is borne by the public. This also reduces the temptation to leave the dispute to the fact-finder rather than resolving it through bargaining.

Many authorities contend that fact-finding should be an open-ended technique for dealing with bargaining impasses; that is, compulsory arbitration should not be available if fact-finding fails. They argue that while mediation and fact-finding are a logical extension of the bargaining process and the most satisfactory substitutes for the strike, compulsory arbitration adds a new and undesirable dimension to the settlement procedure.

Compulsory Arbitration. Compulsory arbitration, as a third method of resolving a dispute with the help of outsiders, is much like fact-finding except that the parties are bound by the award of the arbitrator and there is less likelihood the arbitrator will engage in mediatory acts during or after the hearing.

Many public employers and employees believe compulsory arbitration destroys real collective bargaining. Extremist strategies develop in the bargaining process as the parties prepare to submit an issue to the final and binding authority of an outsider. In spite of this, compulsory arbitration is being given more and more serious consideration.

Grievance Arbitration

In the public sector the concept of sovereignty holds that public employers may not delegate their discretionary authority and so may not agree to be bound by the award of a third party arbitrator. This has deterred the development of binding grievance arbitration. Consequently, advisory arbitration, which might be more appropriately called grievance fact-finding with recommendations, has been frequently agreed to by public employers and employees at the state and local levels in jurisdictions where the enforcement of binding grievance arbitration clauses are in doubt. Some state legislatures, *e.g.,* Massachusetts, New Jersey, and Rhode Island, have provided for binding arbitration.

Where the parties agree on some form of arbitration, they generally agree to share the costs of arbitration equally. *Ad hoc* arbitrators are the rule; an exception is the New York City teachers agreement which, beginning in 1965, called for a permanent panel of three arbitrators. The principal appointing agencies, when used, are the American Arbitration Association and state mediation or labor relations agencies.

The Administrative Organization

An analysis of public employee bargaining laws and their underlying policy considerations provides little insight for a model administrative organization. Similarly, the functions of any administrative organization—unit determination; election proceedings; disputes concerning representation and contract terms; mediation, fact-finding and arbitration services; enforcement of the policies of the act, including strike penalty provisions—do not dictate a single most appropriate administrative body.

The advantages of utilizing existing state labor relations and mediation boards lie primarily in the use of available expertise, economy, and administrative efficiency. The advantages must be weighed against the likelihood that these agencies might overstress the similarities between the bargaining process in the private and public sectors to the neglect of the differences that exist and, consequently, try to shape bargaining in the public sector to the established private sector process. In addition, it is argued that utilization of existing labor agencies ignores the deeply entrenched adverse attitudes of some professionals in the public sector toward becoming a part of the labor process. A new public agency, it is said, would not carry any labor stigma and should attract trained and well qualified experts in labor relations to the challenge of new concepts in public employment relationships. The contended advantage of the professional agency, such as the state department of education, is grounded in the "all one professional family" concept. Even if this concept were generally accepted by all members of the teaching profession (and it is not), there exist cogent disadvantages in reposing the foreign functions of a labor relations administrative agency in an office which must otherwise effectively perform educational functions with the full cooperation of those engaged in the collective bargaining process.

The Future

The divergent approaches illustrated here suggest that great diversity may arise among the states with the development of public employee labor relations. Such diversity and experimentation can, in the long run, provide us with a superior model, but one may question whether those states that have forged another model will be able to abandon their own handiwork. Will established attitudes and interests then prevent a unified approach for public employee labor relations at the state and local levels? At the moment, the differences primarily present difficulty in the adjustments that must be made in organizational efforts and bargaining strategies. But, as public employer-employee relationships develop, conflicting established attitudes and interests may result in serious disruptions.

Educator Attitudes and Value Differences in Collective Negotiations

"The clash of doctrines is not a disaster, it is an opportunity"
Alfred North Whitehead,
Science and the Modern World

Patrick W. Carlton

It has been pointed out with some frequency that there are two contrasting images of teachers in American society, one of docile bureaucratic bawcocks controlled by a monocratic administrative structure, and the other of more dynamic individualists increasingly espousing the autoregulatory norms of their emergent profession. The latter image assumes sufficient competence and ability on the part of the teacher to render possible his meaningful participation in areas of decisional activity which have traditionally been presumed to be the

The High-School Journal, October, 1968. © 1968, The North Carolina Press. All rights reserved. By permission. Dr. Carlton is Associate Professor of Educational Administration, New York University.

exclusive bailiwick of administration. Such dual images tend to promote a division of attitudes and values on the part of teachers, on the one hand, and administrators and school board members, on the other.

Corwin has indicated that the current drive toward teacher decisional involvement is symptomatic of the rapid professionalization currently taking place in education. He states "... whatever else it is, professionalization represents the drive of a group to control its own work; and conversely it represents dissatisfaction with the traditional forms of control."[1]

Collective negotiations presages the shifting of the intra-system focus in administration from one of idealistic informality toward one of pragmatic formality. The ideology that teacher-administrator concerns are identical has been rapidly eroded by this shift, a matter of considerable concern to numerous educators. Likewise, the argument that the use of collective negotiations and strikes is unprofessional and that such activities tend to place educators in an infra dig position[2] has lost considerable credibility during the past several years. Iconoclasticism is apparently the order of the day, so far as militant professionalism is concerned.

Collective Negotiations Defined

The movement of teachers, as a power bloc, to gain for themselves additional influence in the operation and control of public schools is well established as a form of objective reality. The activities characterizing the movement are similar in some respects to traditional collective bargaining.[3] Called variously collective negotiations, professional negotiation and collective bargaining, it is a process whereby school boards and their administrative representatives discuss and make mutual determinations of educational policy, economic policy, and working conditions in conjunction with the teaching staffs.

Negotiations is a bilateral, as opposed to a unilateral, technique for settling matters of mutual concern involving the use of proposal,

[1] Ronald G. Corwin, *A Sociology of Education* (New York: Appleton-Century-Crofts, 1965), p. 262.

[2] Patrick W. Carlton, "Labor Psychology and Educational Planning," *Educational Leadership*, 25 (February 1968), p. 423.

[3] Patrick W. Carlton, *Teacher Salary Negotiations: A Case Study and Analysis* (Portland, Oregon Education Association, 1968), p. 58.

counter-proposal, compromise and concession. Negotiations is based upon the assumption that there are issues upon which school boards, administrators, and teachers lack preceptual congruence, and that it is better for these matters to be resolved through rational bargaining processes than through organized militancy.

Negotiations as a process has been labeled on occasion "the blatant usurpation of administrative prerogatives"; "the erosion of the legal authority of that traditional arm of the state—the school board"; and "a significant step toward the attainment of true professional dignity and status for American teachers." The reader will have little difficulty in determining which of these value-laden statements are attributable to a superintendent, a school board member, and a doctrinaire member of a teacher organization.

Indicators of Militancy

A dramatic indicator of the disparity in the attitudes and values of American teachers, administrators, and lay school board personnel is the strike tally for 1967-68. Between 1956 and 1966, there were only 35, but between September, 1967 and February, 1968, there were almost 100. Braulio Alonzo, then President of the National Education Association, forecasted a possible total of 300 by the end of 1968.

In early 1968, strikes took place in San Francisco, Albuquerque, Pittsburgh, Montgomery County, Maryland, and the state of Florida. In addition, teachers staged protest demonstrations before the State houses of Pennsylvania, South Dakota, and Oklahoma, and in the Nation's Capitol, Washington, D.C. At the time of this writing, statewide sanctions were underway in Colorado, Pennsylvania, Idaho, and Florida. New Orleans, La., and the states of Delaware, Maryland, and West Virginia represented potential "hot spots."

Causes of Militancy

The current unrest is predicated upon a number of socio-economic factors which are interrelated and, to an extent, complementary. A major source of militance is the economic problem. The necessity for allocation of scarce resources in the form of tax dollars for public educational services has existed since the organization of America's first public schools following passage of the "Old Deluder Satan" Act of 1647. Horace Mann provided vivid descriptions of the inadequate state of teacher remuneration during the years immediately preceding the Civil War. Mann pointed out that in a certain Massachusetts town all journeymen and craftsmen received more than teachers—some received twice as much money as the average teacher. Mann's own comment on the situation would be humorous were it not so tragic in implication. "We pay best, first, those who destroy us—generals; second, those who cheat us—politicians and quacks; third, those who amuse us—singers and dancers; and last of all those who instruct us—teachers."[4]

Salary conditions have improved to a considerable extent since Mann wrote. The average teacher's starting salary in 1967-68 was $5519 for nine months work, or $6745 for 12 months, depending upon the mode of calculation. The 12 month figure compared favorably with 12 month starting salaries for all liberal Arts graduates—$6780. However, it was considerably below the composite figure representing the starting salary for "other fields"—$7644. The Conference on Economic Progress reports that, compared with financial requirements for a Moderate Standard of Living Budget for a family of four, starting salaries for public school teachers in the U.S. at large averaged 36.1% below the stated minimum requirement in 1967.[5]

There are those who would argue that current teacher salaries represent about all that the taxpayers will stand for at this time, and that other concerns are more pressing. Where such sentiment exists, teachers in many areas of the country have attempted through democratic processes to change it, such actions being based (or so it is claimed), upon the First Amendment guarantee of freedom of assembly to petition for redress of grievances. Sanctions, coupled with withdrawal of services, are indicative of the teacher's changing frame of reference with regard to the use of political pressure as a means of satisfying his felt needs.

Most authorities concede that some form of sanction, economic, political, or otherwise, must be available to the teaching staff if negotiations are to be successful, since the process assumes relative power equivalence on the parts of the protagonists. The strike has

---

[4] *Common School Journal,* Vol. 9 (1847), p. 367, as quoted in Willard Elsbree, *The American Teacher* (New York: American Book Co., 1939), p. 280.

[5] Conference on Economic Progress, *Goals for Teachers' Salaries in Our Public Schools* (Washington: The Committee, 1968).

increasingly come to be used by teacher groups as the means of gaining the requisite power equivalence. Only last year (1967), the National Education Association, long vehemently opposed to the use of the strike, promulgated a policy which pledges support to striking affiliates where conditions are sufficiently serious to warrant such teacher action. The organization's overall attitude has been shifting toward a teacher welfare orientation, as demonstrated by a set of eight priorities adopted at the National convention. Seven of the eight relate rather directly to matters of self-interest.[6]

A second cause of current teacher militancy is an intense organizational power struggle between the American Federation of Teachers, with some 165,000 members, and the National Education Association, with over one million members. The beginning of this militant escalation was marked by the New York teacher strike and representation election of 1965, in which the AFT defeated a much larger NEA contingent.[7] Since that time, AFT has made consistent membership gains, particularly in the nation's larger cities, while the NEA, highly stimulated by these activities, has moved with great rapidity into a stance that is militant to such extent that it is virtually indistinguishable from that of AFT. (A major issue in both the Florida (NEA) and Pittsburgh (AFT) strikes was the question of exclusive organizational representation rights, for instance.) As one biased sage put it, "The AFT is the best thing that ever happened to the NEA. If the AFT hadn't come along, the NEA would have had to create it." Such a judgment would have been considered heretical ten years ago. Today, it qualifies as being only mildly irreverent.

Next on the list of militant antecedents is the newly developed political potency of the schools which has arisen as a result of passage of the National Defense Education Act of 1958 and the Elementary and Secondary Education Act of 1965. These acts, which made available to education larger sums of federal money than ever before, have been accompanied by an increased level of both state and local support to public education. Education has, virtually overnight, become one of the nation's growth industries. Partially as a result of increased support levels and partially as a result of increased education and level of sophistication, teachers have been caught up in a revolution of rising expectations. However, expectations generally exceed fulfillment, and teachers have increasingly chosen to organize

6 *Education News,* 2 (March 4, 1968), p. 25.
7 AFT received approximately 20,000 votes. NEA received 9800 votes.

for direct group action rather than to await the tide of events, which they apparently believe has passed them by in the past.

The change of teacher leader attitudes from conservatism and conformity to militant liberalism has no doubt been influenced by the value orientations of the social protest movement that is developing in the U.S. The non-violent civil rights activities of the early 1950's gave proof of the efficacy of civil disobedience in protesting unjust social conditions.

The widespread social protests of the 1960's have tended to reinforce the feeling that militant protest is both a respectable and, indeed, a virtuous and appropriate form of extracurricular activity for teachers to espouse. Many of the nation's teachers have accepted the premise that direct social action is an effective means for challenging the status quo, and for gaining those things they deem appropriate in today's society.

Another cause of teacher militancy is the increased size and impersonality of the educational bureaucracy. Today's teacher often perceives himself as a small faceless cog in a bureaucratic machine—unknown and unnoticed. Also, as the management role in education becomes successively more complex, the principal tends to be perceived as being less the master teacher in the school and more the representative of absentee management. He becomes less and less one of the teachers. This, of course, is even more true of the superintendent, who has been conceded by employee associations to be management.

Compounding the problem of identity loss is the fact that growing numbers of teachers no longer perceive themselves as being closely tied to the communities in which they teach. Some cannot afford to dwell in the high taxing areas surrounding their places of employment—others are afraid to live in the school neighborhoods because of the increasing incidence of violence and intimidation directed against teachers by certain segments of the community. This is, of course, a major problem in the core cities.

All these factors, increased size and bureaucratization, the changing role of management, and the lack of community identification promote the alienation of teachers from both the institution of education itself and the community served. Alienation results in the development of a "we-they" syndrome, the logical outcome of which is self-interested protectionism on a group basis (i.e. group action).

This alienation has been stimulated, in addition, by the presence of various poor working conditions—over-crowded classes, unrealistic curricular expectations, racial unrest, and the presence of monocracy in administrator-teacher relationships. The latter refers to that attitude of over-protection or paternalism on the part of administrators the outcome of which is lack of teacher decisional involvement in operational and policy matters. Such monocratic tendencies are no longer acceptable in an age when professional employees increasingly are pressing for collegial pluralism in organizational operation.

Teachers, as a group, are changing. They are brighter, younger, more self-assured, and less likely to accept non-professional duties and arbitrary decisions than was previously the case. Increasing numbers of males have entered the teaching ranks, also. (1965–35% of the teaching force male as opposed to 17% in 1925.) Newer teachers tend to be more pragmatic, less dedicated in the "anything for the good of education" sense, more willing to accept as appropriate the tactics of organized labor in their struggle for improved conditions of employment.

Values, Strikes and Sanctions

As would be expected, collective negotiations and the use of strikes and other forms of sanction have been vehemently and formally opposed by the National School Boards Association since 1961. The American Association of School Administrators, on the other hand, produced a statement in early 1968 which proclaims the fact that collective negotiations are here to stay, and which outlines procedures for engaging in effective collective negotiations.[8] The AASA position on sanctions is one of cautious endorsement, but strikes are condemned as inappropriate under all circumstances.[9]This is apparently the result of a desire on the part of AASA to support the NEA, as opposed to the AFT, line in these matters.

At the 1968 AASA meetings, value reorientation was evident as school administrators took an exceptionally hard line in their references to teachers and their negotiators. The fragile veneer of brotherhood was badly tattered in a number of statements made.

---

[8] American Association of School Administrators, *The School Administrator and Negotiation* (Washington: AASA, 1968), *passim.*
[9] American Association of School Administrators, *Administrators View Professional Negotiation* (Washington: The Association, 1966).

Sup. George Young, of Canton, Ohio, offered a resolution calling for withdrawal of AASA support for any form of NEA sponsored sanctions. Supt. D. P. Whitmer, of Pontiac, Michigan, stated: 'We can no longer live under the same roof with those who sit across from us at the negotiating table."[10] He called for AASA withdrawal from NEA. Both his motion and Young's resolution failed. From the general tone of the AASA meeting, it seems safe to predict eventual withdrawal of AASA from the NEA, since the two groups are rapidly diverging in their ideological configurations.

The American Federation of Teachers, on the other hand, has become increasingly complimentary in its remarks concerning the NEA's recent actions. President Cogan, writing in the March, 1968, *American Teacher,* looked forward to the day when " . . . AFT-NEA unity may become a reality. Heaven knows, we badly need a strong unified, militant, and labor-oriented teachers union . . . ," he stated. It seems likely that these overtures are a direct result of the NEA's increasing espousal of the general value configuration of the union, operationally speaking.

Attitude Evolution in Negotiations

The current militant revolution within the educational corpus has induced strains, tensions and to some extent, dysfunctions of a previously unknown and rather alarming nature. It seems only natural that such a state of affairs should result in the manifestation of differential perceptions on the part of various role-incumbents involved in the process.

The teaching staff in an average school district tends to experience several identifiable stages in the process of negotiatory growth. Initially, there is a good deal of hesitancy and uncertainty on the part of the staff with regard to the implementation of negotiations, since the process is quite foreign to the experience of the average teacher. Having accepted the process, which may take only a short time or a more extended period of orientation, teacher groups generally embrace a period of hard-nosed militance, which activities can be described as being legitimating in nature.

[10] *Education News,* 2 (March 4, 1968), p. 1. In 1969, AASA members voted to become an associated organization in the NEA framework, the loosest of all possible relationships short of total separation.

Legitimating activities are usually necessary to overcome the board's initial reluctance to deal with teacher groups on a power equivalence basis. During this period, teacher demands are often somewhat extreme, and frequent recourse to the press for purposes of acrimonious attacks is made by both parties to the relationship.

Following the intransigence stage, or period of adolescence, the teachers, having gained major economic concessions, move into a balance of power, or "balance of terror," steady state. Such homeostasis is illustrated by today's situation in San Diego, California, where overt militance is not the usual activity—mutual respect and a spirit of compromise prevails.

From the administrator-board point of view, the initial stages of negotiations are equally traumatic. A common initial reaction on the part of board and administration is one of utter shock, accompanied by organizational decisional paralysis for a short time. More often than not, this state of affairs soon gives way to an adolescent stage characterized by intransigence, indignation, and hard-nosedness. During this period hostility and frustration are often the order of the day. The "we-they" syndrome is evident at this point. As time passes, however, and experiential background in negotiations increases, a more positive attitude tends to develop. Mutuality of educational concern tends to emerge on both sides of the bargaining table, and the "we-they" syndrome becomes somewhat less pronounced, although it does not completely disappear. This is the stage of negotiatory maturity. Arrival at the third stage does not insure maintenance of negotiatory homeostasis, it should be pointed out. Changing personnel in leadership roles and changing economic and political conditions can cause a regression to stage two or even stage one. (Figure 1.)

In stages one and two, distributive bargaining takes place, involving the resolution of issues in which substantial conflict of interest inheres. Such issues generally involve the allocation of scarce resources. Negotiations over salary and other economic benefits fall within the context of distributive bargaining. In stage three, integrative bargaining can occur, predicated upon resolution of issues in which complementarity of interests exists.[11] The nature of the issues must, of course, permit solutions advantageous to both parties. An example of such an issue is the improvement of teaching facilities of of the curriculum.

[11] Richard E. Walton and Robert B. McKersie, *A Behavioral Theory of Labor Negotiations* (New York: McGraw-Hill Book Co., 1965), pp. 11-13.

	Teacher Attitudes	Negotiatory Descriptors	Board-Administration Attitudes
Stage 1 (nativity)	guilt-hesitance	confusion-negotiatory ineptness	utter shock—temporary decisional paralysis
Stage 2 (adolescence)	hard-nosed demands	hostility-frustration "we-they" syndrome-distributive bargaining	intransigent refusal or grudging acquiescence
Stage 3 (maturity)	spirit of accommodation-mutuality of educational interests emerging	homeostasis balance of power integrative bargaining	recognition of mutual educational interests—spirit of accommodation

Figure 1: Attitudinal Evolution in Negotiations

The attitudinal tendencies displayed by the public at large are less easily pinpointed, due to lack of empirical data in this area. In general, the attitude of the public is overtly one of permissiveness until the point at which the question of increased funds for support of education is forcibly raised through the presentation of a tax levy. This statement is supported by a recent Gallup poll, which revealed that nearly 60% of the public surveyed believe that teachers have the right to engage in collective bargaining.[12] There are, of course, less favorably inclined interest groups such as the taxpayers association, which keep close watch on board-teacher relationships, but such groups do not represent the effective configuration of the general public. At the time of the tax levy, taxpayers often display irritation followed by 1) grim determination that the needs of education shall be served or 2) a general damnation of the taxing structure and of the schools. It is fair to state that, in general, group one tends to be younger and to have children in public schools while group two tends to exhibit more advanced age and normally provides a minimal number of school enrollees. This observation furnishes an insight into the differential motivations of the two groups.

The Gallup poll mentioned above indicated that 57% of the public surveyed disapproved of teacher strikes while 36% would allow such militant tactics.[13] Receptiveness to this type of extreme activity is

---

[12] NEA Journal, "News and Trends," 57 (May, 1968), p. 4.
[13] Ibid.

increasing among the citizenry, possibly as a result of the rising incidence thereof. As the public's non-rational fear of teacher strikes subsides, based upon increased experience with such activities, receptiveness apparently increases.

Functions and Dysfunctions of Institutionalized Conflict

Former justice Fortas, of the United States Supreme Court, makes this cogent statement in a recent publication: "We are a great nation . . . because of our protection of the freedom to criticize, to dissent, to oppose and to join with others in mass opposition—and to do these things powerfully and effectively."[14]

Fortas has, it is felt, enunciated a crucial point *vis a vis* collective negotiations in public education. Recently educationists have, with some regularity, acclaimed or deplored the process of collective negotiations, depending upon individual value structures. In general, their reasoning has been based, in the case of the former, upon sanguine belief in the salutary outcomes of the process and, in the case of the latter, upon amorphous forebodings and general negative predispositions toward teacher power. In neither instance has sufficient thought been devoted to the functions and dysfunctions of institutionalized collective negotiations.[15]

School administrators and board members are, by and large, proponents of the melioristic school of social thought, a major premise of which is that essentially all educational problems are amenable to resolution through the application of rational analytic processes (i.e. problem solving and persuasion).

This is in line with March and Simon's paradigm, a major premise of which is that, because of the potentially disruptive effects of bargaining, administrators initially tend to respond to such potential conflict as though it were subject to the aforesaid analytic processes even though these processes are evidently inappropriate, and that administrators (and board members) tend to place greater explicit

[14] Abe Fortas, *Concerning Dissent and Civil Disobedience* (New York: Signet Books, 1968), p. 12.

[15] Institutionalization refers to the process of establishing as an accepted *modus operandi* the formal negotiatory relationship called collective negotiations. Institutionalization brings with it the advantages of regularized procedures and predictability of action, plus the disadvantages of increased tension and opportunity for misunderstanding on the part of the parties to the relationship.

emphasis on common goals where these goals do not, in fact, exist than where they do.[16]

The melioristic school of thought has become an increasingly inappropriate frame of educational reference due to the numerous clashes between boards and teachers over the allocation of scarce financial resources. Where resources are inadequate to meet demand, rational processes often give way to the exercise of political power in the form of hard-nosed bargaining, sanctions, and strikes.

The social conflict school of thought, one much less respectable in this day of sensitivity training, integrative behavior, and empathetic socialization, is generally deemed antithetical to the melioristic school. Too often, it is felt, the social conflict school has been cursorily dismissed as completely dysfunctional in an educational context.

Research indicates that conflict is both necessary and desirable for the maintenance of a viable educational organization. It is a fundamental component of social structure, which one ignores at the risk of seriously misrepresenting objective organizational reality, as was recognized by a number of early sociologists. Cooley, writing in 1918 stated that ". . . . conflict and co-operation are not separable things, but phases of one process which always involves something of both."[17] Small stated that ". . . the social process is . . . prompted by interests that in part conflict . . . and in part comport . . . ."[18]

Simmel's theme is that conflict serves a socializing function, that no group can exist in total harmony except it be devoid of process and structure. He states that conflict is an essential element in the life of an organization or group, and that conflict helps to establish and maintain group identity.[19] It can be posited, then, that collective negotiations serve to bind teachers closer together and to build *esprit de corps*. Such group cohesiveness is not incompatible with the professionalization of teachers.

Furthermore, it is through conflict that change in organizations is accomplished, albeit with less than optimal frequency. As has been

16 James G. March and Herbert A. Simons, *Organizations* (New York: John Wiley and Son, 1958), p. 131.
17 Charles H. Cooley, *Social Process* (New York: Scribner's Sons, 1918), p. 39.
18 Albion W. Small, *General Sociology* (Chicago: University of Chicago Press, 1905), p. 205.
19 George Simmel, *Conflict*, trans. Kurt M. Wolff (Glencoe, Ill.: The Free Press, 1955), *passim*.

noted,[20] organizations demonstrate an almost unbelievable ability to absorb conflict and innovative attempts without manifesting homeostatic upset. Nevertheless, conflict-based relationships such as collective negotiations do represent a potentially viable means of effecting organizational evolution or, more drastically, revolution. Proceeding upon the above assumptions, it is reasonable to view noncongruence of attitudes and value structures within the educational community as both a desirable and normal state of affairs generally, and specifically to conceive of teacher militancy as a potentially salubrious process, one that is capable of contributing not only to the further professionalization of teaching, but also to the development and implementation of more enlightened administrative practices, and to the general enhancement of the quality of American education. Whether the potential inherent in the process is realized remains to be seen, and will depend in large measure upon the basic sincerity and educational commitment of those involved in the relationship.

[20] Vernon Haubrich, "The Rhetoric and Reality of Education," in *Reason and Change in Elementary Education* (U.S. Office of Education, 1968), p. 95.

The Tough New Teacher

J. Douglas Muir

Just because you're a member of a school board, don't allow yourself to become too comfortable with the idea that the real power decisions about the schools are likely to remain the exclusive property of you and your fellow boardmen.

Teachers have a different idea. Backed by one of two powerful organizations—the National Education Association or the American Federation of Teachers—they are organized, financed, trained, determined, and in a fighting mood to win higher (much higher) salaries, improved working conditions, and a strong say in what you might think is your responsibility, policymaking.

Reprinted, with permission, from the *American School Board Journal,* November, 1968. © 1968, The National School Boards Association. All rights reserved. Dr. Muir is Assistant Professor (on leave) in the faculty of business administration, University of Alberta, Canada.

AFT was the first of the two groups to get tough about higher salaries and better working conditions for teachers. It took NEA a few years to get the idea, but it, too, caught on—to the tune of calling this year for a teacher salary range of $10,500 to $21,000 and for a hand in the establishment of all school board policies on recruitment, evaluation and personnel.

If you think it all happened fast, it's because it did. Only a couple of years ago, it was possible to distinguish clearly between the actions of the "teacher union" (AFT) and the "professional association" (NEA). That distinction is no longer easy to make. In just eight years, there's been something like a 350 degree turn in NEA's position concerning collective action. The remaining ten degrees needed to complete the about-face probably will be turned next year when NEA members vote on whether to establish a million dollar "defense fund" to tide teachers over a walkout.

This report will attempt to describe how it all happened and what school boards might expect from teachers in the near future now that not one but two forces of teacher militancy have been unleashed on public education in the United States.

If you want to grasp what's happened to the National Education Association and the more than 50 percent of American teachers it represents, watch the dowdy spinster on the beer commercial, who drops her inhibitions along with her cello and comes alive at a swinging party. NEA has shed its image of an aging sisterhood of spinster teachers and has come alive to the will of its members, 80 percent of whom are teachers, a group that is getting younger and bigger all the time.

Nowhere is the big change more visible than in NEA's development since 1960 of "affirmative action" (my phrase) policies on collective bargaining, strikes and sanctions. They represent a complete turnabout from the days before 1961 when NEA opposed *any* procedure that might interrupt school operations.

What caused the about-face? Two of many factors stand out: (1) demands by NEA's teachers that the association assume responsibility for improving their occupational needs, and (2) the ominous example provided by the American Federation of Teachers, which has been demonstrating what can be obtained from school boards by use of the big stick.

How was the change accomplished? Carefully and completely: through a series of aggressive policy maneuvers—sparked mainly by NEA's teacher members—that has seen NEA change gradually from an association unwilling to concede that the word "strike" was part of the language to an action organization that backs its striking locals with money and muscle.

Professional Negotiations

In 1960 NEA's assembly turned down, strongly, a resolution suggesting that "representative negotiations" are "compatible with the ethics and dignity of the teaching profession."

So a new resolution, which avoided the term "negotiations," was introduced and passed in 1961. That was NEA's first policy on negotiations; it stated simply that NEA believed that professional education associations should "be accorded the right . . . to participate (with school boards) in the determination of policies of common concern," including salaries.

The resolution ruled out "arbitrary exercise of unilateral authority" by boards of education or strikes by teachers. In case of an impasse, a board of review of professional and lay educators—something calculated to preclude the use of state labor mediation or arbitration boards—should be called in.

It was the year 1962 that unquestionably marked the turning point in NEA's attitude toward collective bargaining. By 1962 NEA was "insisting" on the right of teachers to negotiate with school boards—even though the word "negotiation" had not yet crept into official wording of the policy.

Strikes were still anathema, as were labor mediation boards: "Under no circumstances," declared the 1962 resolution, "should the resolution of differences between professional associations and boards of education be sought through channels set up for handling industrial disputes." The rationale: "Industrial-dispute machinery which assumes a conflict of interest and a diversity of purpose between persons and groups, is not appropriate to professional negotiations in public education."

This resolution passed in spite of objections from the floor of the delegate assembly that it focused too much attention upon the professional-union controversy, that it could be interpreted as being directed against the union movement in general and the American Federation of Teachers in particular, and that it handicapped affiliates that were required to support local mediation efforts.

The 1962 resolution didn't spell out how boards and teachers were to reach agreement in impasses, except to recommend that "procedures," including "provisions for appeal through designated educational channels," should be established.

The delegates, in 1963, decided these still-undefined procedures "must" be established, and this was the only change made in the negotiations resolution. The urgency of setting up workable negotiations machinery may have been somewhat in reaction to a speech by the president of the National School Boards Association, who pointed out that NSBA policy urged all boards "to refrain from compromise agreements based upon negotiations or collective bargaining," and to avoid mediation or arbitration.

The 1964 assembly cleared the way for NEA affiliates to resolve disputes with school boards through mediation and arbitration boards originally designed for resolving industrial disputes. The entire section outlawing such action was deleted from the previous year's negotiations resolution. Affiliates were called upon to make a greater effort to develop negotiations procedures and adopt written agreements.

One small but significant change was made in 1965. The word "strike" was deleted from that section of the resolution which previously banned the use of strikes along with "arbitrary exercise of unilateral authority" by school boards. The revision read: "The seeking of consensus and mutual agreement on a professional basis should preclude the arbitrary exercise of unilateral action by boards of education, administrators, or teachers."

A strong plea was made by the 1965 delegates for an amendment to the resolution in order to allow local associations of classroom teachers to negotiate with school boards separately from administrators, but it was defeated. Had it passed, it would have established a bargaining group of classroom teachers within NEA parallel to that of the AFT membership. This could have opened the door for an AFT-NEA merger, or it simply may have helped AFT raid NEA affiliates.

In 1966, William G. Carr, then NEA's executive secretary, reported that the association's push for development of legislation governing teacher-board negotiations had been successful—11 states had passed statutes covering them. From the floor of the 1966 delegate assembly came a motion to write some sort of grievance procedure into the negotiations resolution. "To have one without the other is going half way"; NEA must protect teachers through the right of appeal of grievances, argued the delegate.

A majority agreed. The title of the resolution was changed from professional negotiations to professional negotiations and grievance procedure, and this paragraph was added:

"The National Education Association insists on the right of individual teachers, through officially adopted professional grievance procedures and with the right to professional association representation, to appeal the application or interpretation of board of education policies affecting them through educational channels which include third party appeal if necessary, without fear of intimidation, coercion, discrimination, or other forms of reprisal."

Everything NEA either had condemned or avoided saying about negotiations in the early 1960's was included in the completely revised resolution presented to the 1968 assembly in Dallas. Negotiations agreements, says the latest resolution, "must" be established between teachers and school boards. These agreements "shall provide" for negotiations, mediation, fact-finding and appeal of impasses, and for grievance procedures that include binding arbitration.

The resolution also calls on NEA members and affiliates to push for state bargaining laws.

Sanctions

Just as 1962 ushered in a marked change in NEA negotiation policy, so, too, did that same year see the NEA delegate assembly adopt the first resolution supporting sanctions (blacklisting of school districts) "as a means for preventing unethical or arbitrary policies or practices that have a deleterious effect on the welfare of the schools." The resolution called on NEA affiliates to help develop guidelines for invoking "professional sanctions."

A few points about this revolutionary resolution bear mentioning. It came from the floor, not from the NEA executive, suggesting perhaps that the NEA hadn't intended taking the big step then. It came directly on the heels of heated debate over a negotiations resolution that may have influenced the delegates' thinking. And it came at the end of a long morning after two motions for adjournment, a fact probably influencing its quick, uneventful passage.

At their 1963 convention, NEA delegates decided that complete authority for imposing and removing nationwide sanctions should rest with the executive committee. The guidelines established that the executive committee would impose sanctions only after a request by a state affiliate was received and after the NEA Commission on Professional Rights and Responsibilities had made an investigation.

Nationwide sanctions against all the school districts in Utah were invoked by NEA in May 1963 on grounds that the governor had refused to increase the education budget. No major change was made in the sanctions resolution that year, but the NEA board of directors provided a little more insight into the use of sanctions: They should be applied only "when the total conditions in a district are such that the professional people there cannot perform the services in the interests of the children for which they have been trained."

In 1965 the sanction against Utah was lifted after 300 days. But sanctions were imposed that year against Idaho (only briefly) and Oklahoma. The tactics, initiated in the Oklahoma case, were clear: *censure*—wide publicity on education conditions in the state; *notification*—informing placement services throughout the country of the sanction and conditions in Oklahoma; *warning*—to active and student NEA members that accepting employment in Oklahoma might be considered unethical conduct; *assistance*—helping teachers in Oklahoma leave the state.

Speaking to delegates at the 1965 assembly, NEA executive secretary Carr laid down some specific sanctions ground rules:

"Before sanctions are invoked," he warned, "the educational deficiencies should be established by an impartial study. These documented deficiencies must be serious enough and general enough in scope to warrant so drastic a measure. The profession itself must be substantially united and resolute. The group against whom the sanctions were directed must be legally and financially capable of removing the deficiencies which led to the sanctions. Sanctions should be applied only after due warning, and with a complete absence of threats or vindictiveness. They must be preceded and accompanied by a persistent campaign of public information."

A 1965 addition to the sanction resolution gave the association, for the first time, some effective control over members who ignore sanctions: ". . . violation of sanctions by a member of the profession is a violation of the Code of Ethics of the Education Profession. Therefore, the offering or accepting of employment in areas where sanctions are in effect should be evaluated in terms of the code . . ." The NEA delegates also changed the association's by-laws to give the "Committee on Professional Ethics power, after notice and hearing, to censure, suspend, or expel" violators.

The 1966 NEA convention brought no change in wording of the sanctions resolution from 1965. Recommending use of sanctions over strikes, Carr assured delegates that sanctions do not violate contracts or encounter court injunctions. They are directed at legislatures and other public bodies, not against students. "They [sanctions] constitute," he said, "a procedure which is more powerful, more respected, and more successful than any other."

Worried about that section of the resolution making it unethical for a superintendent whose school district is under sanction to offer a position to a teacher, delegates to the 1967 convention revised part of the resolution to read: "the offering, without informing the prospective employee of sanctions, or the acceptance of employment in areas where sanctions are in effect should be evaluated in terms of the code . . ."

Somewhat surprisingly, this entire section on violation of sanctions was deleted from the resolution presented to the 1968 assembly in Dallas. It is possible that this represents a change in the association's policy concerning the internal disciplining of its members who fail to adhere to an NEA-imposed sanction.

Otherwise, the 1968 sanctions resolution remained as revised through the years, affirmatively stating when sanctions should be invoked, how they should be imposed and lifted, and calling upon affiliates to apply the guidelines.

Strikes

By far the greatest change in NEA collective bargaining policies has come on the issue of teacher strikes, sometimes euphemistically called "withdrawal of services" or "professional holidays" by NEA.

Only eight years ago the teachers recognized an "obligation to maintain the uninterrupted operation of the public schools." Between 1961 and 1964, NEA policy followed this general line, emphasizing that seeking of agreement between teachers and school boards "should preclude . . . the use of strikes . . . "

All reference to the word "strike" was deleted in the 1965 collective bargaining resolution. Whether this change was designed to pave the way for strikes in the future or because of an aversion on the part of many teachers to the word "strike" isn't known.

Although they hadn't condoned teacher strikes, there's no question that NEA leaders recognized the importance of the developing teacher militancy to strengthening the association. Carr said so publicly before the 1966 delegates, warning that such newfound power must be exercised with responsibility, within the framework of the Code of Ethics, and with due regard for public interest. He emphasized that strikes or threats of strikes shouldn't be a requirement for successful professional negotiations. Legislation on bargaining rights and impasse settlements, he added, would lessen the need to resort to strikes—a step some affiliates already had taken on their own.

In 1967 NEA's board of directors took a new position toward striking affiliates. While continuing to recommend that strikes be avoided, the directors decided that, in the future, NEA would "offer all of the services at its command to the affiliate concerned to help resolve the impasse."

The directors' position on the support of affiliates' strikes was upheld by the 1968 assembly. This support was possibly influenced by an NEA research division survey showing teachers who believe in striking rose from 53.3 percent in 1965 to 68.2 percent in 1968. Although the 1968 resolution still recommends that impasses be resolved with procedures other than strikes, it actually calls a strike a strike, admits they will occur, and pledges association support to the striking affiliate.

In part, the resolution reads: ". . . under conditions of severe stress, causing deterioration of the educational program, and when good faith attempts at resolution have been rejected, strikes have occurred and may occur in the future. In such instances, the association will offer all of the services at its command to the affiliate concerned to help resolve the impasse."

The resolution also clarified NEA's attitude toward use of strike breakers: The association "denounces the practice of staffing schools with any other personnel, when, in an effort to provide high quality education, educators withdraw their services."

To leave no doubt that teachers intend to use the strike weapon in the future, the resolution also urged NEA affiliates to work toward the repeal of state laws that prohibit strikes.

The last hurdle probably will be jumped next year when delegates vote on a proposal, tabled this year, for a $10 per year increase in membership dues for a "defense fund" to "prevent reprisals and unjust actions against teachers" and to meet "other" needs.

Throughout the 1960's—the period when these dramatic changes took place in NEA collective action policies—the specter of NEA's rival, the American Federation of Teachers, rose high over the association. Indeed, it's fair to conclude the AFT indirectly but significantly influenced the changes in NEA:

In an historical discussion of teacher-labor movement relations before delegates to the 1962 assembly, Carr expressed worry that the AFL-CIO "after decades of cooperation with the NEA suddenly moved in on the teaching profession" by supporting the AFT.

Concern may have been nurtured when James A. Cary, president of the United Electrical Workers, told delegates the NEA had failed, and would continue to fail, to win wage increases for teachers unless it took on more of a "trade union" relationship with school boards. Unless the basic position of the NEA was changed, he theorized, janitors would get more money and job security through their union than teachers would through NEA.

After hours of heated discussion about the place for trade union activities in NEA, delegates resolved:

"Certain actions of this convention have been misinterpreted as action designed to sever the long-standing friendly and cooperative relations of the National Education Association with the American labor movement. Such misinterpretation could seriously damage the effectiveness of American public education. The National Education Association therefore declares its intention to continue its friendly and cooperative relations with the American labor movement, as it shall with all other segments of American society, in an atmosphere of mutual respect while retaining its identity as an independent professional organization."

But by 1964 NEA had become jittery over the activities of AFT and the support AFT was receiving from the AFL-CIO. A warning came from Carr: Through "substantial financial resources" and "considerable political influence," challenges in local representative elections, and opposition of labor councils to increases in school taxes, organized labor—namely the AFL-CIO and the AFT—was making jetlike headway in its move to overtake the teaching profession. NEA affiliates, he reported, won 12 out of 15 representative elections in 1963-64, but the AFT won the big ones—Detroit and Cleveland.

Definite steps would have to be taken, Carr warned, to counteract the AFT or else the "AFL-CIO program, as defined by its leadership, would, if successful, destroy the National Education Association and its state and local affiliates." Some of those steps were to take the form of cemented collective action policies.

Why this fear of the AFT? Statistics on membership, representative elections, and strikes hold the answer.

Membership. Although NEA members outnumber AFT members almost seven to one, comparative growth of the AFT has been greater. Since 1963, NEA membership has increased only at the same rate as the U.S. teaching force; for the past five years, NEA has represented 52 percent of teachers. Membership of the AFT, while representing only 8 percent of U.S. teachers, has jumped an average of 18 percent yearly since 1959—and most of that growth is in cities. Result: NEA started a membership drive and has "unified" local, state and national membership.

Another reason for AFT influence on NEA policy: Many NEA members—especially the more militant-minded classroom teachers[1]—find AFT occupational objectives most attractive. And NEA cannot afford to snub its Association of Classroom Teachers, which accounts for 80 percent of its membership.

Representative Elections. Between 1961 and 1965, there were 35. NEA won 17; AFT, 18. NEA added 14,600 represented members through these elections; AFT, 76,000. AFT also came away with the bigger victories—New York, Milwaukee, Detroit, Cleveland, Philadelphia. Since 28 of the elections took place in 1964 and 1965, it's understandable that NEA delegates were especially concerned about AFT activities during those years.

Teacher Strikes. Strikes by teachers, especially under NEA auspices, were virtually unheard of before 1966. The 33 strikes held in 1966 alone—followed by another 11 in the first quarter of 1967—nearly doubled total strikes from 1960 to 1965. NEA affiliates initiated 11 of the 33; AFT, 20; independent organizations, 2. These strikes averaged 1.8 classroom days compared to 14.1 employee days for all strikes during 1966. Reasons for the teacher strikes, according to the Bureau of Labor Statistics: salaries or hours, 16; attempts to organize, 9; school conditions and policies, 8. It would appear that NEA's move toward strikes stems, in part, from AFT's successful use of the tactic in the past (substantial salary boosts resulted from 14 of the 16 strikes over salaries in 1966).

What does the development of these stronger collective action policies mean for the future of NEA?

Most importantly, the new policies and their development show clearly that classroom teachers hold the upper hand in NEA. Had it not been for their insistence that the NEA become concerned with occupational objectives, they probably would have defected to the AFT, causing NEA membership to decline drastically rather than merely level off. Acceptance of classroom teachers as the association's strong arm hasn't come easy to administrators and supervisors.

More stress will be produced within the NEA membership as the

---

[1] Obvious differences in policy objectives between NEA's teacher and administrator members have produced serious problems within the association. At the 1968 convention in Dallas, a walkout by school administrators was only narrowly averted.

association struggles to function as an occupational as well as an educational organization. Experience in industry and other professions has shown there's an inherent difference between the occupational views of those who manage and those who are managed. That being so, NEA can expect even more conflicts—not easily resolved—between administrators and supervisors, on the one hand, and classroom teachers on the other.

To deal effectively with these differences, it's going to be essential that NEA establish an organizational structure that goes beyond the internal reshaping the association approved in Dallas in July.

Somehow NEA is going to have to devise an umbrella structure that will allow classroom teachers to bargain separately from administrators and still maintain an educational tie with them. It will have to be a structure that will satisfy not only NEA's educational interests but also its divergent occupational interests. How else will the same organization be able to serve the needs of groups who find themselves on opposite sides of the bargaining table?

The change in basic NEA policies, started in 1962, is not yet complete. The next couple of years are critical for NEA and for teachers. The decisions NEA makes in the immediate future will not only determine the association's ability to enforce its occupational demands on school boards, but also will establish the organizational structure of NEA, which in turn will affect the future strength and unity of teachers.

Implications of the Coming NEA-AFT Merger

Myron Lieberman

A merger of the National Education Association and American Federation of Teachers will probably be negotiated in the near future. Such a move will have far-reaching national implications for teacher militancy. Perhaps because very few educators realize how imminent merger is, our professional literature is virtually devoid of

Reprinted from *Phi Delta Kappan,* November, 1968, by permission. Mr. Lieberman is Professor of Education, Rhode Island College, Providence.

any consideration of the likely conditions and consequences of merger. Inasmuch as organizational rivalry plays such an important role in teacher militancy, it would be unrealistic to consider the dynamics of teacher militancy without serious attention to the effects of merger upon it.

In the following comments, I am going to assume that merger will take place within a few years. This assumption is based largely upon what appears to me to be the practical logic of the situation. My purpose here, however, is not to demonstrate what appears obvious to me, i.e., that the merger will take place in the next few years at most, but to call attention and scholarly inquiry into what is problematical, the conditions and consequences of merger. These are the crucial problems, not whether or when the merger will occur.

Without question, the organizational rivalry between the NEA and AFT has been an important stimulus to teacher militancy. At all levels, the two organizations and their state and local affiliates have come under much more pressure to achieve benefits than would be the case if there were only one organization. A representation election almost invariably causes the competing organizations to adopt a more militant stance in order to demonstrate their effectiveness in achieving teacher goals. For the same reason, any failure to press vigorously for teacher objectives becomes a threat to organizational survival. State and national support are poured into local elections and negotiation sessions in order to protect the interests of the state and national affiliates. Thus at the local level organizational rivalry has led to a vastly greater organizational effort to advance teacher objectives. This development is consistent with the experience of competing organizations in other fields.

The crucial importance of the NEA-AFT rivalry in stimulating teacher militancy raises the question of whether the merger of the two organizations will reduce such militancy. Probably, the merger will simultaneously encourage some tendencies toward greater teacher militancy and some toward less militancy; the overall outcome is likely to vary widely from district to district and time to time. To see why, it will be helpful to review the issues involved in merger.

Historically, two major organizational issues have divided the NEA and AFT. One was the fact that local, state, and national education associations typically permitted all-inclusive membership, i.e., these associations enrolled administrators and supervisors (hereafter referred to as "administrators" or "administrative personnel") as well as teachers. The other issue was the AFT's affiliation with the AFL-CIO. It is becoming evident, however, that these issues no longer divide the organizations as they did in the past.

In the first place, a number of teacher negotiation laws and/or state administrative agencies have settled the issue of administrator membership substantially along the lines advocated by the AFT. True, in a few other states, such as Connecticut, Washington, and Maryland, state negotiations legislation permits or even mandates the inclusion of administrative personnel in a teacher bargaining unit; but this aspect of the statutes is either ignored in practice or is creating too many practical difficulties for all parties. In any event, the Michigan experience is likely to be the predominant pattern. In that state, many superintendents withdrew from, or did not join, local associations after passage of the Michigan negotiations statute in 1965. In 1966, the Michigan Association of School Administrators withdrew from the Michigan Education Association and joined with the Michigan School Boards Association and Michigan School Business Officials to form a new organization. In 1967, the state organizations of elementary and secondary school principals pulled out of the Michigan Education Association.

It should be noted that in the collective negotiations context, administrator membership in the teacher organization (which is not the same thing as membership in the same negotiating unit as teachers) is dangerous for the school board as well as for the teacher organization. Such membership, especially if the administrative personnel are active in the teacher organization, could lead to charges of employer support or domination of the employee (teacher) organization or to other unfair labor practices. In other words, administrator membership may jeopardize both the organization's right to represent teachers and the legitimacy of the board's approach to teacher bargaining.

The Michigan pattern concerning administrative membership in teacher organizations is still a minority one in the country as a whole. Nevertheless, it is likely to prevail eventually because of the difficulties inherent in maintaining all-inclusive membership in a negotiating organization. School boards will increasingly resist situations in which personnel assigned to administrative duties are represented by an organization controlled by the teachers they administer.

At the present time the issue of administrative membership is being debated at all organizational levels. In some districts the issue is seen as pertaining only to local organizations; it is assumed that administrative personnel can and should retain membership in state and national teacher organizations. In other places it is already

46

accepted that administrative personnel cannot continue as regular members of local and state teacher organizations, but it is thought they should continue as members of NEA. Nevertheless, it is clear that even at the national level all-inclusive membership poses many sticky problems; the American Association of School Administrators, National Association of Secondary-School Principals, Department of Elementary School Principals, and Association for Supervision and Curriculum Development are some of the NEA departments already considering the need for modifying their relationships with the NEA in the near future.

The existence of these different approaches is understandable only in terms of intra-organizational perspectives. A state association leader might reluctantly accept the demise of all-inclusive membership at the local level but seek desperately to retain it at the state level. For one thing, he will naturally be unhappy at the prospect of losing dues revenue from administrators and supervisors. And if, as is often the case, such personnel play important roles in recruiting teachers to state membership, the loss of administrative personnel involves much more than the numbers of such personnel. In this situation the state association leader easily convinces himself that all-inclusive membership in the state association is still desirable. After all, he tells himself and others, the local association, not the state, is the negotiating organization. Furthermore, both teachers and administrators have a common interest in more state aid, an improved retirement system, and so on.

As plausible as these arguments are, they ignore the pressures toward separation at the state as well as at the local level. How will administrators be represented in the state association, if not through local associations? What will happen to administrators in districts too small to establish local organizations of administrators? Since the state organization will invariably support teachers in showdowns at the local level—to do otherwise would be organizational hara-kiri—how will administrators be able to work vigorously for their objectives inside the organization? How will school boards react to administrative membership in organizations supporting teachers' strikes or other militant action against the board and its representatives? Will administrators be willing to pay dues to state organizations that support teachers in militant anti-administration activities?

In their frantic efforts to maintain the status quo, some state association leaders have overlooked these hard questions relating to administrative membership in state teacher organizations.

Nevertheless, administrators are taking the initiative in withdrawing from the state associations as often as or more often than they are being excluded from them by militant teachers.

The same kind of wishful thinking characterized the outlook of NEA leaders until the recent past. For several reasons, NEA leaders did not want to adopt a position on administrative membership at local and state levels. There was concern that the exclusion of administrators from NEA would be damaging in terms of NEA membership, and again, the fear was related to administrative help in recruiting teacher members as well as to the loss of administrators per se. There was an emphasis upon the common interests of teachers and administrators at the national level, e.g., in getting more federal aid. There was also a failure to grasp the inter-dependence of local, state, and national organizations in a negotiating context.

An even more difficult problem was the tremendous regional, state, and local differences relating to negotiations. Association experience in Michigan or Massachusetts meant nothing to association leaders in Alabama or Mississippi. A membership policy *vis-à-vis* administrators that would have seemed sensible in Michigan would have horrified association members in Alabama.

The resolution of this difficult organizational problem was deceptively simple. The NEA's *Guidelines to Professional Negotiation* (1965) proposed that the inclusion of administrators in the negotiating unit and the negotiating organization be left to local option. This was not very helpful to local associations who wanted guidance on what their policy should be, but it was probably the only feasible way to avoid the issue until the pro-negotiation forces were stronger and there was a wider understanding of the problem throughout the association structure. Certainly, some NEA leaders realized from the outset of the negotiations movement that local option on administrator membership, without limits or guidelines, was a hopeless long-range policy; but a realistic policy had no chance of acceptance in the early 1960's.

A merger between the NEA and AFT will unquestionably accelerate the flight of administrative personnel from the merged organizations at all levels. First, the very fact that merger talks are taking place will confirm the feelings of many administrators that the associations are becoming "just like the union"—if not worse—and hence that administrators have no business in the association, with or without a merger. A more important point is that the AFT will demand some type of administrative exclusion as a condition of merger. Such a demand would actually make more sense from a propaganda than from a substantive point of view. The reason is that the inclusion of AFT membership in a new organization would tip the organizational balance in favor of administrative exclusion. Thus even if the exclusion of administrators were not a condition of merger, such exclusion would be organizational policy anyway within a year or two after merger. I suggest this independently of any conclusion about the desirability of excluding administrators from teacher organizations; the point is that a sincere belief in the importance of such exclusion does not necessarily justify setting it as a condition of merger.

Note that the issue here is not whether administrators have or should have the right to join teacher organizations. Most assuredly, they do have the right and will continue to have it, insofar as teachers permit it. The real issue is whether a teacher organization which includes administrators should have the legal right to represent teachers on terms and conditions of employment. Teachers and administrators have a constitutionally protected right to join the same organizations, but organizations enrolling both teachers and administrators do not have a constitutionally protected right to represent teachers in negotiations with their employers. Organizational rights to represent teachers are conditioned by law upon a number of public policy considerations. One such consideration is whether the organization can represent employees effectively. In private employment, this consideration has led to the mandatory exclusion of managerial personnel if the organization is to retain negotiating rights. The alleged differences between public and private employment, professional and non-professional employment, and between education and other fields are not likely to weaken the public policy arguments for exclusion of administrators from organizations seeking to represent teachers.

Experience in other fields strongly suggests that administrative membership in state and national teacher organizations will probably not survive collective negotiations by teachers. If such membership is to survive, which is doubtful in any case, it is essential for the NEA and its affiliates to examine the issue by some sort of high-level task force in which teachers and administrators alike could have confidence. Such a task force would have to include experts in collective negotiations and public administration who clearly had no vested interest in the outcome and who could propose a feasible structure for all-inclusive membership. Otherwise, the forced exclusion or voluntary withdrawal of administrators from state associations and the NEA will increase rapidly, and the makeshift arrangements to hold everyone together will continue to ignore important practical considerations. One comprehensive study of the problem, adequately staffed and financed, would have served better than the hasty and improvised studies that have been made thus far. In any event, no task force of the kind envisaged has been or is in prospect; since such a group might well conclude that the separation is desirable and inevitable, perhaps little has been or will be lost by the absence of such an effort.

We should recognize, however, that many of the arguments for or against separation are oversimplifications of a complex problem. Teachers and administrators do not have to be in the same organization in order to communicate and cooperate with each other. Likewise, the fact that they are in the same organization would not necessarily reduce tensions or disagreements or conflicts between them. In other words, equating all-inclusive membership with cooperation, or separate organizations with conflict, is an oversimplification. In any case, the most probable outcome is a sort of confederation of educational organizations, in which each controls its own membership, budget, and policies. There could be joint financing and support of activities commanding the support of all organizations while the organizations go their own way in areas where their views or interests clash. Obviously, we can expect such clashes in the areas of collective negotiations and teacher militancy.

The upshot seems to me to be this: Regardless of the formal membership structure of the merged organization, teachers will control the state and national organizations that merge. The emerging organizations will put great pressure on teachers to join, and we can expect a dramatic increase in teacher organizational membership at all levels. With greatly increased membership and resources—none of which are needed to fight a rival teacher organization—and without the internal constraints inherent in administrator membership or control, the new organization will probably pursue more militant policies in behalf of teacher interests and views than anything we have experienced thus far in either NEA or AFT.

I say "probably" because some aspects of merger will tend to reduce teacher militancy. Thus it is often thought that merger will reduce teacher militancy by eliminating competition between the two organizations. So long as two organizations are competing for members, there is great pressure on each to achieve significant results. With merger, this pressure, and the militancy it generates, will disappear. Interestingly enough, many leaders in both organizations, as well as experienced observers familiar with experience in other fields, share this expectation.

Undoubtedly, organizational rivalry typically results in greater organizational militancy. Even if this were not the case in other fields, it is clear that the recent sweeping changes in the NEA and its state and local affiliates would not have occurred (at least not so soon) except for the challenge of the AFT. This conclusion is not questioned, privately at least, by many NEA leaders.

Nevertheless, although organizational rivalry increases teacher militancy, it does not necessarily follow that merger will reduce such militancy, or that every aspect of merger will have this effect. For example, in many school districts, neither the local association nor the federation can afford full-time local leadership. With merger, the teachers may be able to support full-time local leadership with adequate facilities; much of the time and resources that were devoted to fighting the other teacher organization may now be directed at the school board. One of the certain consequences of merger will be a substantial increase in full-time representation of teachers and in their organizational resources, facilities, and support at all levels.

The increase in organizational capability may not fully offset the loss of dynamism inherent in two competing organizations. The crucial point, however, is that merger will not necessarily end the kind of competition and rivalry that has undergirded so much recent teacher militancy. In short, we must consider the possibility that competition *within* the merged organization will result in as much teacher militancy as competition between the present separate organizations.

I have noted that enrolling everyone in the same organization does not automatically eliminate differences or conflicts of interest among the members. In negotiations where there are rival organizations, the minority organization may criticize the results in order to persuade teachers to vote for and join the minority organization and give it a chance to become the bargaining agent. With one organization, the objective is to persuade teachers to change the leadership of the organization instead of to change their organizational affiliation. However, from the standpoint of teacher militancy, the dynamics of the situation can be much the same. In both situations, there is pressure on organizational leadership to achieve results, and there is also a leadership need to arouse teacher militancy for the same purpose.

The crucial difference between competition between two organizations and competition within a single organization relates to the capacity of those not in control of the organizational machinery to wage an effective campaign against the incumbents. To be specific, NEA publications are controlled by persons independent of AFT control, and vice versa. Thus, regardless of which organization is the bargaining agent in a given school district, there is a rival organizational apparatus not controlled by the bargaining agent. This rival apparatus constitutes a source of information, criticism, and opinion whose very existence places greater pressure on the bargaining agent to achieve every possible gain.

If, however, there is a merger and therefore only one organization, how will critics and opponents of the incumbent leadership get their views publicized? They will no longer have an official organizational publication for this purpose. They will no longer control organizational conventions, conferences, news releases, and other means of disseminating their views. As a result, the incumbent leadership comes under less pressure to achieve results, with a consequent diminution of teacher militancy.

Merger per se will tend to weaken effective capacity to oppose incumbent leadership, and such weakening will inevitably lessen teacher militancy. However, appropriate action could be taken to insure that this does not happen. The appropriate action would be the introduction of the caucus system in the merged organization. Because the long-range effects of the merger will depend on how soon and how effectively caucuses are established in the new organization, and because the existence and effectiveness of caucuses will be the major influence on teacher militancy in the merged organization, it is necessary to analyze their role in some detail.

A caucus system is essentially a system of political parties within the organization. Organization members may join a caucus, pay dues to it, attend its meetings, participate in its deliberations, and perhaps represent it in official organization proceedings. It is essential that caucuses be financed and operated independently of the organizational machinery; otherwise there is the danger that the caucus will lose its ability to function as an independent source of information, criticism, and leadership. The crucial point is that in the absence of a caucus, individual members or convention delegates are helpless before the organizational machinery. To change organizational policy or to launch a campaign to change organizational leadership, collective action is needed. First, there must be a forum not controlled by incumbent leadership in which the opposition has full opportunity to state its case and generate support. Floor fights (hopefully, only verbal ones) must be organized, fall-back positions established, and strategy coordinated. Signs, posters, and other literature may have to be printed and disseminated, and so on. These and other essentials of effective organizational leadership or influence cannot be initiated effectively by ad hoc committees or organizations, which are formed—usually over one issue—at a particular convention and then wither away. At all times there must be an organizational mechanism which can serve all the constructive purposes served by a rival organization. Such a mechanism, however, must be as independent of control by incumbent leadership as is a rival organization.

The incumbent leadership will also need a political mechanism independent of the organizational machinery. The elected officers of the organization should not be able to use organizational funds to finance their election campaign. As in most such situations, the incumbents will have certain political advantages accruing from their incumbency, but they too will have political needs which cannot legitimately be met by using official organizational machinery. It would, therefore, be erroneous to regard caucuses solely as a means for helping the "out's" clobber the "in's." Neither democracy nor militancy will flourish in the merged organization unless there exists practical means of exerting organizational influence and leadership which are not dependent upon the official organizational structure. Policies and leaders must be forged in the caucuses, and thence into the official organizational structure. If this is done, and I believe it can and must be done, we can be optimistic about the level of internal democracy in the merged organization. We can also expect a continuing high level of teacher militancy under these conditions.

Affiliation as a Merger Issue

For all practical purposes, the forthcoming merger will end teacher affiliation with the AFL-CIO. The AFT will need some face-saving concession on this issue, such as a national referendum on the question within the merged organization or local option to affiliate with the AFL-CIO; but the issue is already a dead horse for all practical reasons. The fact that AFT leaders are already proposing a referendum, knowing full well that it would be overwhelmingly defeated in the merged organization, ought to be signal enough for anyone to see. There is even reason to doubt whether such a referendum confined to the present AFT membership would support affiliation. Certainly there is very little sentiment in the AFT to insist upon affiliation at the cost of preventing merger.

Allowing local option to affiliate with the AFL-CIO might be a viable solution, since it would ease the transition problem, support the principle of local autonomy, and quickly lead to disaffiliation anyway. Affiliation with the AFL-CIO is not important to most AFT members, but it is important to some AFT leaders in some large urban centers. If local option is permitted, only a few locals will affiliate with the AFL-CIO, and the impracticalities of such a relationship will lead to their disaffiliation soon afterward. Furthermore, it is doubtful whether the AFL-CIO would find it advantageous to enroll a few teacher locals, even a few relatively large ones.

Since the teacher organizations choosing to be affiliated with the AFL-CIO would not be a rival to the merged teacher organizations, affiliation would not constitute an organizational issue as it does now. Actually, there is no constitutional reason now why an NEA local affiliate cannot affiliate with the AFL-CIO. Such affiliation would probably lead to expulsion by the NEA Executive Committee under present circumstances, but such a reaction would be overkill if there were only one teacher organization. At any rate, despite the enormous importance of the issue in the propaganda war between NEA and AFT, it is not a very important substantive issue, and it will not hold up merger as long as it takes to read this paper.

What will be the impact of disaffiliation on teacher militancy? A popular view is that AFT militancy is due to its affiliation with the AFL-CIO. This seems very questionable. Affiliation has contributed to AFT militancy, in specific communities under specific circumstances; likewise, affiliation has often been a conservative influence in many situations. The teacher stereotype of labor bosses inciting teachers to strike is far removed from the facts, as is the notion that the AFT depends largely upon the AFL-CIO or the IUD (Industrial Union Department, whose main function is recruitment) for support. The AFL-CIO did play an important role in the early stages of the AFT's drive for collective bargaining, but it is not a decisive factor now. Surely, there have been enough teacher strikes, boycotts, sanctions, and other pressures by associations in recent years to end the fallacy that affiliation with the AFL-CIO underlies or is an essential ingredient of teacher militancy. In fact, nonteacher members of the AFL-CIO at any level may view teachers' strikes more critically as parents and taxpayers than favorably as the justified efforts of fellow wage earners. Realistically, there is no strong reason to believe that disaffiliation will reduce teacher militancy in any significant way.

The major problems of merger are not philosophical or ideological; they are practical, such as who gets what job in the merged organization. The practical problems will be complicated more by the political implications of any settlement than by the equities from a strictly organizational or employment point of view. To be candid, there are enough resources to take care of everybody reasonably well. The more difficult problems will arise over the inevitable efforts by the negotiators on both sides to place their political supporters in as many of the key positions as possible. These efforts will create internal problems on each side which may be more difficult to resolve than the issues dividing the negotiators along organizational lines.

It would be naive to underestimate the importance of this problem. Beyond the broad social factors affecting teacher militancy, the quality of teacher leadership is necessarily a crucial factor in the dynamics and future of teacher militancy. For this reason, my concluding comments will relate to this matter.

The most immediate effects of merger upon leadership will be at the state level. In a number of states, federation locals dominate the large urban districts, whereas other districts are largely association-dominated. Especially where the AFT-dominated districts include greater proportions of all the teachers in the state, the impact of merger may be truly traumatic at the state level. In fact, there are states where federation members have no significant reservations about affiliation at the national level but object strenuously to state association leadership. This is especially true in states like California and Minnesota, where state association leadership—to the obvious chagrin of many NEA leaders—has vigorously opposed effective negotiation legislation.

Another point here is that the NEA's national staff is much more oriented to collective negotiations and teacher militancy than is the leadership of many state associations. Many state associations are oriented more to lobbying in the state legislature than to effective support of locals at the bargaining table. It appears that the NEA has had to establish regional field offices to assist local associations in negotiations partly because of state association slowness in responding to the negotiations movement. The state associations in Massachusetts, Michigan, New Jersey, and Rhode Island were the quickest to adapt effectively to negotiations, but in many states the local associations must still look to the NEA rather than the state association for significant help in negotiations. Indeed, this is still necessary occasionally in the states mentioned as having made the most rapid adjustment. The point is, however, that merger will sometimes change the constitutency of the state organization more than it will the national; hence changes in leadership and policy in some of the state organizations may emerge rather quickly.

At the national level, full-time leadership in the merged organization will be largely as it is now in the NEA, at least for the near future. This is not only due to the arithmetic of the situation, i.e., the NEA's much greater membership and national staff. It will also be due to the fact that most of the NEA's present leadership is negotiation-oriented. Merger, therefore, will not be seen as a threat but as a step forward toward a more militant organization. On this score, it must be conceded that changes in the NEA within the past few years, and especially since its top leadership changed in 1967, have been truly remarkable.

In the early 1960's, one New York City law firm (Kaye, Scholer, Fierman, Hays, and Handler) provided the national leadership and the expertise which saved the NEA and its affiliates from organizational catastrophe in its competition with the AFT. It is a little known but singular fact that a New York City law firm, which ordinarily represents management in its labor practice, negotiated the first association agreements, trained the association staff, and guided the NEA to an acceptance of, and commitment to, collective negotiations. Ironically, corporation lawyers succeeded in convincing NEA leadership (correctly, it appears) that the NEA had to cease rejecting collective negotiations and demonstrate its determination to negotiate better agreements for teachers than those negotiated by the AFT. As this view prevailed, those who supported it became more influential in the NEA; today, NEA leadership is clearly committed to collective negotiations and includes a capability in this area which is not inferior to the federation's.

Without getting into personalities, therefore, it seems to me that one of the most encouraging aspects of the present situation is the tremendous improvement in the quality of teacher leadership and in the likelihood that merger will strengthen the tendencies in this direction. If this is the case, teacher militancy will continue to increase and will be increasingly devoted to constructive public policy as well as teacher objectives.

Part Two

The Practitioners

Those who practice the art of collective negotiations are involved in what is at once both a stimulating and frustrating occupation, their successes and failures being, respectively, sweet and bitter as circumstances dictate. Negotiators serve as "power brokers," representing as they do the various sub-systems of the educational power structure. These sub-systems can be identified as follows: 1) the organized teachers; 2) the school board; 3) the administration; 4) the community. While tradition holds that the school board represents the community, practice has established boards of education as independent centers of power.

Part Two as a whole is designed to give the reader an initial perspective on disparate viewpoints held by the parties to collective negotiations, and to demonstrate some of the results of these viewpoints through the presentation of case analyses. It is composed of three sets of articles. Section A sets forth the teacher-employee viewpoint. Section B is devoted to the viewpoint of management, here defined as including both administration and school boards. Section C is composed of four case analyses descriptive of the state of negotiations around the country.

Teachers View Negotiations

Teachers, as association and union members, constitute one party to the all-too-often adversary or "zero-sum" relationship that has developed in public education.* The ideology of teachers turns upon three major points: 1) teachers are professional persons, and as such know what is best for the schools; 2) teachers have the best interests of children at heart; 3) teachers are entitled to a bigger share of the economic "pie." There are numerous variations on these themes, but most teacher arguments, voiced by their paid representatives, or "teacher administrators," turn on these points.

In the first article Cogan describes the developments and successes of the American Federation of Teachers during the past decade. He discusses the More Effective Schools Program, stressing the Union's interest in "professional as opposed to traditional economic aspirations." Herndon describes the changing attitudes of teachers toward questions of decisional control in education, from the point of view of an official of the National Education Association, and points out some of the realities—as opposed to the mythology—of collective negotiations between teacher-employees and management.

Pindara describes the development of collective bargaining in the Canadian provinces and suggests the presence of an "evolutionary ladder" in negotiations, beginning with right to petition and ultimating in true collective bargaining. His statements serve as possible descriptors of the American situation within the next decade. Shanker analyzes the concept of "professionalism" and cites points of union-management disagreement.

---

* For a thoughtful explanation of "zero-sum" vs. "variable sum" games, see Richard E. Walton and Robert B. McKersie, *A Behavioral Theory of Labor Negotiations* (New York: McGraw-Hill Book Co., 1965).

The American Federation of Teachers—Force for Change

Charles Cogen

We have been on the verge of a revolution in teacher-administrator-school board relations. That revolution climaxed in recent years in New York City. This great breakthrough brought the revolution to a head—a revolution of teachers demanding and *getting* not only equality of bargaining across the table, but other benefits right down the line. These were things they had never dreamed of before, like class size and control sharing. The revolution in this situation was initiated and the breakthrough came in New York City. That revolution has taken the format not only of a content breakthrough in regard to what the teachers are getting, but also a breakthrough in the bargaining *procedures*.

There were several factors that helped to bring about this revolution. We have the factor of a greater proportion of men coming into the profession in recent years. Men are a little more militant than women, who somehow have the habit of taking things on the chin. Also, the great lag in conditions of work and fringe benefits that teachers were suffering in comparison to industrial workers, who had made great gains over the years. Since the New Deal put the National Labor Relations Act on the books, sooner or later teachers had to get wise to themselves. In addition, you have the tremendous demands for improvement in the slums and ghetto areas. The terrible conditions there, and the difficulty that was created in teaching under such circumstances, helped bring about greater teacher militancy. It was impossible for teachers to get any satisfaction out of the job.

There was, as a result, a great increase in demands for a change in the situation. But it was not until the New York local went out on strike that we got collective bargaining. Until then the Board of Education was playing around with us and saying that no one knew whether it was legal. The strike convinced them that it *was* legal, so we began collective bargaining and arrived at a milestone in education—the collective bargaining agreement between the United

Reprinted from Harold I. Goodwin and Patrick W. Carlton (Eds.), *Above the Salt: Militancy in Education* (Morgantown: West Virginia University Press, 1968). Mr. Cogan was formerly President of The American Federation of Teachers, AFL-CIO.

Federation of Teachers, our local, and the Board of Education. That contract became a model for teachers throughout the country. The mood of militancy and the demand for collective bargaining and conditions of work that you could live under with dignity and self-respect was achieved.

I have given a little background of how we became a force for change, and some of the fundamental changes that have come about as a result of what was done in New York and other areas. The American Federation of Teachers locals are now the elected collective bargaining representatives in practically every large city in the country and in a number of smaller communities.

Another of the changes, interestingly enough, is that brought about in the National Education Association. The National Education Association has been revolutionized in its attitude toward collective bargaining and strikes. When we had our first election in New York City we were by far the underdog in the situation, having a very small membership. The National Education Association came before the teachers at that time saying that it is unprofessional to belong to a union, that unionism leads to strikes, and it is against the interests of the teachers, the community, and the children for teachers to strike. Therefore, according to the National Education Association, teachers must vote against the union. On the contrary, we in the union had a long list of useful demands, perhaps as many as 150. To everybody's surprise, including ours, we won that election by a vote of 2 to 1.

Let us consider the various contracts that we negotiated in New York, and elsewhere. I will mention, in sort of outline form, some of the things that have developed. Great improvements in salaries—take that for granted for I do not place salaries first. You have fringe benefits, for example, such as insurance, welfare, improved sick leave, improved sabbatical leave and what not. You also have working condition improvements such as the elimination of non-teaching chores, providing for duty-free lunch periods—that inhuman and totally undignified situation where elementary school teachers were required to perform supervisory duties in the lunch room. We have had improvements in tenure laws. We have had the strengthening of academic freedom in many respects. As a result, we brought about grievance machinery which includes impartial third party arbitration.

There is the area of educational policies—the "gray area." I suppose some of them are even beyond the "gray area." They are things one would say do not belong to teachers at all. Let me name a few of them. First, there is class size, which has already been mentioned. Is it a working condition or an education policy? It is a little bit of each, I suppose. Second, we have bargained in several cities on the question of integration of textbooks. Those of you who are familiar with history books know, and those of you who are familiar with problems pertaining to the Negro know, that our textbooks until very recent years have been propagating sheer falsehoods about the Negro. There have been falsehoods through various statements in regard to their activities. There have also been falsehoods by the omission of African history, including its very rich cultural activities.

We also have discipline treated in some of our contracts. The Detroit contract, for example, specifies not only what teachers have to do to keep the children quiet and well-behaved, but what the administration has to do. You know what the usual thing is. If you have a troublesome child or children you are told by the supervisor that it is all your fault. You do not know how to teach. In the first place you do not know how to motivate. If you motivate, kids will be interested. You are told that every child wants to learn. So in the Detroit contract there are specified provisions for the duties and responsibilities of the teachers and of the administration in regard to disciplining youngsters. It spelled out what the administration *must* do in order to participate and assist the teacher in the disciplining of a hard-core problem. This is certainly an educational policy area into which we have entered, and this has spread.

There is the matter of curriculum, too. I have mentioned textbooks. There are many other curriculum areas that we have entered into, for example, the teaching of what is now called Afro-American history. The history of the Negro both here and in Africa has been one of our concerns. This is spreading. I know of several classes teaching that subject in New York City. This movement is taking place in other cities and the AFT has been a great influence in bringing that about.

And finally, I think that we have had a tremendous impact on the whole teaching-learning process. I will mention only very briefly something I hope you have heard about, namely, the More Effective Schools Program. We initiated this while I was still in the New York City local as president. The program offers a total approach to the educational process, not a little gimmick here and a little gimmick there. The More Effective Schools Program is not just compensatory education as we generally understand it, but a *total* program. I am not going into details, but just imagine anything that you think is necessary to bring about good education of the particularly underpriviledged, and that was included in the More Effective Schools Program.

After some resistance on the part of the die-hard Board of Education, the Superintendent and the Board of Education agreed that we should all sit down together—representatives of the AFT, the supervisors, and the Board of Education—and map out this More Effective Schools Program based upon the union's proposal. To the credit of the Board of Education, it must be said that they recognized this initiation of the American Federation of Teachers by adopting the name of the program. We are now pushing that program throughout the country. We have a man whose heart and soul is in this program. As the chairman of the National Committee on Effective Schools he has been traveling all over the country for the past couple of years speaking with superintendents, boards of education, state legislators, and community groups. After we get through with our disadvantaged areas we can use the same idea in our more priviledged areas because they, too, can stand some improvement.

These have been some examples of the educational policies in which we have had a great share as a force for change. But I would add change in teacher-administrator relationships. There was a time, as you know, when all decisions were made unilaterally. The teacher came, hat-in-hand, to the board and might or might not be permitted to speak for five or ten minutes. When he was through, just as somebody said today, the board said thank you for your contributions. Then behind closed doors, they made their decisions. Likewise, on the lower levels within the school systems and within individual schools, decisions were made unilaterally by the principal.

Now we have changed all that. We started out in New York City with a provision, for example, that the superintendent of schools is mandated to have monthly conferences on policy matters with representatives of the union. I have not kept up on that sufficiently, but from what I read in the papers and union publications, these monthly conferences have become more or less permanent ones. And on the school level, the principal is mandated in the contract to have a conference at least once a month with the representatives of the union chapter in the school. They have to be real give-and-take conferences, not just one of these listen-and-goodby sort of things. There has been a real revolution, and we have been the force for change.

There have been tremendous changes outside the school system—changes in the multiplicity of social problems that we face in our nation. These problems seem superficially related to the business of the teacher or superintendent, but really, when you come down to it, nothing influences the education of our children more than what the teacher does in the classroom. Among these are: extreme poverty; slum conditions; and joblessness, particularly among the adolescents who roam the streets with nothing to do and who are open to natural temptation of delinquency and criminal activities. There are also problems in regard to segregation and racism.

All these problems are ones in which the American Federation of Teachers and its locals have had very deep and active concerns, as indicated by our freedom schools in southern communities where the schools were shut down by the white citizen councils.

But mainly I would say that we have made our contribution through our affiliation with the labor movement, the AFL/CIO, for which we have been attacked from various sources. As President Johnson has said on several occasions, "The one organization that has contributed most to the improvement of the conditions of the common man in our country, not only of union men but of all the common people in the country, has been the AFL/CIO." We are very proud to have that affiliation and to be able to work with them to bring about these improvements. In conclusion, I think it is quite obvious, or should be, that the American Federation of Teachers and their various local and state affiliate bodies have certainly been a most vital and significant force for change.

The Future of Negotiations for Teachers

Terry Herndon

Teacher negotiations is inseparable from the modern day phenomenon of a new kind of teacher organization. Teachers are saying things and doing things they have not said or done heretofore. They are deploying themselves to new objectives that in the past have been pretty much neglected. It is difficult to talk about teacher objectives without talking about teacher militancy and work

Reprinted from Harold I. Goodwin and Patrick W. Carlton (Eds.) *Above the Salt: Militancy in Education* (Morgantown: West Virginia University Press, 1968.) Mr. Herndon is Assistant Director, Division of Urban and Field Services, of The National Education Association.

stoppages—strikes of one kind or another. It is even more difficult to sort them out and see what are causes and what are effects and what are produced by the same forces. I do not suppose I will be able to do that, so we will consider them as not separable.

The most significant thing taking place in many school districts where there is some experience with negotiations is a maturation in relationships. The relationship between the union or the association in the respective school districts is maturing. We can see growth in these relationships as we look at those districts that have had several consecutive years of experience. It is in looking at such relationships that we can more clearly assess what the future is going to be in negotiations.

One thing that *cannot* be overlooked: there will be no reprieve in the aggressive behavior of teachers. Teachers will intensify what has been known as "teacher militancy"—their aggressive efforts in negotiations. They are going to bring forth *more* intensive demands than they have in the past. We find much written about the race riots and various revolutions. One of the things the writers seem to agree on is that people who have arrived at the *brink of hope* are the most aggressive, most militant, and most effectively organized for mass action. This seems to be the case with teachers today. They are working in a new situation in which they have greater opportunity. They are in a culture with unprecedented affluence. They will become *more* militant in their drive to have greater control of their own professional destinies. And they will become *more* militant and *more* aggressive in asserting their *right* to have some full measure of partnership in deciding upon the new directions and revisions of educational planning. This is a fact of life with which we have to live.

There are probably some who will say, "It is different where I come from." When I go out to work with teacher locals, I always know that I am in trouble when the teacher organization starts telling me how it is different in their particular case. I think of the many occasions where this has been said; and yet we find in reality it was not different at all. Somebody had a grossly distorted perception of reality. The leadership in Kentucky said, "What is all this talk about collective bargaining and negotiations and strikes? We do not have this problem here!" One month later they tried to open schools and found they did not open in one county. A month after that they found them closed again in Pike County.

Even more prevalent than among teacher leaders, we find it among superintendents and board members. When I call upon a school system in Texas or Oklahoma or Iowa, I get invited first of all to the superintendent's office and advised that "Things are different here. Our teachers are happy. We think there will be professional negotiations someday and I will point out to the teachers when the time is right. It all depends upon patience and tolerance. *You* have a major responsibility today because if you can go away causing our Board of Education to fall in love with teachers, it will hasten the right time for professional negotiations." This is *not* reality!

The realities, I think, are quite simple. They can be perceived as we look at this maturing relationship of which I spoke. The over-riding trend seems to be some measure of peace or coexistence followed by a period of adjustment that is very traumatic and frequently resulting in disruption of the school operation. But generally this is followed by a new kind of coexistence and a new kind of peace which I think is more productive than the former. We move from peace to discord to peace. It appears that identification of this pattern could help by short-circuiting it. We may be able to arrive at what the future holds in negotiations without going through the turmoil and the trauma of the discord.

One of the things that seems to be happening is an emergence of a new kind of leadership pattern. You are all familiar with the tradition of public education. There was active support for, or acquiescence in, the notion that the administrator was the educational leader. The superintendent was the leader of the district; the principal was the leader of the school, etc. This no longer exists. People are coming pragmatically to accept the fact that teachers, like everybody else, will appoint, designate, or elect their own leadership. This is not to say that there are not some administrators who have performed admirably in the leadership role. But teachers are *demanding* that *teachers* articulate the point of view of teachers. I think this will find wider acceptance. It will become a new part of the educational scene.

There is a growing understanding that, as power positions are balanced, conflict becomes rather inevitable. We used to talk about one happy family—about everybody being on the same side. One of the dimensions of the future of teacher-board relationships will be the recognition of the fact that in a family where people speak from positions of relatively equal authority or equal power, conflict is nearly inevitable. It is far more sophisticated to recognize this, and to provide an orderly means for dealing with conflict, than it is to pretend there is no conflict. A quiet family is one in which at least one party is being suppressed rather than speaking as it would like to speak.

One dimension related to impasse resolution is the whole matter of grievance processing. They cannot be separated. Grievance processing is no longer feared, but is accepted as meritorious. We know that problems exist. The whole spirit of negotiations is to get problems out of the teacher's lounge and onto the table where they can be dealt with and provided for. Procedural agreements are being drawn to provide for expedient resolution of dissatisfactions and frustrations. We are shortening grievance procedures. We are providing more absolute protection for the teacher alleging to have been wronged. We are finding a much higher frequency of binding arbitration as the final step in the machinery. This offends some boards of education, but it does provide an orderly method for dealing with conflict. We are finding it is more satisfactory to solve problems than it is to allege victory. It is more important to deal with the conflict and to manage it than it is to decide who won.

We find less talk about board prerogatives and administrative needs and demands. We find that there is great expansion in the scope of negotiations. I find in situations where there is conflict that the board of education or the administration says, "No, we do not want to talk about that." In one recent strike five hours were spent deciding whether or not two simple items should be placed on the negotiations agenda. Of course, they ultimately were. There is less concern about what I refer to as the "divine right" of boards of education to rule. I think that is *basically* what the conflict is all about. Boards are saying, "We will rule. We are autonomous. We have powers vested in us by the legislature which we will not compromise." But teachers are saying that "divine right" does not exist. This is the basic conflict. Conflict will not be resolved until an effective dialogue replaces the defensive posture taken by those who protect the status quo.

So I see wider acceptance of negotiations as a part of the future. There are those referred to as "harbingers of doom" who talk about the terrible consequences of teacher negotiations. But as we move through the trauma of the discord to the bliss of a new, more productive interaction, we find that contracts have been written which provide for an expanded scope of negotiations. They provide for building-level negotiations to solve those kinds of problems. They provide for joint committees to study and make recommendations regarding those provisions that have long-range and complex implications for district managements.

What does this say about the future. In many places there will be a more intense trauma because I find that teachers, boards of education, and school administrators are very slow learners. They do not like to learn vicariously. The typical position is that it will not happen here—it is different here. Inevitably we find that it is not so. So we must learn directly. A board of education very recently told me that *everything* in the contract must be qualified to provide for the best interests of the school district. Who will determine the best interests of the school district. The board of education, naturally, since they are elected by the people to do so. This is inviting trouble. This kind of board resistance to the process of effective dialog with employees, and to the formulation of policy, is an invitation for conflict. For example, after three weeks of strike a board continued to hold to the position that it *would not* negotiate under the threat of a strike. It *could not* negotiate under the threat of a strike. But it *did* negotiate—in secret. The negotiations took place in the back room of a roadhouse. There was a problem that both parties had an interest in solving and that mandated some negotiations.

We find boards in many places taking the position that negotiations are not legal. When enough pressure is applied, it becomes legal. A board recently told us it was not legal to submit grievances to binding arbitration. In the face of my very cursory brief, and I am not an attorney, they conceded, publically, that they took their position only because they did not want to submit grievances to arbitration. This is a position with little integrity. It is a perfectly honorable position to say, no. It is a perfectly honorable position to say, maybe. But to hide behind a law that does not exist is to invite conflict.

The worst mistake administrators make, because they will not learn vicariously, is to suggest throughout the negotiations that they have more valid insights into teacher aspirations and objectives than the elected leadership. Invariably in the first round of negotiations you have such responses as: "Do all the teachers feel that way?" "I do not think the teachers feel that way." "I had a phone call the other night." or "I met with four teachers over here the other day." The Board constantly challenges the elected leadership of teachers. When peace returns, when the conflict and the hostilities are over, there generally is acceptance of the fact that elected teacher leadership does truly speak for the majority of the teachers.

What, then, do I see in the future of negotiations. First, a much improved economic status for teachers because there will be hostility and there will be conflict until that comes about. Teaching must become economically desirable—not economically competitive—but economically desirable. Teachers have embarked on that course. They will be satisfied with nothing less. Second, there will be an expanded scope for negotiations. I see this in many places already. If there is a problem, if there is a frustration, if there is an aggravation, we must deal with it. Perhaps the answer will not be affirmative, but we must discuss it and explain why the answer is such. We *do not* strike it off the list and remove it from consideration.

I see in many places where negotiations are successful that boards of education no longer say the answer is negative. In the face of a demand for rigid class size, perhaps the response would be, "This causes problems X, Y, and Z in the administration of the schools. Is there any way we can satisfy the teachers' problem and accommodate our problem at the same time?" Through an effective dialog it becomes possible to work out a compromise position on this demand. The future will be marked by altered power positions. Teachers used to engage in "collective begging." The board of education's position was rather well known and it was here that the teachers did all that they could via begging. That will not be a characteristic of the future. Collective bargaining is distinctly different from the collective begging that has characterized public education.

Further, there will be a sharp definition of leadership and authority. Our tradition has been to confuse them. Principals are saying that we are restricting their opportunity for leadership. I see no way this can be done. We are restricting their *authority* and thus creating a situation where they must rely more heavily upon *leadership*. They have confused their roles, authority, and leadership. They have talked about leadership in the past in terms of going to the teachers' lounge and finding out who is on bus duty. This was leadership because it solved the problems as to who supervised the bus. When they can no longer do that; when they must rely upon influence and persuasion to get the task done, then they will exercise true leadership. Yet they say that we have restricted their leadership capacities. This is not so, and I think in the future we will understand that there is a difference between authority and leadership. Authority *will be* restricted. The opportunity for leadership that emerges from a situation because of a person's ability to help a group achieve its goals will not, and cannot be, restricted via a written document.

Unfortunately, as I look ahead, I see some separation in the professional organization between teachers and administrators. For purposes of negotiations or collective bargaining, teachers will be an entity unto themselves. Teachers will speak for teachers. The principals' point of view will reflect the management perspective.

They will be the adversary of the teachers in the negotiations process. One important difference between my feelings and those that are often articulated is that I do not believe this is the death knell for a united, comprehensive, and professional organization. I think that future negotiations will open more doors than they close. There is more effective interaction. Problems that arise are being solved. Contracts will continue to include restrictive language to prohibit those practices that have been offensive to teachers. What they do mean is that movement away from the rigid restrictions of the contract will be *bilaterally* agreed to, not that there will be no restrictions.

I think that local negotiations will begin to interact more dynamically with state-wide legislation. I don't feel that state-wide negotiations will supplant local negotiations. But I do know that in Michigan the results of negotiations are creating needs and pressures that are going to force the legislature to take certain kinds of action. Uniformity of practice across the face of Michigan will bring about more pressures upon recalcitrant districts to fall in line or to go out of business for want of personnel. There will be an influence here to greater uniformity in work practices across states, and even across the nation. Like national testing programs, the foundation programs, and other kinds of nationalizing influences, I look for negotiations to be one of these. Because of the role that the state associations, the national association, and the Federation play, there will be a more uniform demand coming from teacher organizations across the country.

Negotiations in Canada:
Implications for the American Scene

Wally Pindara

In Canada we have never had an opportunity to sit down to talk about negotiations for teachers and school boards. Our situation up

Revised from Harold I. Goodwin and Patrick W. Carlton, *Above the Salt: Militancy in Education* (Morgantown: West Virginia University Press, 1968.) Mr. Pindara is Field Representative for the Manitoba Teachers Society, Canada.

there, like Topsy, just grew. Many developments arose out of a pragmatic approach, discarding things that did not work and using things that did work.

The determination of salaries, working conditions, and other decisions influencing education may be achieved by one of two means—unilaterally or mutually. Unilateral determination may be either by the employer or by the employee. This does not exist much anymore. The second method is mutual or joint determination involving two parties. This means of negotiations may be achieved through one of two ways—through individual bargaining or collective bargaining. Individual bargaining is rather unrealistic in public education. That leaves collective bargaining.

Collective bargaining is the process for determining salaries, working conditions, or any other matter to the mutual satisfaction or agreement of the two parties concerned. It is a mechanism used to minimize or resolve the differences between two positions. Bargaining is collective since the determination is for and by a *group* of individuals who are united so as to provide the strength necessary to conclude a bargain. The process might be called the art of friendly persuasion. The techniques of the process are essentially pragmatic. No one technique works in all cases. People must develop the techniques that meet their needs and work for them. It would be presumptious for me to tell you that if you do *x, y* is what *might* happen. But the techniques you must develop yourself.

In our organization we define a "teacher" as one who may be in a classroom or may also have a responsibility for some supervision, or who may happen to be an administrator. The only group of people that our organization does *not* include are the superintendents who seem to be somewhere out in left field. They are not sure where they stand. It is a problem for them, and it is a problem for the teachers.

At any rate, the teachers in Canada believe in collective bargaining. We are opposed to a "cap-in-hand" relationship with our boards of education. We are opposed to a paternalistic approach or attitude on the part of the boards. But I have run into many examples where such an attitude prevails. I speak of the attitude, "Why are you concerned? We will do the best we can for you. Haven't we always been good to you?" There is no case that I know of in our country in which a board of education has given something to the teachers on a platter and said, "You have done a fine job. You deserve a 10 per cent increase in salary. The working conditions are a little grim in this situation. We will clear it up by doing this." I have not seen it happen.

As teachers we believe we have the right to participate in the determination of our salaries and working conditions. We are selling a service, and we must participate in determining the price of this service, and the conditions under which this service can best be rendered. This is *our* decision. We want to participate in determining the conditions under which we feel we can give the best service to the students. As such, we believe that we must meet and discuss and negotiate with our employers, boards of education, and not some intermediary group. Our position over the years has been this: We want to talk to the organ grinder and not the monkey. This belief requires a similar belief on the part of the other party. This is where we run into difficulty. The extent to which the other party has accepted this belief in Canada varies. But before looking at the situation in Canada, there are two other points that I would like to discuss with you.

The General Secretary of the British Columbia Teacher Federation has suggested the thesis that there is an evolutionary ladder a teacher organization must climb in seeking to represent effectively the interest of its members. The rungs of the ladder are: The right to petition, the right to consultation, the right to negotiations, and the right to collective bargaining.

The first step in the ladder towards true collective bargaining is petition. This is a one-sided decision in which the teachers present their case and then wait and wait for a unilateral decision to be made by the board of education. The second rung is again a one-sided decision—consultation. Here the teachers present their case, the board of education consults with the teachers, asks for suggestions or reactions, and then says, "We will call you, don't call us." They then make a unilateral decision. These two rungs have been often referred to as "collective begging." The third rung in the ladder is negotiation. Here the two parties get together and by negotiation try to come up with the best solution but in the end the teacher group accepts what is being offered. The last step is collective bargaining, a two-sided decision-making process in which your case is presented and negotiated. *But in addition you have the ability to apply pressure for a better deal if you are not satisfied.* These stages may evolve over a period of time.

I suggest that some of these steps are being short-circuited. A jump from the bottom rung to the top rung is possible when a teacher group is prepared to force the issue. It involves the use of pressure and requires unity, strength, and determination. I would suggest that such a jump was made by the New York teachers in

1962. They wanted an equal voice in what was happening in education in the determination of the conditions under which they worked, and the salaries they received. A jump is now being made in British Columbia. Civil servants have taken strike action for the right to bargain collectively. The rallying cry for unity and bargaining and power and strength is not money. It is the principle of collective negotiations that is involved.

Now we come to the top rung—true collective bargaining. What conditions are necessary for it to exist? I would like to suggest six conditions necessary for true collective bargaining. The first condition is the right of association or the right of individuals to join or form their own organization. The second is the right to determine the bargaining unit and certification of *one* agent for it. Third is the implementation of the bargain into a written collective agreement which is broad in scope. Fourth is the need for a formal structure of procedures. This structure of procedures may be either in statute or may be traditionally determined. Fifth is the need for a conciliation and/or mediation provision to assist the parties if agreement cannot be reached.

Lastly, we need provision for a method of resolution of disputes. Sometimes our thinking about collective bargaining is not focused on the *process* but on this one and last condition, the provision for the settlement of disputes. I am willing to bet that if you talk to people on the street and ask them what they think about collective bargaining, they will either be for strikes or against strikes. This is the equation collective bargaining so often means. Either you strike or you do not strike. But we have to distinguish between the process and the last step, albeit we do not use it very often and should not use it very often. If this process is overused its force and effectiveness is diminished.

What is the story in Canada? To see our situation we must look at the British North American Act, which is our Constitution in which the exclusive right to bargain in the field of education was given to the provinces.

In Canada in recent years, the federal government has become more and more financially involved in post-secondary vocational and manpower education so that they do have a voice. The provinces in turn delegated much of their responsibility for education to school boards at local levels of government. Though the costs of education are shared by the provinces and the local boards, and it varies from about 50 per cent in some cases to 100 per cent in the case of other provinces, the responsibility for education, including the hiring and firing of teachers, rests with the local boards. In the past couple of years where financial responsibility has been removed entirely from local boards and assumed by the provincial governments, this general responsibility of education at the local level tends to exist in name only.

Teacher organizations began to take shape in Canada before World War I on a provincial or a local base. In the case of my own province, the Manitoba Teachers Federation was formed in 1919 with a total membership of 60 teachers. It became the Manitoba Teachers Society in 1942 and membership was compulsory or automatic. The early years in the life of the teacher organizations across the country saw some accomplishments although a good portion of the efforts were devoted to just staying alive as organizations. It was not until the depression years when the economic struggle to survive became paramount that teachers first grew more aggressive and better organized in their attempts to strengthen their organizations. In 1935 a significant breakthrough was made by the Saskatchewan teachers when the government legislated compulsory membership for the Saskatchewan Teachers Federation. Now we had two organizations in the country with 100 per cent membership. This provided the solid base for later efforts seeking to improve the welfare of the teachers. With the example of Saskatchewan and Alberta, the other provincial organizations followed suit. Between 1942 and 1944 Manitoba, New Brunswick, and Ontario obtained statutory membership. The other provinces obtained their legislation in the late 1940's. Nova Scotia, however, did not get automatic membership until 1953.

Each province in Canada has one teacher organization in which membership is compulsory or automatic and which speaks with one voice for the teachers in the province. There is a distinction between compulsory and automatic membership. Compulsory membership means that you must belong to the organization. In automatic membership you are automatically a member as soon as you get a teaching certificate but you have the privilege of writing yourself out. This is the type of membership we have in Manitoba, and we have virtually 98 per cent of the teachers as members of our organization.

The compulsory-automatic membership feature of the provincial teacher organization has relieved the organization of the unpleasant task of soliciting membership, provided stable incomes through fees deducted at the source, and has allowed the organization to get on with the job of improving the economic lot and professional status of the teachers. Subsequently the teacher organization intensified efforts to obtain laws permitting collective bargaining on behalf of their members.

Rights to bargain collectively under the law were obtained during the late 1940's and early 1950's, but they were not obtained for *all* provinces. The eastern provinces—Newfoundland, Prince Edward Island, New Brunswick, and Nova Scotia—by and large do *not* have full collective bargaining. Newfoundland and Prince Edward Island petition and consult with the government. They are under government scales and are completely centralized. New Brunswick had local collective bargaining, but eighteen months ago the government took over education completely. The teachers are now involved with attempting to set up procedures for bargaining collectively with the provincial government. Nova Scotia has a combination of both of these. Until February 17, 1967, Quebec had some of the best legislation for bargaining rights for teachers in Canada. In 1967 the provincial government assumed full financial control over education and the teacher association is now bargaining collectively with the government. It remains to be seen how successful they will be. Ontario is a case apart. For years there was a paternalistic attitude on the part of the employing school commissions that came down from the church to the school boards. Ontario has no statutory provisions governing collective bargaining. But teachers bargain collectively at the local level and have done so for years. In Ontario procedures have been established from practice and tradition and Ontario teachers make use of sanctions as opposed to strike in the final settlement of disputes.

All four of the western provinces—Manitoba, Saskatchewan, Alberta, and British Columbia—have statutory provisions for collective bargaining. They have provisions for writing collective agreements signed by both parties. They have provisions for conciliation and/or mediation. And they have some provisions for the final settlement of disputes. But there are some differences in this last area. Manitoba is the only province in Canada where the teachers are *expressly forbidden* to strike. The last strike in Manitoba was in 1921, and it was completely unsuccessful. Alberta is the only province in Canada that *expressly has* the provision that teachers *may* strike. Two years ago there was a lot of furor over a strike. The legislation was reviewed by a commission and briefs were submitted. The government commission's recommendation was that there be no change in the legislation that governs bargaining rights for teachers in

Alberta, and especially that the teachers not be denied the right to strike. British Columbia has compulsory binding arbitration and a series of time limits. They operate under a very restrictive legislative pattern. In Saskatchewan legislation is currently being rewritten.

I believe that it is safe to say that the Western Canadian teacher organizations have the most highly developed structure for collective bargaining, both in terms of their own organization and their statutory rights, of all teacher organizations in Canada. The cooperation between the four organizations has been excellent. Over the past 10 to 20 years, these four organizations have been involved in negotiating literally thousands of collective agreements. In Manitoba alone we were negotiating 300 to 400 collective agreements a year.

At the same time that this was happening with the teachers, strong trustee organizations or boards of education organizations developed in these provinces. This is the way it should be and it must be. Successful collective bargaining cannot take place when the parties attempting to strike the bargain are not equal and respectful of each other's strength. Boards and teachers do not always see eye to eye, but there is a general recognition that the best means for resolving differences is through collective bargaining in which the two parties concerned participate in determining mutually satisfactory solutions.

Though differences exist and will continue to exist, I believe that the practices of the past and present have borne fruit and are bearing fruit as far as education in Canada is concerned. Both parties have been the winners, and the biggest winner has been the children we serve. It may be that as time passes opinion will change. Already there are some who suggest that collective bargaining is an outmoded instrument not compatible with the thinking and the events of the late 20th century. They may be right, but as far as I am concerned, there has been advanced no substitute I am prepared to trade for collective bargaining. You cannot turn back the hands of time. To have any system work effectively, the people involved in the system must have a voice. That voice has been supplied and will continue to be supplied through the process of collective bargaining. We may have many battles to fight. For the present, I have made up my mind; the teachers in Canada have for the most part made up their minds. We believe in collective bargaining.

I would like to conclude by a simple statement. I don't recall where it came from but I think it is very apropos: "Professional employees, and that includes teachers, are treated collectively. The only choice they have is whether it will be with or without representation."

The Future of Teacher Involvement
in Educational Decision Making

Albert Shanker

Before we can speak with understanding about the future of teachers' involvement in education and their role in it, we must first understand the past experience of this group. It is a group that is large, that works in a very important public sector, but that has been to date relatively powerless. It has generally had little voice in the economic, in the political, or in the professional matters that concern it. Now conferences across the country have certified that teachers, like other second-class citizens and members of minority groups, are starting to stir. As a result there have already been some changes in the power relationships that exist within the school system, within municipalities, and within states. Some administrators who have exercised exclusively certain types of power are now compelled to share it with teachers; they find the adjustment uncomfortable.

The nature of the teachers' involvement in the future will be in the large measure an extension of present developments. Several of these are important. First, we must emphasize that teachers for the first time are openly, actively, and unashamedly becoming involved in determining their own economic destiny. The public expresses no surprise or shock when any other group asserts its interest in the compensation it receives. But it does react when a teacher declares that teachers are interested in their salaries and welfare benefits, in the size of their classes, and in the number of hours they teach. This, the public feels, is wrong. Instead, a teacher should express concern with education, with children, with the curriculum, and with the

Reprinted from *Teachers and School Committees: Negotiations in Good Faith* (Cambridge: The New England School Development Council, September, 1967). Mr. Shanker is president, United Federation of Teachers, New York City.

American flag, and — only as an afterthought, and apologetically — then justify his interest in his own economic welfare by saying that it serves the public welfare. Teachers are a unique group in our society in that only they have had to justify a better salary on the grounds that it would serve the public welfare. For this reason, economic impact must be at the very beginning of any list of the characteristics of teacher involvement. It is not a postscript about which to apologize. Teacher involvement in the future will demonstrate the right of teachers to be as self-interested as any other group in our society.

This does not conflict with the ideal of professional service to the public. Other professionals that are well paid are presumed, therefore, to perform well. Nor do the teachers in New York City feel less professional because they have been earning higher salaries over the last five years, or because of other benefits they have acquired, such as a welfare fund that includes a dental plan, major-medical insurance, and other forms of coverage.

Teachers will also press their economic citizenship in an effort to relieve themselves of various non-teaching chores, which impede their efficiency as teachers. A trained teacher should not be required to patrol cafeterias or to place children on buses. Although factory workers are assured by New York law of a fifty-minute luncheon break, teachers have been expected either to eat in the classroom with the children or else to pass the time patrolling the cafeteria. "The right to eat" is a phrase coined some years ago as part of a campaign to obtain a duty-free lunch period.

A very important part of the future thrust of teacher involvement will be directed toward establishing in the school system objective mechanisms for assignment and promotion. At the present time, in the majority of cases there is a system composed of politics, patronage, and petty types of terror. Most teachers feel that if they are outspoken in a faculty conference, they will be much more likely to be assigned to a difficult class the next year. Again, they feel that if they object to a particular assignment, they are likely to be given further similar assignments or, alternatively, their opportunities for promotion will have been undermined. The drive to establish an objective system in which teachers are not assigned by an individual acting on the basis of favoritism or politics encounters much opposition. Opponents advance strong claims for the prerogatives of the principal in this area: They say that he is the most competent person to make appropriate assignments. However, there is no study available that demonstrates that the principal's judgment in these matters brings results that are superior to those of an objective system. The effect of morale upon a teacher's work is especially pertinent in making job assignments, for the improvement in morale that results from an objective system of assignment may far outweigh the benefits realized when a wise administrator correctly appraises the abilities of the persons he is assigning.

Teachers are also becoming more involved in the making of educational decisions. The debate over "professionalism" is a part of this. What meaning for education should be conveyed by "professionalism"? The word itself is becoming more and more a dirty word for teachers. It is a word that the administrator uses to criticize anything to which he objects. He says, "You are not being professional." He implies, "Be good; be obedient; do not rock the boat." The concept of professionalism that is practiced in most of our school systems is more appropriate to a military establishment. George Orwell has shown that the meaning of a word can be turned into its opposite. This is what has been done to "professionalism," which should describe a system in which people who have an area of competence are free to exercise decision-making power in that area—no hospital administrator, for example, tells a doctor how to perform an operation. Teachers are beginning to question in what respects the principal, who may have been a very good football coach, qualifies to observe a French lesson and then to evaluate the teacher's performance. Teachers are evidencing a growing concern about areas of competence. For example, they ask why—if they are supposed to be competent within their area—they must draw lines in a plan book, three inches by two inches for each hour of the school day, for the approval of the principal.

Thus, although school boards and administrators tell teachers to be more professional, they do not really want them to be more professional. If a teacher stood up at a faculty meeting and refused to carry out a proposal of the administration that his professional knowledge and experience showed to be in error, would this display of professional integrity be approved? Would he be rewarded or would he then find it advisable to seek another position?

In the past several years there has occurred a substantial increase in teachers' decision-making power. But this power cannot express itself through such an institution as the senate described by Sperber. This was not a senate such as our national Senate, which has real power and which must approve all legislative bills. The rather powerless advisory body described might better have been called the supreme soviet. Teachers do not want the power to be heard and then turned down; they have long been listened to and consulted. But no matter how hard teachers have argued and demonstrated and reasoned, there has always been a point at which the principal could say, "No." If they then appealed to the superintendent and the school board, the power to affirm or reject has again been in the administration. Now teachers are demanding for themselves the equivalent power of saying, "No." This power intends to ensure decision-making in consort, by working things out together. The adjustment this requires of administrators is not easily made.

As teachers exercise their new power, they must anticipate that it will create new public relations problems. Teachers are very conscious of and sensitive to publicity and public relations. Before they exercise power, the press is very good to them. It repeatedly editorializes about wonderful, dedicated teachers, in editorials that closely resemble the type one gets during "Be Kind to the Handicapped Week." But as soon as teachers start saying "No" and start exercising power, the editorials and the public relations change. Suddenly the dedicated people that worked so hard and that are so underpaid have become power hungry and are fighting against the public and against the children. Even so, there are few teachers that would change their improved position for sympathetic editorials.

Where there are questions of salaries and welfare benefits and working conditions to be decided, there are a number of ways decisions may be taken. Collective bargaining is not an abstract ideal, but the lesser of many evils. Since the 1930's, public policy has essentially proclaimed that the employer should not have exclusive rights in these areas. Nor has society accepted the proposition that employees determine all of this unilaterally. Yet another position argues that if neither employers or employees can do it, then a third party ought to be brought in to make these decisions. That system, which may be useful during a strike, has great shortcomings. Our American tradition favors letting the employees and the employer fight it out among themselves; whatever decision they reach, both parties will concur—both parties can view the results of their negotiation affirmatively.

The possibility that both parties may not be able to agree raises the matter of the strike. I believe that there is no substitute for some form of withdrawal of services, whether this means a strike, or resignations, or something else. The argument has been advanced that the strike has become relatively obsolete in private industry. I believe that the strike in the public sector is a completely different kind of weapon than in industry. A strike in the Ford Motor Company represents a substantial amount of money through unpaid salaries. The reason that teacher strikes are effective is, that most people believe that teachers are not revolutionaries who seek to undermine their government, that there must be some very substantial reasons for their actions. In this instance the strike is not an economic weapon, but an act of violent political embarrassment. Although the public may not approve the strike, it will, nevertheless, register much sympathy for the cause of the teachers. The strike is, therefore, a weapon that has been successful, a weapon for which no substitute will be found.

The issues that we have discussed to this point are descriptive of the present. What are the issues of the future likely to be? The scope of negotiations will certainly be among them.

The upcoming battlefield will be the board of education. The board will accept the idea of sitting down with teachers to discuss and negotiate matters of salary and working conditions, narrowly defined. But as soon as teacher groups assert a claim to be involved in teacher evaluation, in selection of textbooks, in curriculum, in the construction of new buildings, the boards of education will say: "That is none of your business. You are here to represent the employees and to get them higher salaries; it is our job to run the school system." One hears the criticism that teachers are insufficiently involved, but in situations in which teachers have stepped forward and asked to be involved, no school board or school administration has been willing to relinquish any part of its present responsibilities to teachers. Teachers will have to fight for this. An involvement in which the teachers have no power to implement their recommendations will quickly result in a stalemate and a confrontation between the teachers and the administration.

The increase in teacher power will mean that teachers are going to be deeply involved in solving some of the major school problems. When teachers were powerless, nobody challenged them to do something about the slum child, or the ghetto child, or the non-reading child. Now parents continually address themselves to the Teachers' Federation, and ask how it is directing its powerful organization to the solution of the problems in which they are interested. To illustrate how we have responded, let us consider what happened four years ago when the Superintendent of Schools in New York proposed a bonus for teachers in disadvantaged areas. The phrase "combat pay" was developed by myself and one of my colleagues to describe this bonus; we intended it to be pejorative because we wanted to defeat the proposal. The bonus is a device to get teachers to serve time in intolerable schools. We do not believe that merely by placing a teacher with five or more years of experience in a ghetto school we can give any more education to the children within those schools. This is not an educational solution. The Teachers' Federation appointed a committee composed of psychologists, teachers, and social workers to seek other solutions. The committee brought out what is now known as the "More Effective Schools Plan," the components of which are quite simple: It is a saturation program that ensures that teachers will have a maximum opportunity to teach and that provides help to the teacher whenever special problems arise. This is not accomplished by paying a bonus to the teacher, but by spending an additional $550 per child. We believe that this expenditure is justified. If the child does not learn how to read or write and ends up on welfare, we will spend much more money on him for the rest of his life than this. An investment of $550 more a year for four or five years at this time is preferable to sending him into the Job Corps at a cost of $2400 a year later, when the chance of success averages about twenty-five percent. This example demonstrates how teachers have assumed responsibility in this area and have come up with answers that will enable children to live useful lives within society.

Again, agreements that reduce class size and teacher load are contributing to tremendous teacher shortages. Three contracts with the Board of Education in New York City, by reducing class size and the number of teacher periods, created over eight thousand additional positions. In an effort to relieve the acute shortage of teachers, the union has suggested that the method of certifying and licensing teachers be changed. We propose an internship program that will give beginning teachers help on the job instead of assuming that, because they have amassed a certain number of college credits, they can be thrown into a classroom to sink or swim on their own. We also insist that teachers participate in the evaluation of the beginning teacher. In addition, we have proposed separate facilities for disruptive children who cannot benefit either themselves or other children or the teachers by remaining within a regular classroom. The union has committed itself to aid in reducing the shortage of teachers because it acknowledges that it could not otherwise press for reduced class size.

We feel that department chairmen and principals should be more sensitive to the needs of the classroom than to the wishes of the administration. We are proposing that department chairmen, assistant principals, and principals be elected for a specific term of office by the tenured teachers within a school. This method need not result in a less competent administrator than the present system in which favoritism and patronage determine progress in the administrative hierarchy.

Teacher organizations have to develop alliances with a variety of parental and community groups. Negotiations are in the public realm, and in that realm, the Board of Education has claimed to represent the children and the public against the teachers. We are developing in New York City, on a school by school basis, joint action programs with parents directed to specific goals. For example, Public School 66 in the Bronx was experiencing such a teacher shortage that in the event of a teacher's absence, classes had to be broken up and the students reassigned. The teachers and parents resolved to close down the school unless more teachers were assigned to it. We have met with parents and civil rights groups in each individual school, and we have agreed on the things that teachers, parents, and community groups must do, and then together we have faced the Board of Education. I submit that this partnership between parents and teachers is inevitable in every large urban area. Teachers and parents will either be hostile to each other as children continue to fail, or will unite in understanding what is wrong with the schools and what has to be done to improve them. There are real problems here that are being worked out with great effort. Teachers and parents are not used to working together, and are to some extent afraid of each other.

A vigorous teacher organization will confront the issue of uncertified teachers, whose number is very great throughout the country. In New York City at the present time, twenty thousand out of fifty-four thousand teachers are not fully certified. In forthcoming negotiations there will be for the first time a contractual clause intended to prevent the Board of Education from hiring any teachers that are not fully licensed. We have always believed that they should hire only fully-licensed teachers, but we first had to resolve the conflict within the union between certified and non-certified people. The non-certified teachers believe they should get pensions, should reach maximum salary, on the basis of the work they are doing. The teacher that took all the courses and examinations and attained the credits disagrees. This problem, internal to the teacher organization, will have the incidental consequence of raising teaching standards.

Teacher participation in bargaining and entry into the power relationship will guarantee that emphasis and priority will be given to improving classroom performance. What has resulted from the widespread lack of attention upon the classroom? Large class size has prevented the teacher from doing an adequate job, from giving sufficient individual instruction, so that a lot of children have fallen behind. After we have ruined these children, we then set up a series of extremely costly salvaging operations to undo past mistakes.

The conflict between teachers and administration that is going to take place cannot avoid some unpleasantness. But from this conflict will come great improvements within the school system. Some of the problems of our schools today result from the lack of enough conflict of the right kind in the past. People within our schools have been challenged to come up with new ideas. The result of the conflict between the union and the school board in the City of New York, for example, has produced ideas that have helped stabilize the staff within the disadvantaged schools and that have developed a creditable transfer policy.

Finally, I would like to suggest, as a teacher, what value all this has for education and for the children. When the children have left the teachers and schools behind them, they will remember more what the teacher has taught by his actions than what words have come out of his mouth. I think that the ultimate goal toward which teachers must direct their new power is to have children come out of their schools having learned that their teachers are men and women of knowledge who are not afraid, who have a personal dignity, and who deserve their respect. They may not remember the derivation of Pythagorean theorems and the names of the capitals of all the states, but the chances are that they will remember whether they had a teacher that stood on his feet or that crawled on his knees.

Section B

Educational Management:
A Redefinition of Functions

The collective negotiations movement has caused realignments in the thinking and actions of all parties to the relationship. It has served to delineate more clearly the relationship of the superintendent to teachers and school board. Whereas, prior to the development of organized teacher militancy the superintendent claimed to represent both the interests of teachers and board, it is rapidly becoming apparent that under current circumstances the superintendent is the "board's man." This is as a direct result of the pressures being applied by board and teachers.

Furthermore, the current ambiguity concerning the role of the principal is fast being resolved, with the principal accepting a management role. Principals now claim that they should be represented by the management team at the bargaining table, either through membership on the team or through regular consultation with members thereof.

Section B sets forth the thinking of various segments of the management team toward the negotiations process. Metzler discusses the role of educational management (i.e., administration and school board) in the operation and governance of school systems. He sets forth the argument that negotiations forces administrators closer to boards of education so that their role becomes more clearly managerial and subordinate in nature. Metzler differentiates between the teachers' employee relationship with the board and their professional relationship with the educational community. Jamieson places emphasis in his article upon the legal and historical prerogatives of school boards, but recognizes the necessity for and desirability of involving teachers in the decision-making process. He provides suggestions for state legislation favorable to school boards and suggests negotiatory procedures for school board members to follow.

Young discusses the teacher drive for decisional authority in matters of educational policy, pointing to this as the overriding issue in collective negotiations. He documents the potential for ill-will and divisiveness inherent in the bargaining process, drawing upon the Michigan experience for his examples. He also discusses the various roles the superintendent is necessarily called upon to play in negotiations. Epstein discusses the growing trend toward and desirability of separate negotiating units for teachers and principals, and follows with a discussion of alternative models for the involvement of principals in collective negotiations. Epstein favors the withdrawal of principals and other administrators from teacher organizations.

The Role of Management in Negotiations

John Metzler

Before beginning an analysis of the role of management in negotiations, it is necessary to determine (a) what does management do in education? and (b) who is management in education? Unfortunately, these are terms too frequently avoided. It is much more pleasant to think in terms of professionalism, professionals working together for the common good of children, professionals with one pure over-riding goal which transcends all selfish interests and conflicts, professionals who, by their very righteousness, purity and logic, will convince and explain, thereby making unnecessary the giving and following of orders and the other trappings of industrial management.

The essential question is this: Is there something so unique about education *and* those who are professionals in education that its process can function without some individual directing others, some individual coordinating the work of others? This is the work of a manager: planning, organizing, directing, coordinating and controlling.

Can this function in education be accomplished as a partnership? Both major teacher organizations insist that all educational questions be subject to negotiations by co-equals—the board on one hand and the teachers on the other. Partnerships do function in industry—two parties who own the business and have one over-riding concern—a profit. In education the partnership will not be joined to make a profit but to perform a service. Can the pressure of performing a service to society be equated with the pressure induced by the profit motive? It is doubtful.

Reprinted from Gerald Ubben, ed., *Collective Negotiation in Education,* Report of the Superintendents' Conference, University of Tennessee, 1967. By Permission. Dr. Metzler is Associate Chairman, Department of Industrial Relations, Newark College of Engineering, New Jersey.

What is the role of management in education? It is only as this role is understood and accepted that the role of management in negotiations becomes clear. The role of management—whether in education or elsewhere is to make sure that the goals of the organization are met. The educational manager both devises a set of guidelines to aid him and performs specific tasks to accomplish it.

E. Wight Bakke, Professor of Economics and Director of Labor and Management Center, Yale University, has differentiated between the employment relationship of the teacher to the board and the professional relationship of the teacher to the educational system. He points out that an employment relationship, from the employer's point of view, imposes certain organizational and managerial responsibilities and to meet them the employer must pay primary attention to the following operating principles:

(a) the principle of efficiency
(b) the principle of authority
(c) the principle of minimal cost and opportunity cost
(d) the principle of discriminating supervisory evaluation

He insists that these four principles, whether in school or elsewhere, are the "... concern of managers prior to any principles of operation concerned with satisfying the human interests or declared professional interests of the people they employ." Dr. Bakke goes on to say, "The operating of an organization, be it school or factory, is.... the result of a necessary condition for getting cooperation in the production of goods or services with limited resources that have to be allocated among many alternative uses for those resources."[1]

Robert L. Saunders, School of Education, Auburn University, states that the role of the administrator includes the following tasks: "...(1) budget making, (2) staffing, (3) administering pupil personnel, (4) administering staff personnel, and (5) planning and maintaining school plants."[2]

The outline of both the necessary guidelines and the necessary tasks begins taking form. The manager in education, following guidelines such as those of Dr. Bakke, performs the tasks itemized by

[1] E. Wight Bakke, "Teachers, School Boards and the Employment Relationship," *Employer-Employee Relations in the Public Schools,* Robert E. Doherty (ed.), New York State School of Industrial and Labor Relations, Cornell University, Ithaca, New York, January, 1967, pp. 41-59.

[2] Robert L. Saunders, "The Role of the Educational Administrator in Negotiations," a speech prepared for presentation at UCEA-UT Regional Graduate Student Seminar, University of Tennessee, April 29, 1967 (mimeographed).

Dr. Saunders. This is what the manager does. The answer to the second question becomes obvious. It is only necessary to ask, "Who does this?" to answer the question, "Who is the manager in education?"

In theory and usual practice, those areas of the managerial function in education which fall within the policy-making sphere are performed by the board of education. The tasks of management which entail carrying out the policy are performed by the administrators. Management in education is, therefore, jointly performed by the administrators and the board.

It seems apparent that the pressure of teacher militancy will have the inevitable effect of forcing the board and administrators more closely together. It doesn't seem probable that the mantle of management can be assumed and removed by school administrators as circumstances make desirable. If the teachers select representatives, the administrator cannot hold a dual leadership role with the teacher selected representative. Nor does it seem probable that administrators can perform the managerial function required of them while continuing to be represented themselves by the organization which must militantly lead the teachers. The desires of the administrators, the teachers or the teacher organizations cannot control the forces released by the process of collective bargaining, nor can an exercise in semantics disguise the result.

Dr. James Kuhn, Columbia University, believes that the unilateral managerial function of the school administrator will be sharply curtailed. He says, "I would argue that to try to limit the scope of collective bargaining is useless." Kuhn points to the history of labor-management relationships in industry and says he has seen nothing that would suggest ". . . any chance of growing limits and saying 'collective bargaining will go this far and no further.' " He indicates his belief that the limits presently existing on the scope of negotiations in the private sector are related to the reluctance of unions to become involved in the managerial function rather than to the difficulty of expanding the limits in the face of a law which reads "hours, wages and working conditions."

Dr. Kuhn insists that any claim to any absolute unilateral right to manage is an empty claim and that it is impossible to separate our educational policy as something that does not affect conditions of work. I am not in agreement but he does emphasize the problems involved. He has one statement which I wish to quote in full and with which I am in total agreement:

Further, even under the best of circumstances, to maintain management's right to manage, you're going to have to have very able managers and you're going to have to be on your toes all the time. Any poor administration, any poor enforcement of the agreement, any ill-advised or poorly prepared arbitration, or poorly prepared grievance settlement, any loose supervision or hasty negotiations can result in a wider scope if the teachers want to move in that direction. Whether the administrator likes it or not, he's going to have to defend his preserve constantly.

Dr. Kuhn concludes that while there are no boundaries to the scope of negotiations, there are probably real limits because of the practicalities of what the teacher organizations want to negotiate and the problems they wish to assume or avoid.[3]

Dr. Bakke, in his article, posed the question: "Is it inevitable and is it appropriate that teachers participate through collective representatives in joint determination and administration with superintendents and school boards of the terms of their employment relationship?" He answered his own question with a simple, "Yes." However, recall that he differentiated between the employment relationship of the teacher to the board and the professional relationship of the teacher to the educational system. His answer of "Yes" clearly referred to the employment relationship, for he added later; "Whatever may be the ultimate arrangements by which . . . due weight is given to *consultation* with teachers in the development of overall educational programs and educational policy, the point on which we are now focused is how the terms of employment of teachers shall be determined."

Dr. Oscar Knade and I, in separate articles in the April, 1967 issue of *School Board Notes,* the official publication of the State Federation of District Boards of Education, New Jersey, and also in a jointly authored article, laid out a procedure by which the teachers could be guaranteed consultation on educational programs and policy, while at the same time removing these as issues to be settled by the pressure-cooker of negotiations.[4,5]

[3] James Kuhn, "The Scope of Negotiations," *Teacher-Administrator School Board Relationships,* published by Educational Research and Development Council of the Twin Cities Metropolitan Area, Inc., and the Department of Educational Administration, University of Minnesota, January, 1967, pp. 44-54.

[4] John Metzler, "A Journal of Collective Negotiations," *School Board Notes,* April, 1967, Volume 12, No. 7, pp. 32-35.

[5] Oscar Knade, "Resolving Educational Disputes Outside Negotiation," *School Board Notes,* April, 1967, Volume 12, No. 7, pp. 35-38.

The purpose was to provide a system which would permit the managerial function to be performed as efficiently as possible for the ultimate good of the educational process. The legal prerogatives of the board and of the administrators, in and of themselves, have no value except as they add to the educational process. The contribution of the teachers to the educational process is manifest. Unquestionably, their means and methods of making that contribution changes and will continue to change over the years. Collective negotiations or bargaining is going to be one of those means by which they make their contribution.

However, there is a tremendous difference between issues involved in the employment relationship and those in the professional relationship of the teacher to the educational system. Negotiations function in only one manner—by the use of pressure, whether overt or covert. The process by which two equals reach a decision is the same, regardless of whether those equals are husband and wife, father and son, Johnson and Kosygin, union and management, or teachers and boards. Visualize the old mill wheels which exerted a pressure upon each other and produced flour from wheat. Each wheel had some source of power to cause it to operate and each had some form of friction which restrained it. The grinding wheels operated against each other, resulting in a jointly produced product which differed from that which began the journey between them.

The reaching of an agreement between co-equals operates in the same fashion. A variety of forces flow through and are exerted upon each party, creating pressure which results in agreement. The pressure is the essential point, not the logic of argument nor of discussion. This is the manner by which co-equals reach agreement and there is no other way—not love nor affection, professionalism nor ethics, nor any factor other than pressure.

That which Bakke defines as the employment relationship very readily lends itself to the pressure of negotiations. It is doubtful if the professional relationship does so. Mixing and confusing the two relationships cannot but produce anguish and conflict by which the educational process may be harmed. The essential role of management in negotiations, therefore, is to make every effort possible to separate these relationships, to negotiate upon the problems of the employment relationship and to devise a means by which the demands of the teachers in the professional relationship are satisfied.

Bakke points out that this is "... going to be hammered out and choices made to meet the particular circumstances, to satisfy the kinds of people who make the decisions in particular localities, and in accord with the relative skill and power they have to make their decisions stick."

To the same point, Kuhn said, "... if some issue is very important to you, fight very hard to preserve it. When I say fight, I think you're really going to have to use some of the strong techniques and attitudes. The teachers, if they feel very strongly, and I think you're going to have to try to gauge how strongly they feel, are going to respond, probably, in very much of the same way. Get it down to a specific situation, decide whether you want the scope wide or whether you want it narrow, and then work very hard to see that you keep it where you want it."

Performing this role of management in negotiations requires a series of tasks:

(a) preparing for the organization of the teachers in the school district;
(b) preparing for the negotiating sessions;
(c) preparing for the continuing board-staff relationship within the new form.

Preparing for the organization of the teachers in the school district takes several forms. One, of course, is that of attitude. Administrators and boards alike must learn to live with the fact that their decisions will be subject to question, as will their actions. They must learn to live with the fact that demands will be pressed and that the allocation of available funds will be argued. Finally, they must learn to live with the fact that this does not necessarily work to the detriment of the educational process, it merely adds a new dimension.

Robert E. Doherty, an Associate Professor at the New York State School of Industrial and Labor Relations, Cornell University, points out that "It may be that formal bilateral determination of the conditions of employment would have a meritorious effect." He emphasizes the managerial problem that collective negotiations will add to the factors now weighed by the administrators and boards, with this statement:

> The problem is how to balance the interests of teachers, which certainly include their right to influence school policy and the conditions of their employment, with the interests of a society which is relying on the public schools, today

more heavily than ever before, to help bring about broad social improvements.[6]

Preparing for the negotiating sessions requires many considerations. One is the make-up of the negotiating team for the school management. Should it be comprised of board members, of the school administrators, or a mixture of both? One point is evident. The agreement should never be negotiated without administrators available constantly to the management negotiating team to discuss the ramifications of any demand or proposed solution which entails the tasks necessary to carry out the managerial function.

Obviously the policies established by the board must be reviewed and considered. Regardless of the issues to still be settled concerning the scope of negotiations, the following policies are almost certain to be questioned:

Salaries and Schedules	Fringe Benefits
Assignment	Extra-Curricular Duties
Rating	Working Conditions
Promotion	

The school management must constantly consider the continuing board-staff relationships, and evidently, must achieve their improvement within the collective negotiating process. When a legal solution is sought to a problem posed by the inability of the parties concerned to resolve that problem, all other efforts stop until that legal solution is achieved. It is rare, if ever, that quality education is an outcome secured by a legal solution to a board-staff problem.

The best theories of management and supervisory practice must be sought out and applied. The research accomplished by those psychologists concerned with the forces in existence between those who manage and those who are managed must become known and utilized. The school administrators must learn new skills to perform their managerial functions—skills which can no longer be based upon authoritarian assumptions. None of this is impossible, but it does require change. And change, unfortunately, is always met with resistance.

[6] Robert E. Doherty, "The Impact of Teacher Organizations Upon Setting School Policies," Reprint Series Number 193, New York State School of Industrial and Labor Relations, Cornell University, originally published in *The Clearing House*, Vol. 40, No. 9, May, 1966.

To summarize, the role of management in negotiations is this:

(a) to make every effort possible to separate the employment relationship of the teacher to the board from the professional relationship of the teacher to the educational process and

(b) to negotiate upon the problems of the employment relationship and to devise means by which the demands of the teachers in the professional relationship are satisfied.

To perform this role, management must:

(a) prepare for the organization of the teachers in the school district;

(b) prepare for the negotiating sessions, and

(c) prepare for the continuing board-staff relationship within the new structure of collective representation.

Minimizing Problems in Professional and Non-Professional Staff-Board Negotiations

Robert A. Jamieson

Many of our major problems in education today are discussed *too much* in terms of emotion and *too little* in terms of reason. This, too, is the danger inherent in teacher-board relationships. We, as boards of education, must preserve and extend our capacity for a *rational* persuasion about the most important questions facing us as we sit around the board table. In times of conflict we must avoid both *ignorant change* and *ignorant opposition* to change. When we lose our capacity to debate rationally, we also solicit disaster and lose community confidence. The world is changing rapidly and some adjustments *are* necessary. How to make those adjustments without diluting our responsibility and authority, and at the same time enhance the welfare of the children entrusted to our care is the goal we must establish. There is no question that teacher organizations

Revised from Harold I. Goodwin and Patrick W. Carlton, *Above the Salt: Militancy in Education* (Morgantown: West Virginia University Press, 1968.) Mr. Jamieson is an experienced school board member and was Vice-President of the Illinois Association of School Boards.

have moved faster than most boards have been willing to accept, and engulfed in the climate of social reform, new concepts of school administration are finding their place in the educational systems throughout our nation.

The tragedy is, like many teacher groups, we have arrived at these changing concepts without sufficient preparation and are trying to re-group for sensible and responsible action. Unfortunately, we are receiving more heat than light in the process. Many organizations we encounter use objectives the way an old man uses a lamp post—for support and not illumination.

Basic to this reasoning is the acceptance of the philosophy that the legal responsibility for the operation and the management of the public schools is vested in boards of education and this responsibility cannot be abrogated. However, in meeting this responsibility, it *is* desirable that a climate of mutual trust and dependability between the board and the staff be established and maintained, and this can be achieved best by maximum involvement of board and staff in the cooperative development and evaluation of the educational program and personnel policies.

The role of the teacher in our modern society is not an easy one. In present day-to-day operations, teachers are asked to solve problem situations over which they have little or no control. The rapid growth of school districts creates an impersonal relationship and subsequent problems of communication between teachers and decision-making personnel. Furthermore, schools have become the arena for such volatile issues as federal aid, civil rights and racial imbalance, separation of church and state, and war on poverty. Because teachers have been given little protection in this cross-current, their effectiveness has been reduced. There is academic pressure for quality education and, at the same time, an emphasis on the total education of *all* children. There are technological pressures for new math, teaching machines, television, language labs and computer programming. Finally, there are financial pressures which result from an archaic system of school financing, from demands to utilize the money available for new buildings to meet the population explosion, and from competition for the tax dollar by all governmental bodies.

Militancy of teachers is decidedly increased by the developing conflict between the two organizations representing the teachers, which both depend on dues income and large representative memberships for their power. Boards have been led to believe that contract negotiations are needed to relieve universal dissatisfaction and solve problems that exist in education. Most of us who have been involved in the day-to-day operations are aware that communication problems exist. However, throughout our land there are *many* boards which have highly satisfactory working relationships with teachers without formalized collective agreements. Efficient and effective boards have always operated in this manner. The power play by competing unions which uses boards of education as the catalyst for conflict, ridicules the fiscal responsibility and conservative attitudes of boards, and makes charges, demands and promises, many without a foundation in truth or realistic hope of accomplishment, has had a divisive effect upon the total school effort. Under these conditions immaturity has been misinterpreted as militancy and has caused serious results in the attempt to cultivate rapport between boards of education and teachers they employ. As Dr. Louis Pollak, Dean, Yale Law School, so aptly expressed it, "Whether a teacher's organization is a union or is a professional association, seems to be an important matter of mythology. The issue of whether an organization with which we deal, calls itself a union or calls itself not a union, is not of sublime importance. Whether an organization represents people who regard themselves as professionals—as I think our teachers do and should do and should be—whether an organization can properly claim to be active in a professional way for persons who are professionals—seems to me not a matter of labeling. It *is* a matter of how maturely, in fact, people behave."

Boards of education are caught in the middle in their attempt to effect mutually beneficial settlements which reduce these pressures, keep teachers relatively happy and at the same time fulfill the responsibility delegated to them by law. For those who are attempting to maintain the status quo, the battle is fierce—and for those who are attempting to influence the direction of change in this new challenge, the difficulty is our legitimate desire for discretion and flexibility in face of the desire of the teachers for certainty.

What, then, is our challenge and our role in meeting the challenge? Our challenge is to find the delicate balance between meeting the demands of teachers for more consideration in decision making and the demands of our constituents for not only educational but also social leadership. Most of us share the major objectives of teachers, and confrontation takes place only when priority must be established in relation to the funds available for their implementation. This problem of delineation is complicated, but its solution is a major answer to the conflict.

It may be difficult for some board members to accept, but the handwriting is on the wall everywhere for eventual legislation for either permissive or mandatory bargaining with public employees. Now is the time to refrain from opposing all legislation to permit collective bargaining with teachers and actively influence, institute and mold, the kind of legislation you can support. When legislation is not in the common interest, oppose it with all the forces you can muster. There are basic principles which can be applied to all legislation under consideration in many states, and for those areas where future legislation is only a matter of time. These principles should place emphasis on preserving the informal, cooperative voluntarism in local school districts, avoiding when possible intervention by outside agencies or persons, and minimizing costs in establishing and maintaining the formal relationship. It is hoped that by following these principles, school districts can evolve their own procedures without a complex, highly restrictive, formalized document which retards the desire or opportunity of some districts to develop their own relationships.

Proposed legislation should apply exclusively to teachers and boards of education and not group them with other employees; operate within the framework of the state educational agency or any agency created for this purpose other than the department of labor; cover all certificated personnel actually engaged in full-time positions which are not administrative or supervisory in nature; provide for exclusive representation by one organization; permit exclusive recognition by majority designation where no competing organization files in opposition; provide for negotiations on salaries, fringe benefits, complaint processing procedures, and related economic matters; prohibit strikes and provide penalties for non-compliance; provide mediation, fact-finding, and arbitration on non-binding recommendations; require a waiting period following passage to allow boards of education to prepare for the assumption of new responsibilities inherent in the legislation; provide a definite terminal date for salary negotiations; and finally, provide for a written agreement between the parties involved.

These items do not all meet acceptance by either group but in the desire to obtain legislation and to recognize the value and right of teachers and professional staff to be heard on matters affecting the operation of our schools, there must be some framework within which to begin the process. In discussions that follow legislation, boards of education and teacher groups must demonstrate their belief that school policies, programs, and solutions to problems can best be developed by working together in harmony and with respect for the roles of each.

Regardless of whether there is collective bargaining legislation or not, boards are responsible for creating a climate which encourages good educational experiences both for teacher and child. Management means more than authority—it means leadership. How long you will maintain your ability to manage will depend on how effectively you display courage, wisdom, vision and understanding of the feelings and aspirations of those whom you employ to carry on the affairs of the district. Keep in mind that no matter how well you execute the initial agreement, it is not a substitute for creating satisfactory relationships on a day-to-day basis, in every classroom, in every building and from the central office. Only in its exercise of sound management through human understanding does a system acquire the respect and confidence of its faculty. When we, as school board members, have an election within our school district to select the bargaining representative for the teachers, the results of that election will be determined more by the record of our performance to date than what we promise to do in the future. Keep open the lines of communication without interfering with established lines of authority. Collective bargaining is the result of a situation, not the cause of it. Tolerance and patience are the order of the day. Real bargaining only takes place after each side has had an opportunity to "explode" as a part of the preliminaries. Once this experience is out of the way the day-to-day process of resolving the agreements takes place.

I would like to be very specific and practical in outlining a procedure in the preparation for negotiations. The difference between successful negotiations and those that result in confusion and ill will on behalf of both parties often lies in the preliminary planning which precedes the bargaining sessions. Preparation is the most important aspect of collective bargaining.

If teachers have not already demanded collective negotiations, the school board should take the *initiative* and *make* teachers aware that their representatives can bring their problems to the board for discussion through recognized channels. This does not mean, however, that the board should aid and abet employee organizations or create a type of company union.

If the teachers have already demanded that the board bargain collectively, the board should listen to these demands with a sympathetic ear and maintain an attitude of reasonableness and cooperation. The board should exhibit an awareness of the problems that exist and a desire to mutually resolve these problems. School board members with the proper attitude toward employee organizations will be infinitely more successful than those who regard the employee organization as a threat to the board's authority. Board members should demonstrate a desire to be fair and reasonable. There are times when a board member will think that the teachers or their representatives are being unfair or unreasonable in their demands. This is not the time for the board to compromise its own standards, for to do so would only create more ill-feeling and justify further behavior of this nature on the part of the teachers. All parties need to take negotiation seriously and spend the necessary time to arrive at agreement.

The selection of the negotiator must be considered in any discussion of the preparatory steps in the negotiation process. There are many factors which affect the choice of negotiator, including the employee's choice and the size of the school system. The possibilities that are available include the school board as a whole, a committee of the board, the superintendent or one of his assistants, a principal, or a group, or an outside negotiator. Regardless of what group is chosen to conduct the actual negotiations, there must be unified control. One person should be placed in charge, and other members of the negotiating team should make suggestions to him and not to the opposite side. Any agreement or difference of opinion should be resolved in caucus so that the board can maintain a unified position. It is also of the utmost importance that the negotiating authority of the team be clarified so that the representatives of the teachers have confidence in the words and promises of the negotiators. It is also advisable, especially in the case of a neophyte school board, to obtain the assistance of an expert in this area even if that expert is not included on the bargaining team.

All boards need to be aware of dates which are of paramount importance if negotiations are to be conducted both properly and legally. Negotiations should be concluded on a date which will allow the school board a sufficient amount of time to issue and receive the teachers' contracts, which, in turn, must be accomplished a sufficient amount of time before the beginning of the school year. Another crucial element in the time factor is the legal procedure concerning revenues, which must be followed by the school board. The school board, being governed by the State statutes, must submit its budget during a specific period. The teacher organization will have to submit its proposals in time to allow for negotiations to take place before the school board budget is submitted. An adequate amount of time must be allocated to the negotiations themselves and sufficient time must also be allocated to preparation. Almost invariably both school administrators and organizational personnel underestimate the time needed for negotiations.

In order to insure a sufficient amount of time to meet all deadlines, an agenda should be developed. This agenda should be worked out cooperatively by the board and the teachers. It should contain a list of items presented by the teachers and a list of board demands as well as the amount of time allocated to each and the date on which it is to be discussed. The agenda must be somewhat flexible, yet firm enough to allow the negotiations to proceed at a steady pace.

The negotiating committee of the board should meet to discuss the board's proposals on anticipated issues prior to the meeting with the teachers. At these meetings, the team should identify and analyze each anticipated issue relative to cost, workability and degree of importance to the teachers. The team should then agree on its own proposals and establish a priority for each. It should also prepare counter-proposals to the teachers' demands and set forth its reasoning on every issue.

It has been suggested by some that the board decide beforehand what it considers bargainable items. It is my opinion that a board which tells its employees that it refuses to discuss certain issues will be creating an atmosphere of resentment which will destroy the relationship and result in undesirable consequences for both the board and the school system. The better approach would appear to be a willingness to discuss any and all items with the understanding by both parties that school boards are *subject to* and *controlled by* the State legislature which restricts their authority in certain areas by statute. This approach will result in a more responsible attitude on the part of the teachers and a more harmonious atmosphere in which to conduct negotiations.

Among those who have had successful experience in the collective negotiations process, it is recognized that an informal procedure for improved board-administrator-staff relationships is available and when it is used, the scope of collective negotiations may be narrowed.

Teachers have special competencies which enable them to make significant contributions to the purely educational aspects of the school. Machinery may be established where the board, the administration and the staff consult on a regular basis concerning "What is good education for the district." These sessions occur in an informal setting and can result in improved education, board-administrator-staff relationships and school-community morale, and no formalized agreement is signed.

If such a procedure is successful, the scope of collective negotiations can be reduced to specific areas primarily concerned with staff welfare—salaries, fringe benefits, the processing of grievances and a procedure to resolve an impasse.

After identifying probable issues and clarifying negotiating authority, it is necessary to collect and assemble factual data on each issue. Such data should include salaries in neighboring districts and in comparable districts across the country, costs or savings of proposed changes, the board's ability to pay, economic conditions prevalent in the neighborhood and community, agreements recently negotiated in comparable communities, working conditions in the particular school district, cost of living, the classroom and curriculum needs, etc. The negotiating team will also be interested in data pertaining to the teachers' representatives who are conducting the negotiations. What are their points of view, their arguments in the past and pressures on them? Since, very often, both the teachers and the school boards may need to have identical information, it may be feasible to conduct joint research. Such research may include sending out a questionnaire, agreeing to study other districts, etc. Such cooperative endeavors should be encouraged. This type of activity has a unifying effect and helps to reduce suspicion concerning information obtained by each party. In addition, the results obtained probably will prove to be more reliable. The chief goal is to reach an agreement, not to win an argument.

It should be strenuously emphasized that the board's negotiating team should not come to the bargaining table merely to respond. It must be prepared to *initiate* proposals of its own. The wise administrator will work with his staff and be prepared to request changes in personnel policies to strengthen the system. He will also have anticipated teacher proposals and be prepared to respond to them.

The school grounds probably is the best place to hold the negotiation meetings. Although there may be some advantage to a more neutral location, there is also less convenience, especially for people living in a smaller community. The meeting place should be equipped with adequate facilities to handle both the negotiations themselves and provide space for caucuses, i.e., a separate meeting area for the committee to use during negotiations.

It is strongly recommended that the actual negotiations take place in private rather than subjecting them to the public view. Although phrases such as "the public business must be conducted in the public eye" receive favorable response from the press, they have been found to be unworkable in a bargaining situation.

Paramount in developing policy through negotiations, the fundamental considerations of teachers, administration and board *must be* the *educational welfare of the children*. Policies regulating board-teacher-administrator relationships must be predicated upon this common interest. An atmosphere of cooperation and mutual respect will usually result when the joint efforts of all parties are focused on this objective and when reasons are given for recommendations made and for actions taken.

The grievance procedure is the core of the collective bargaining agreement. When handled properly, it is an effective safety valve in the discussion of employee problems. It is a protection not only for those in the bargaining unit but also for those on the board. For those districts which have failed to meet and confer with their teachers, the grievance procedure is a mandatory means of communication and an unique means of becoming informed about the problems of the district. The board should not seek a confrontation with teachers during the implementation of the grievance procedure. Although the board cannot abdicate its responsibility to be a source for a final decision, entering the process at an earlier stage reduces the effectiveness of the procedure and limits the scope of the authority involved.

In the area of board relationships and in the anatomy of negotiations, semantics play an important part. There is a tendency to revert to industrial bargaining terms such as management rights, protective clauses and others that do not accurately reflect relationships and further induce antagonisms. Board prerogatives are those rights, or that authority, which enable it to successfully carry out its function of managing the school system. This functional rather than legal view of board prerogatives or authority is much more acceptable to teacher groups. I believe a board has sounder arguments when it regards itself as required to exercise functions in order to fulfill its responsibilities rather than having a divine right to manage. Delineation of terms is always difficult. We must, however, be able to differentiate between educational policy and terms of employment. Without this distinction, arguments and not agreements, will occur. Seeking a middle ground requires compromise which is the essence of collective bargaining.

Credence must be given to the "third party" in the agreement—the taxpayer and citizen who is ever-vigilant to your actions. He is never at the bargaining table except through you as his representative. The teacher and the board member are only partial participants and have authority for only partial claims. The "third party," the community, is also involved in the process of policy making. George W. Brown, Superintendent at Webster Groves, Missouri, had an interesting comment. He said, "it may seem peculiar, and unfair, but the general public will only support education if it benefits their children. They do not object if it also benefits teachers, but they will not pay the bill just to benefit teachers." Some changes may be necessary to bring professional goals and community goals closer together.

Collective negotiations can be as valuable for boards as for teachers. There is an opportunity during negotiations to press for your own demands and obtain changes which have been impossible for years but are now subject to bargaining procedures. Some boards have even questioned the propriety of tenure laws. If a bargaining agent has been selected for the first time, what former practices are to be maintained and what shall be a subject for bargaining?

Morris E. Lasker, Counsel for the New Rochelle Board in his article *The Influence of Bargaining on the Quality of Education*, notes a favorable aspect of collective bargaining in addition to the improvement of teacher morale and the introduction of creative educational ideas. "The requirements that teachers through their representatives must, if they share power, share responsibilities, for making choices, imposes on the teachers and their representatives the necessity of considering the needs of the district as a whole. Collective bargaining should, and in my opinion, does force the parties to articulate a scale of values if for no other reason than the demands put forward almost inevitably exceed the resources available."

As in the grievance procedure, do not enter into direct contract negotiations. The superintendent or chief administrative officer of the district or anyone delegated by him is your agent. Again, the position of the board is weakened by participation at a level which violates sound administrative procedure. Let us make it clear, school administrators can no longer equivocate as to where they stand in relationship to their role as agents of the board. Failure to accept this responsibility should result in the early termination of their services.

I would hope we would take careful stock of our past experiences. An unfortunate experience is not pleasant, of course, but it is less pleasant if we fail to understand it and use it to improve our future relationships. In this sense, we must maintain the rapport between boards and teachers without reducing the flexibility and interaction which are necessary in a professional effort, to a staid, restrictive agreement for collective negotiations. As Mrs. Radke, past president for the NSBA remarked, "It is time for teachers to decide whether they are *calling for joint responsibility* with boards of education—or whether they are saying we have *joint concern* with boards of education, and we want our opinions to be heard and our counsel to be carefully considered before decisions are reached by the board. If it is the latter, boards can give this their support."

The Superintendent of Schools in a Collective Bargaining Milieu

Charles R. Young

It is difficult to know what tomorrow's optimum superintendent will need to be. But of one thing I am certain; whatever he is, whatever is expected of him, whatever he hopes to become will be profoundly influenced by the manner in which he comes to grips with the historic collective movement of teachers. The burden of my remarks will rest on that simple premise about this relatively new phenomenon in American education as we consider the superintendent's identity crisis. My remarks are predicated on several assumptions. They are:

1. Teacher militance will continue at an accelerated rate and intensity, and it will manifest itself in reasonably predictable patterns as it reaches all regions of the country.
2. Teachers' organizations and state statutes will obligate the educational community to use the collective bargaining model patented by the private sector of our economy.
3. The single most significant determinant of the character of the superintendency in the foreseeable future will be teacher militance and its chief instrument — collective bargaining.

Dr. Young is Superintendent of Schools in Glencoe, Illinois. Text of speech presented at the annual meeting of the Pennsylvania School Boards Association, Dec. 21, 1967.

It is now patently clear that the collective action of teachers is radically altering the social, political, and emotional climate within which schools operate, and as a result the superintendent's role is undergoing major redefinition. Easily among the most crucial questions before today's boards of education is whether or not their superintendent can grasp the essence of teacher militance and collective bargaining and if he can respond in such a way that he remains a central figure in the district's decision-making process. Failure to answer these questions affirmatively may well be a forerunner to the decline of local and lay control of public education in the community.

Teacher militance has not come about overnight, and it represents considerably more than a cruel twist of fate to torment our generation of administrators. It is evolutionary and the product of a long and determined struggle for economic justice for public employees. Looking back, we note that each decade since the 1930's has seen the enactment of at least one major law dealing with labor relations. The Wagner Act of 1935, the Taft-Hartly Act of 1947, the Landrum-Griffin Act of 1959 — all excluded government employees. The 1960's, now three-quarters over, have earned the right to go down in labor relations history as the decade of the public employee. Across the country policemen, firemen, teachers, and garbage collectors are organizing, bargaining, submitting grievances, striking, and for the most part acting like their counterparts in the private sector. Of equal significance, legislators are passing laws which accord public employees rights won by workers in the private sector thirty years ago.[1]

Those boards and administrators thinking only in terms of teacher negotiations are headed for some very unpleasant surprises. Most Michigan superintendents today are administering schools through the constraints of five separate master agreements covering custodians, secretaries, bus drivers, cafeteria workers, and teachers. The Michigan statute is not as monstrous as its interpreters would have you believe. In practice it seems to matter very little whether the law is labor oriented, such as Michigan's, or a professional practices act, such as Connecticut's. When teachers decide to move, euphemistic terminology and intonations of professionalism—will not add up to operational differences.

---

[1] Jack Stieber, "Organization and Collective Bargaining in the Public Sector" (Paper prepared for American Assembly on Collective Bargaining, October 27-30, 1966).

We are wrong when we reserve all of our wrath for the law-makers whom we feel led us into this predicament. Michigan's school boards and administrators and many teachers will tell you they were unconcerned and unassertive at critical times. Furthermore, we must honestly acknowledge that laws did not usher in the collective action of teachers, and I dare say laws will offer no appreciable deterrent to the teacher's historic move to prominence in educational policy making. Objectively viewed, the Michigan law is but a manifestation of the community broadly defined and served primarily to institutionalize what was already happening or about to happen.[2] It was, of course, no legislative accident that Michigan wrote a labor-oriented law and did it in the first wave of state statutes. For years Michigan, a highly industrialized state, has held a pro-labor outlook.

There are worse things that can happen to education than a law compelling "good faith" bargaining. If conflict exists between employee and employer (and it usually does), then the bargaining process offers a reasonably authentic way to resolve it. Don't delude yourself about the presence of conflict in your district. It's there. For in every district someone supervises and someone is supervised. In that relationship resides the potential for conflict. The teacher is not a free agent. He works within the framework of institutional laws.[3] And he now is telling us that he must have a voice in shaping those laws, or he is going to raise hell until he gets it.

Michigan has gradually recognized the potential of collective bargaining in extending teachers a needed sense of security and offering a legal and orderly framework within which conflict is expressed and constructively resolved. I consider it healthy and encouraging that education has decided to wash some of its dirty linen. The supreme irony of all of this is that teacher frustration with the traditional bureaucratic structure which presumably precipitated much of their militance has now been replaced by what many teachers are recognizing as an even more monstrously frustrating and impersonal bureaucracy within their own ranks.

We now know that laws which fail to give teachers enough freedom to act will eventually lead to extra-legal action. But lack of

---

[2] Daniel H. Kruger, "The Teacher In The Decision Making Process" (Address by Daniel Kruger, Professor of Industrial Relations, Michigan State University, before the Detroit School Administrators Workshop at Michigan State University, August 11, 1966).
[3] *Ibid.*

latitude alone cannot account for the ugliness. In Michigan it was ignorance! The law was implemented before teachers, boards, and administrators could grasp the meaning, ritual and tactics of collective bargaining. As a consequence the state is still attempting to recover from the unnecessary ill-will our original ignorance generated.

It is well that we do not deceive ourselves about the issues being raised by teachers. They are not what they appear to be on the surface. The real issues are not wages, hours, and conditions of employment. Very few boards or administrators will deny the need for vast improvement in all of these areas. The bedrock issues are concerned with bi-lateral policy determination between boards and teacher organizations. They are concerned with the dilution of the delegated authority of the administrative staff. They are concerned with the extent to which a board can give way its ability to respond to the wishes of the community. They are concerned with the weakening or elimination of local and lay responsibility for education.

For superintendents the matter quickly reduces itself to the stark reality that the decision-making centers and process are no longer under their exclusive control. Much of the formal authority traditionally reserved for our status position is in this realignment process passing to officers of the teachers' associations. Before we know it, our management rights narrow to those which have not been surrendered in negotiations. When teachers negotiate on issues such as class size, promotions, length of students' day and when seniority clauses and not the principal's judgment determine room assignment, course assignment, transfer, and parking space assignment, then it becomes clear that discretionary actions of administrators are being curbed.

Today's bargaining tables accommodate a bewildering range of topics, and yet the subject matter falls conveniently into three categories: money, time, and rights. Interestingly enough, in that order boards are inclined to give ground. Some beautiful clauses have been written into master agreements. One of the all time greats is a "matters not covered" clause which in effect says that any current practice or policy not covered by the master agreement cannot be altered by the board or administration unless it is first reviewed with teachers' association to determine if they want to negotiate it. Rank and file teachers are just as amazed and often amused as we are at such antics but have come to accept them as by-products of the bitter NEA-AF of T struggle for membership. Michigan has demonstrated beyond a doubt that neither group will overlook or surrender any weapon which would prevent it from out-demanding and out-delivering the other.

Last spring Dave Seden, assistant to the president of the AF of T, and I were on a program together. I still enjoy and find truth in his statement that the best way to influence NEA policy is to join the AF of T. In East Lansing we subscribe to the *American Teacher,* published monthly by AF of T, just to give ourselves lead time on the next move of the NEA and its state affiliate. Frankly, until the NEA altered its strike position last summer, we in Michigan viewed their entire professional negotiations position as either incredibly naive or an outright fraud and delusion.

With two bitter, costly years under their belts, most Michigan administrators blush as they look back on their naivety. For too long too many of us harbored hopes that the harsh rules of collective bargaining would somehow not apply to education. We were far too late realizing that a cooperative posture at the bargaining table was not winning friends and establishing rapport which would, as we reasoned, moderate teachers' demands. The formal withdrawal of Michigan's principals and superintendents from the MEA was not an impulsive act. It grew out of two years of frustration and abuse. I personally felt reconciliation would in time be possible, but the superintendents vote was overwhelming. The mood remains angry and irrational. The wounds will be long in healing. Most Michigan administrators and boards will now tell you, in the most adamant terms, of the absolute necessity for a hard-nosed adversary posture at the bargaining table if you intend to leave it with your shirt and any semblance of control of the district's operations.

Michigan today is no place for the faint-hearted nor for the superintendent who needs to feel loved and revered by his teachers. The greatest distress has been reserved for senior superintendents whose dearest policies and practices have come under withering attack. The ugly, discrediting, unwarranted innuendo unleashed against boards and administrators has been a necessary device of negotiating teams to rally the troops when it appeared they might be losing interest. Those teachers, administrators, and board members unable to go through the process with emotional detachment have suffered greatly.

My greatest concern is that such teacher behavior will lead to a decline in the quality of board membership. Superintendents are paid to take that kind of flak; boards are not.

For three years, then, Michigan has been unpleasant and, in terms of child benefits, far less productive than it should have been.

Within the school setting we witnessed an almost total preoccupation with the law. We must report that teachers have turned time and attention from children and their own professional growth. We report that essential services to children have been set aside because of monies being diverted to teachers' salaries and fringe benefits. We know that implementation of promising programs has been stalled awaiting the purchase of teacher good will at the bargaining table. In some instances we know that teachers have ignored the law and provided our young people with a shoddy example of lawlessness (but a potent economic lesson in use of collective power). We know that deep divisions have been created within teacher ranks. Highly professional teachers who protest the recklessness of the militants have found that they were not exempt from the innuendo and attack, and with great regret we watched them retreat to less conspicuous positions within the teacher association. There was ample evidence of protecting incompetence for fear of appearing weak in the presence of the competing union. I regret that candor compels me to bring this kind of report.

Having acquainted you with the wretchedness of it all, I now want to reverse my field, for I believe we must assume that collective bargaining will serve us well during the transition. After necessary decision-making prerogatives have been achieved, teachers will return to a more "professionally respectable" stance which will reject or radically alter use of this basic instrument of their revolution. I am confident the long term effects can be viewed optimistically, first because we have something education has never had—an orderly vehicle for resolving conflict. Debilitating, morale-destroying practices and policies will receive searching re-examination, and they will be acted upon promptly rather than allowed to smoulder and erode effectiveness. Hopefully, teachers will be committed more than ever to institutional goals—goals they have had an authentic role in formulating.

Secondly, the new pride and dignity which accompanies the sense of control over their professional destinies should bring us a mature career-conscious teaching profession capable of attracting its fair share of the best minds, and this to me is the most redeeming part of it all. Through the years we have been damned by our own shoddiness, and it is never more apparent, never more damaging than when we place an incompetent person in the classroom alone with children.

Thirdly, once the intoxication of militance and collective bargaining has run its course, I'm confident we can arrive at a collegial relationship which will bring an effective marshalling of teacher and administrator creative energies. The efforts will then be constructive because the question of accountability will apply to the teachers as much as administrators. This is an eventuality which only a few boards and teachers groups have recognized, but doesn't it seem almost axiomatic that teachers insisting on decision-making on a major scale will have to accept a correspondingly major performance burden? Wise boards and administrations are insisting that any new decision-making power gained by teachers is immediately matched by assumption of corresponding responsibility.

Resolution of the accountability question is far from over. It is not at all clear to whom the teachers' organization is accountable. Theoretically and functionally under bilateral decision-making it can no longer be just the board or administration. In theory teachers' organizations are now obligated to the public, but it is far from clear how the public will impose that accountability.

If my faith in teachers turns out to be misplaced, then education faces a bleak and uncertain future. There is within teacher militance the potential to destroy public education as we now know it. The taxpaying public will not remain indefinitely on the sidelines amused by our intramural battles. I already sense their impatience.

Collective bargaining has gained a fair degree of acceptance in our society, but the basic nature of the process remains largely a mystery. Within the public as well as the private sector it is built on several remarkably durable postulates which must be accommodated if the process is to be viable and productive.[4] I will cite four which seem to have particular relevance for education.

First, *a genuine interdependence must exist between the parties.* Said another way, "schools need teachers and teachers need schools." Both must be restrained by the recognition that self-interest is served by keeping the enterprise going. If either party fails to recognize its dependence upon the ongoing enterprise, it will destroy the enterprise. I fear this eventuality is one that reckless and highly militant teacher groups have not sufficiently taken into account.

Second, *we must recognize that the parties have diverse and conflicting interests.* That's what bargaining is all about—resolution of conflicting interests. Teachers want a larger share of the administration-board decision-making power. Administrators and

    [4] Vernon H. Jensen, "The Process of Collective Bargaining and The Question of its Obsolescence," *Industrial and Labor Relations Review,* 16:546-556, July, 1963.

boards want to keep what they have. Teachers want to increase tax rates for salaries and fringe benefits; boards do not. We are unrealistic to expect teachers to cooperate with management on all fronts, and we should not expect them to depart from an adversary posture unless we want them to return to the paternalism of another era. If we assume the teachers have fundamental concern with the educational process (and surely we must), then we ought not discredit confrontation on important policies and issues. We ought to recognize that long-term educational objectives are not well served by quiet acquiescence to a school board's decisions or the taxpayers' resistance.

Third, *both parties operate with certain internal and external constraints.* Internal politics, legal restraints, and public opinion set limits for bargainers. Board and administrators carry a much heavier burden than private sector management because of the public nature of their deliberations and the pressure of accountability to all citizens, including a sizeable number of teachers. Policies and actions of teachers' organizations are getting an increasing amount of visibility, and one of the most serious problems for teachers today is to reconcile their desire for an image of professionalism with the roughhouse realities of collective bargaining.

Fourth, *it must be assumed that over a period of time boards and teachers will find a balance of power.* Any situation in which one party has the power to impose its will arbitrarily on the other is alien to collective bargaining. At the moment teachers seem to hold the trump cards. I doubt that they can be expected to acknowledge any balance of power until they realize the board and community are prepared to absorb their ultimate weapon—strike. There is every reason to believe that teachers will continue to demand and intimidate until the public recognizes that a work stoppage is not the worst thing that can happen to youngsters or public education.

Myron Lieberman, an articulate spokesman on the subject of collective action of teachers, has written in the *School Board Journal,* and he offers an alarming account of the dollar discrepancy between management and teacher efforts to conduct the warfare at the bargaining table.[5] The MEA-AF of T expenditures just for negotiations services are estimated to be more than five times that of the total budget of the Michigan Association of School Boards.

---

[5] Myron Lieberman, "Collective Negotiations: Status and Trends," *The American School Board Journal,* 155:7-10, October, 1967.

Lieberman notes the enormous advantages accruing to the side which is better prepared. He alertly summons us to vigorous action at all levels of management if disastrous consequences are to be averted.

Assuming continued teacher militance and continued but temporary reliance upon collective bargaining as the vehicle most compatible with the elevation of teachers to a prominent role in decision-making, we are now ready to ask what is the response of the superintendent. Of one thing I am certain; if he persists in the notion that it can't happen to him and if he fails to act, his problem will be solved. He will be a non-participant in the essential matters of education, if he is around at all.

My first recommendation to your superintendent is that he not waste energy or time trying to turn back this important and inevitable movement of teachers. Even if I didn't support the movement, and I do, I would alert him to the futility. It is much better that he become a student of the new power relationships, that he grasp the subtleties and dynamics of what must be a temporary adversary relationship. He can either look backward and try to reclaim part of the past and lose, or he can seize this privileged moment in history to shape a truly significant role for himself.

To do that, he must become more of a political animal than ever before, not in a partisan sense, but in the art of analyzing, acquiring, and using power. I suppose great superintendents have always done that instinctively. The desperation and uncertainty of the moment is great enough that he must do it deliberately and consciously.

For your consideration I have formulated what I believe are realistic roles for the superintendent given the hand he has been dealt. They are based upon the daily experiences of Michigan superintendents who for the past two years have had their feet put to the fire.

Role 1. In the collective bargaining setting the superintendent is an agent of management. He must be the one person to whom the board confidently delegates the executive authority to negotiate for what the board judges to be the public interest. Boards must have accurate data and solid counsel on what is essentially educational subject matter. Boards have the right to expect the positions taken at the bargaining table to be educationally defensible and backed up by solid logic and, when appropriate, carefully organized technical data. It may well be that the superintendent's most active significant role is leading his administrative staff and the board through the stages preparatory to actual negotiations. Together they must formulate objectives, guidelines, limits, and tactics from which the board's negotiating team proceeds.

I realize this is contrary to the NEA's announced preference for the superintendent as a resource person to both sides. Neutrality is a myth. Michigan superintendents will tell you the invitation from teachers will never come. Why should it? Their state and national leadership has wisely developed highly sophisticated legal and research services, the allegiance and expertise of which is above question.

Role 2. The superintendent should not be a member of the board's negotiating team. From the standpoint of time alone he will find it impossible to exercise his total leadership role if he is tied to the bargaining table. Perhaps a more important reason is that his presence at the table tends to symbolize for teachers that *he* is the teachers' enemy and adversary—an image no superintendent can be saddled with when one considers the many important relationships apart from collective bargaining that he must maintain with the staff. As a non-participant he is better able to keep his informal communications network open to key teachers. In many districts this has meant the difference between hopeless impasse and a settlement.

Tactically the board's position is weakened when its executive officer is at the bargaining table positioned for the opposition to stampede him into hasty and often ill-considered decisions. Matters which the board's negotiating team can legitimately defer for study or consultation with the superintendent and board are frequently matters which the superintendent, by virtue of his position, would find embarrassingly difficult to side-step if he were at the table.

Role 3. After the master agreement has been negotiated, the superintendent's administrative skill is put to one of its severest tests. He and the board's negotiating team must interpret the language and terms of the contract to those administrative colleagues who will carry the contract back to their buildings and make it work to the best interests of the educational program. It is at this critical stage that a philosophy for administering the contract emerges. It is here that a tone is set which will determine the number and nature of grievances. I have yet to see a contract so well written that is free of widely divergent interpretations.

Role 4. The superintendent must assume major responsibility for helping the community, the board, administrators, and the rank and file of teachers to grow in understanding of the origins, meaning, ritual, and tactics of collective bargaining. It is alarmingly easy for onlookers to hurry to erroneous conclusions about the aggressiveness of teachers or obstinence of boards. Such impressions can have a devastating effect later when teachers and the board join hands and go to the community for more millage.

Role 5. The superintendent must exemplify and demand from subordinates moral and ethical standards of administrative function which remove any doubt teachers may have about the credibility and integrity of administrative motivations and behavior. Until teachers can "make book" on the word of the superintendent and his supporting staff, no district's negotiations are going to be free of real difficulty. In no way am I suggesting that administrators accede to the wishes of teachers or retreat from reasoned firmness. I do mean that administrators must deal from trust built on truth, not duplicity. Those superintendents who persevere the initial excesses of some teacher groups, those who steadfastly resist becoming wheeler dealers themselves eventually will have a positive and lasting effect on the attitude and rationality of teachers in the collective bargaining setting.

Role 6. Finally, and above all, the superintendent must use his unique vantage point to be the consistent champion of the interests and welfare of children. The heat of negotiations tends to blind the combatants to the silent and infrequently mentioned third party, the children. In spite of the union's hard sell to the contrary, not all matters placed on the bargaining table serve the best interests of children. Furthermore, I believe there is a direct relationship between a superintendent's value to his district and his ability to assist others in defining and clarifying the purposes of public education. If he can keep these purposes continually before the participants at the bargaining table, he will have served the children, the teachers, and his community well.

From these several roles I'm brought to one overriding conclusion that many of us in Michigan have reached with great reluctance. It is simply that in the foreseeable future superintendents are going to do much of their business from across the bargaining table. But I consider the situation transitional only. I know we cannot indefinitely pay the enormous emotional price of bargaining with teachers nor can we indefinitely sacrifice our best professional time and talent at the bargaining table. Whether they realize it or not, teachers nationally are now committed to hard bargaining until they have received solid contractual guarantees of a major voice in educational decision-making. There will be many local variations for accomplishing this. The one thing all will have in common is the abandonment of unilateral decision-making by administrators.

Once that phase is settled, bargaining can be confined primarily to salary and fringe benefits, matters boards and teachers may be able to handle without much help from us. If they cannot handle even that without distress and disruption, then it is easy to predict the next step—statewide negotiations with the legislature. One step away is civil service and considerably more mediocrity than most of us could stomach. If the sad day should find us, then we have incurred a serious, perhaps fatal, setback because we will have booted our great opportunity to bring America's bright young people into our classrooms as teachers.

The superintendents of this country are a hardy and resilient breed. They have been tested before. The question of their obsolescence poses no real problem for men strong enough to weather the initial storm of collective bargaining and wise enough to turn its enormous potential into a creative and unified effort by teachers, administrators, and boards. If you can bring it off, American education is assured of experiencing the best of times.

A Principal Shares Some Thoughts on the New Era of Collective Negotiations in Public Education

Benjamin Epstein

There are a number of basic understandings that one comes to learn rapidly when trying to develop broadly general approaches to so complicated a problem as employee negotiations and collective agreement writing in public education.

First, one comes to recognize tremendous variations in procedures and laws that exist between one state and every other,

Reprinted from *Impact,* April, 1967. Dr. Epstein is Assistant Superintendent for Secondary Education in Newark, New Jersey. He was for many years a secondary school principal.

between the administrative practices of respective state departments of education, between systems of selecting school board members, methods of financing education, tenure laws, pension systems, state-mandated minimum salary schedules, sick-leave laws, and standards for certification of teachers. All of these affect negotiations very directly.

Second, it takes very little effort to come to know that within each state, every single school district is a distinctive and unduplicated entity. It is common that two school districts immediately contiguous each to the other often exhibit worlds of difference. One is urban, the other suburban. The tax sources of each are of vastly different dimensions. The ethnic composition of their population is dramatically unlike. The age, number, and adequacy of their school buildings per unit of student population bear little similarity. Their salary schedules, the average age and years of experience of their teachers and curricular offerings are completely different. The social attitudes of their communities towards such things as academic freedom, trade unionism, or the status of teachers are grossly dissimilar. All of these affect what happens at the negotiating table.

Third, the organizations and mechanisms used by teachers, administrators, and other employees in each school district to express both individual and collective requests, attitudes, and criticisms are highly varied in structure, tradition, and operation. They may exist as overall combined units, as separate and separated units of particular segments of the staff, or as loosely or tightly federated groups. Some are strongly influenced, controlled by, or loyal to the administrators of the schools, while in others administrators are rejected and classroom teachers dominate completely. In one district administrators may serve as the membership recruiters for particular professional organizations while in another there is a meticulously maintained policy of laissez-faire. In one school system, the AFT is considered an anathema while the local association is looked upon with approval by the school board, administrators, and teachers alike; in the district next door, the association is either ineffective or defunct, while the AFT local is accepted, respectable, and the recognized voice of the teachers. In one community, the AFT local is a relatively cooperative not-too-militant group that works for harmonious relationships with the school administration while one or two districts away the local association is loaded with fire and brimstone and feels it is most professional to conduct a strike. In a third school district a strong AFT local and a strong association are in a state of almost civil war with each other. All of these are involved in what happens when teachers negotiate with school boards.

Fourth, one reluctantly comes to see that altogether too many of the demands of teachers when they negotiate for written agreements are very often the product of gripes and annoyances which have been occasioned by questionable administrative practices of one or, at best, very few individuals in isolated situations. The one-only eager-beaver principal who conducts a faculty meeting at least once a week for two hours after school in order to review administrative routines or admonish his teachers, generates the demand by all teachers that faculty meetings in all schools be held no more than once a month and may last only 30 minutes. The transfer of a teacher from one school to another as a punitive measure for having disagreed with the principal about the size of a contribution to a local charity drive ends up at a later date at the bargaining table in an elaborate and deliberately clumsy set of teacher transfer rules. The playing of favorites by administrators in assigning teachers results in sections of an agreement which so decrease the discretionary powers of principals that they feel themselves in strait-jackets. When the superintendent or one principal forces a situation in which one-half of a faculty must attend every student evening school event even though only a handful of teachers are really necessary, the net effect may turn out to be a clause in an agreement which makes it next-to-impossible to obtain the help of any teacher who refuses to volunteer—and many refuse! Most principals sensitive to staff problems will easily understand the dynamics by which the teachers, who resent a situation in even only a single school, appear at the local organization meeting and, with vigor, convince their colleagues in other buildings to incorporate measures for correcting their one-school grievance as part of the negotiated policies that affect all schools. After all, they argue with other teachers, "You can never tell. Our principal may become yours."

Fifth, one must sooner or later realize that, while all those who participate in the educating of children—board members, superintendents, principals, and teachers—have a genuine commonness of interest and concern, there are, nevertheless, areas of conflict between these groups—legitimate differences which need resolution. There are the conflicts which arise when school boards try to keep tax costs down and employees seek wage increases. There are conflicts that become apparent when teachers feel that were it not for the raises granted to the administrators more money would have been available to increase their own pay to a higher level. There are disagreements as to what is reasonable in terms of a teacher's work load or class size. School boards and superintendents seeking to staff schools in difficult sociological trouble spots try hard to set up a system of assigning the most experienced teachers to such schools and having those already there remain. When they do make such assignments, they find themselves in conflict with teacher organizations which argue that teachers should not be assigned involuntarily in the reverse order of seniority and should be able to transfer out of any school on the basis of seniority. Principals find themselves in conflict with teachers over assignments of classes, cafeteria patrols, and often even of rooms in the building. Principals have begun to be in conflict with superintendents and school boards whom they feel are too easily permitting too much of their needed authority to be taken away from them during negotiations in which simultaneously their responsibilities are increased. Teachers are in conflict with their supervisors over ratings of their teaching performance.

With few exceptions these conflicts are not at all new and have existed for a very long time. The basic change that has taken place is the fact that the areas of conflict have become more sharply defined in this period of negotiations. They are being more openly and militantly expressed by teachers and their organizations. This in turn is forcing school boards, superintendents, and principals to reexamine and redefine their own roles, obligations, responsibilities, and powers.

There are those in the teaching profession to whom the admission and identification of the existence of significant conflicts make for a very upsetting and threatening concept. If the prophet, Jeremiah, were writing this paper, he would say that these worried people keep crying out, "Peace, peace, when there is no peace!" Such individuals and groups struggle hard to hold on to what are, at best, placebos such as "the one-happy-family," or "all members-of-one-team," or "the united profession" idea. They seem to forget that even within happy families, strong teams, and every other profession there are disagreements and conflicts among its members. And these conflicts have existed from the time there was a first family, team, or profession. Education is not and never will be an exception, nor need it be. May I repeat that the existence of even the strongest community of interest—one which in education is a "sine qua non" if we are to accomplish the tasks for which we are responsible—does not automatically exclude the existence of conflicting interests. It is precisely because there is a common goal that teachers, principals, superintendents, and board members do try to examine and reach productive resolutions of these conflicts. It is because of the differences that negotiations are needed.

But, if differences and conflicts are to be settled, then the representatives of all parties involved must be participants in the search for solutions during "collective negotiations", or "professional negotiations", "collective bargaining" or call it what suits your temperament best. Unfortunately, and too often, those of us who are principals have been excluded from the process although our functions and activities and conflicts are under constant evaluation and decision at negotiations among school boards, superintendents and teachers. This is one of the reasons that many of us feel that negotiations have increased rather than decreased conflicts for principals. Even when negotiations are not successful for superintendents, school boards, and teachers, they may intensify conflicts for principals.

At this point I'd like to try to give some close attention to the relationships of principals with the negotiating process itself and with those groups who are typically part of these negotiations. So that I may be pointedly specific, permit me to pose a series of questions and supply my own answers.

I. At the 1967 convention of NASSP, William G. Carr, then Executive Secretary of the NEA said, "While the NEA has no official preference for one local affiliate organization over another, evidence and experience clearly show that an inclusive approach to negotiations can operate successfully if all parties desire to make it so. *However, individual segments of the organization* should be able to arrive at important policy decisions, *free of the domination or undue influence by other segments."* How does one interpret these remarks in terms of NEA policy attitudes towards the participation of principals in negotiations with school boards?

What Mr. Carr is saying between the lines is that, while the NEA has been trying hard to hold on to its traditional patterns of organization of local associations which have enrolled superintendents and principals as well as teachers, the classroom teachers want to arrive at their own conclusions, make their own demands, and they feel that the presence of administrators in their own internal deliberations creates pressures and duress which unduly dominate their decisions.

Mr. Donald Wollett, an attorney who has represented a number of NEA local associations in their negotiations stated at an institute held at Rhode Island College that no one who gives one-half or more of his time to administrative-supervisory duties, should be included within a teachers' negotiating unit.

One cannot avoid the observation that, in an increasing number of school districts where the NEA association is the prevailing teachers' organization, the desire of teachers to negotiate apart and separate from principals and other supervisors is the growing trend. And this is as it should be since, in part, the demands at the bargaining table will be in the nature of seeking a narrowing of the limits of the authority of administrators over teachers.

In such an atmosphere principals will find themselves increasingly uncomfortable and unwanted. Moreover, even in communities where local associations would like to continue to maintain traditional organizational patterns, the associations are constantly embarrassed by charges of rival AFT locals that they are administrator-dominated, a charge to which they tend to react accordingly. The fate of principals in local teachers' associations is creating much anxiety and is becoming even more difficult.

(Lieberman and Moskow, in their book on Collective Negotiations for Teachers, have this to say: "In the long run, teachers must depend upon effective organizations which represent them, not upon the chief representatives of their employers, to improve their conditions of employment. In education, the implications of this are very unsettling, which is perhaps the reason why there is such a desperate effort to avoid the issue.")

II. How does the AFT feel about the inclusion of principals as part of any of their local negotiating units?

Beyond any question, the AFT, at its convention this past summer made it quite clear, if there had previously been any doubts, that it no longer wanted any more principals or supervisors as members of the organization—let alone, the negotiating units. Principals are regarded as part of management, and the AFT doesn't wish management inside its own councils.

III. Should principals, along with others of the administrative-supervisory staff, have the right to negotiate for themselves and should they exercise such a right?

There is growing recognition, in terms of most commonly accepted definitions in the field of employer-employee relations, that principals must be thought of as part of the management personnel. Any principal who has lived through a teachers' strike in his school district will be acutely aware that this is a role expected of him by teachers, superintendents and boards alike. However, at the very self-same time, principals are also wage-earning employees of school boards. As employees they do not and have not been given the power to determine their own salaries, personal welfare benefits, range of duties, limits of executive authority, and many other conditions of employment. If one agrees that teachers should have the right to negotiate on parallel issues with school boards (and the writer is convinced that they certainly should!), then principals, in their employee roles, also should.

Because, so often their problems are different, in type and dimension, it makes good sense that they, often jointly with other administrators and supervisors, will wish to carry out such negotiations as a distinct unit separate and apart from teachers. Let me give some obvious examples. When a principal is absent for a day's illness, the school board never has to go to the expense of hiring a substitute as it does when a teacher is absent. Shall the sick-leave privileges of principals, then, be no different from that of teachers, especially when a principal is on call to handle any emergency that arises at his school 24 hours every day, all year? Or shall salaries of principals be based upon ratios of teachers' salaries or on some more absolute determination? What shall the rate of remuneration of expenses be for a principal when he is out travelling to seek new teachers for his school? What rights to legal services does a principal have when parents bring suit because of the suspension of a troublesome student? These are but a few of the areas of special concern for principals. Many of these are of small consequence to a teachers' negotiating unit. They are of great importance to principals in determining their own working conditions.

IV. Do administrators, especially principals, have the legal right to negotiate for themselves?

This is a very difficult question to answer. In some states laws have been written in such a way as to make this right questionable. In other states, such as Connecticut, they clearly have such a right. In some they can only bargain as part of an overall professional unit.

It is my belief that, if principals are not included as part of teacher representation units, (and I feel it wise that they should not) since they have problems as employees, since they have no less a right to be heard and to bargain collectively than any other group of employees, and since the act of denying them negotiating rights is an act which discriminates against them by preventing them from exercising the same rights as are guaranteed by law or made available by ongoing practice to other categories of employees, principals should have the right to negotiate for themselves if they so choose.

What then should be done if a school board refuses to permit its administrators the exercise of such a right when they petition to use it. There are several ways to deal with such a situation. One way is to appeal to the State Department of Education or the State Commissioner, requesting that the local school board be directed to afford equal rights to principals as it does to teachers. Or principals may have to resort to litigation which will call upon the courts to protect them from discriminatory denial of equal treatment. Or they may want to go to the Legislature to seek appropriate statutory definition of their rights.

All of these are difficult, time-consuming, and, unhappily, expensive courses of action. The resources of the administrators of any one school system will probably never be adequate enough to pursue the struggle to the end. Those principals who set up a test case will need the support of colleagues all over the state—political, psychological, and, of course, financial. Principals will have to become far more tightly organized in most states than they are at present.

V. When representatives of teachers' organizations sit at the bargaining table with the superintendent and members of the school board, a considerable portion of the items dealt with impinge upon and seriously affect the responsibilities, powers, decision-making functions, and possibly almost every prerogative that principals have in relationship to the staff they are required to supervise. What role do principals have in such negotiations and in what fashion shall they participate in such negotiations?

The answer of AFT members would be simple. They would defend their right to negotiate directly with the school board or its immediate representative, the superintendent. Since all administrators are to them direct agents of the board, there is no need for the principals to have any part in the negotiations. After all, the board and superintendent will, they argue, protect the interests of principals quite adequately. If the superintendent wishes to consult with the administrative staff before or during negotiations, that is his business and not that of teachers. Finally, it makes no real difference what the principals think. Theirs is but to do or die, for their most characteristic role is that of carrying out the policies that come to them from the board and the superintendent.

The NEA seems to suggest another approach. It proposes negotiation through one single, all-inclusive bargaining unit which speaks for all professional employees. But, as was pointed out earlier, local NEA associations are, at an accelerating rate, rejecting this approach. William Carr offers another possibility that unity is possible even where teachers and administrators are acting independently of each other when he says "The diverse needs and interests of various groups should be reconciled satisfactorily before negotiations begin." But this gives us no view as to what would happen if such reconciliation did not occur because the conflicts of interest are too sharp. Nor does such an approach sit well with school boards who consider administrators as their representative executives in each school and resent having principals acting in dual roles with respect to teachers. And the school boards are justified in believing that the coming of collective negotiations has made it questionable as to whether it is proper for principals to be other than a part of management. Principals will have to give up the notion that they are "one of the boys" and they must not become overly exercised by the fact that they are not going to be "loved" by teachers.

Principals will have to have better ways to play a role of influence on items under discussion at board-teacher negotiations. There are several ways in which this can be done. 1. Representatives of principals' associations in larger communities or all principals in very small systems may sit with either the superintendent or the superintendent and the board in order cooperatively to review, analyze, and evaluate the demands of teacher negotiators in terms of their positive and negative effects upon the effectiveness of school management, and, more important, on the quality of education; this joint review and its conclusions should then become the basis for the board-superintendent responses to teachers in negotiations. 2. In a second approach, one or more of the representatives of the principals or joint administrator-supervisor organizations may serve as full-fledged members of the board's active negotiating team, which may even have the power to act on most matters. 3. Still another possibility is the case in which representatives of administrative organizations participate as one party in three-party negotiations— board - administrators - teachers. 4. A fourth procedure, especially useful for larger school systems, is the setting-up of a series of teacher vis-a-vis administrator negotiating units to work out specific and relatively narrow areas such as transfer policies or teacher sponsorship of student activities, etc.; the conclusions reached at this level are then transmitted to the superintendent or the board for final confirmation by the board and the teachers' top negotiating unit.

All of these (and others are possible) procedures are presented to indicate that there are a variety of ways for principals to play a significant role in influencing the outcomes of teacher-board negotiations in ways that can be acceptable and mutually agreeable to all those whose work is directly affected by negotiations. Which of these procedures, or modifications of them, are to be used will inevitably turn out to be a matter of local judgment, expediency, or experiment.

(At this point, a strong word of caution is necessary. In a statement of this kind, it is difficult to avoid highlighting the differences and conflicts. One should bear in mind that, far more often than it would seem, principals will be in substantive agreement with the proposals and requests of teacher organizations during negotiations. At such times principals should have no reticence about applauding and supporting with the full weight of their status and experience the justifiable and positive demands of teacher organizations.)

VI. Shall principals continue their membership in teacher organizations?

Here it is important to differentiate between local, state, and national organizations, and between types of organizations. There is no reason for principals to question their membership alongside of teachers in science, foreign language, physical education, behavioral research, curriculum development, and any of the many other purely professional associations with which American education is so luxuriantly blessed.

The problem of the retention of membership by administrators in local teacher organizations concerned with representing teachers at the bargaining table is quite different. More and more I find that administrators are either not joining or are severing their membership ties—and I think wisely so. Their continuation as members has become an anomaly and an anachronism since the coming of teacher negotiations. It bears within it too many contradictions.

Let me give only one example. Characteristic of all written agreements are teacher grievance procedures. Suppose a principal belongs to the local association and one of his teachers brings a grievance against him. The association comes to the support of the teacher. The principal suddenly and unhappily finds an organization to which he gives his time and to which he pays his dues vigorously carrying out an action directed against him and his stewardship. He appeals to the organization pointing out that, after all, he, too, is a member, and the least it can do is not to act in opposition to him. His appeals fall on unsympathetically deaf ears because after all is said and done, the purpose of the organization when it first negotiated the grievance machinery was exactly for the reason that it would have an effective way of protesting the authority of a principal whenever it felt the need to do so. The principal should have realized that that was the intent right from the outset, but he didn't want to believe that such a thing could happen to him. But it did!

Of course, if administrators decide that the time has arrived when they can no longer be members of local teacher associations or unions, then they must determine that they will have to do a big job of strengthening and improving their own principals' and administrators' organizations if they are to be effective in a new kind of day and age.

The problem of retaining membership within state and national education associations is not a simple one. (Insofar as the AFT is concerned, there is no problem because one can only be part of the state and national organizations by being a member in a local union.) Administrators have, over and above their conflicts of interests with teachers, many important common concerns which affect all of education and its practitioners—federal and state aid to schools, pension systems, tenure, protection of public education from the attacks of extremists, welfare needs of pupils, etc., etc., etc. There is little doubt about the splendid service which has been given and continues to be rendered by state associations and the NEA. Administrators will be most reticent about severing their ties and their participation with organizations dedicated to the welfare of schools and the educational profession on state and national levels.

Yet, these same state organizations, aided enthusiastically by NEA, are now in the business of doing their utmost to promote teacher negotiations. And as this drive intensifies, administrators begin to feel the same discomforts and conflicting relationships, though more diffusely, state and nation-wide as they have in local associations. Will the superintendent or principal who tries to hire substitutes to cover classes of teachers who have chosen to go out on strike be charged within the state association, which is supporting the strike, as having been guilty of professionally unethical conduct? What will the feeling of an administrator be when the state or national association sends an attorney to serve as a consultant or advocate for the local teachers association in a grievance procedure against the administrator?

There are bound to be periods of anger, misunderstanding, and many varieties of irritation in these first years of teacher negotiations. It may well be that new organizational patterns will have to be evolved. State associations and the NEA may have to move from their individual overlapping basis of membership to a federation of organizations (no double entendre is meant here), each with its special interests but united for common purposes, and with individual membership limited strictly to the special interest concerns of teachers, or supervisors, or principals, or superintendents, as the case may be.

At this time, it is too early and too soon to undertake rash and precipitous policy decisions on the subject. What is badly needed is a series of down-to-earth, man-to-man, hard-fact, let's-stop-kidding-each-other dialogues between the leaders of teacher associations, and those of principals and superintendents, which will realistically appraise developments and search for a mutual *modus vivendi* appropriate for a new era in staff relationships in the educational profession

---

Section C

Recent Cases in Collective Negotiations

Section C, which illustrates the uses of power in collective negotiations and the rewards accruing therefrom, is composed of descriptions based upon data collected in several areas heavily engaged in collective negotiations. Each of the articles deals with a different situation in terms of geography, circumstances, and the organizational units involved. Together, the four articles present a composite of current negotiatory reality.

Elseroad describes the tactics employed and mistakes made by teachers and management during the Montgomery County, Maryland, teachers strike which paralyzed the school system of that affluent Washington, D.C., suburb for ten days. Donovan describes the problems he has encountered during his tenure with the New York City schools. Of particular interest are his references to the dissatisfaction of the black community with the schools, and his description of the union-community power struggle that was building at the time he wrote. These difficulties preceded the strikes of 1968 which disrupted the city's educational program for almost a semester, focusing attention upon the issue of community vs. professional control.

Carlton describes the unusual teacher council form of representation provided for in the Oregon statute, analyzing the strengths and weaknesses of the legislation. He then describes the salary negotiations which took place in an Oregon city in recent years. Cass provides a vignette of the political struggle which occurred in Florida during the teachers' strike of 1968. He indicates failures of the teachers' association in public relations, internal communications, and overall organizational control, as well as depicting with considerable clarity the "strike-breaking" tactics of the public and the reprisals against educators which characterized the grim aftermath of the strike.

Professional Negotiations in Montgomery County

Homer O. Elseroad

Montgomery County occupies an area of over 500 square miles on the northwest border of the District of Columbia. We have a mobile population—about 7 per cent of our people move each year. The educational level of adults in the county is high. A recent census indicated the average is about two years of college. We have a lot of bright students in our schools. The median I.Q. is around 115. Many of our parents are employed in technical and professional occupations. The National Institutes of Health, the Bureau of Standards, and the Atomic Energy Commission, plus several large research and development firms are located in the County. The average income per family was reported to be a little over $13,000 in 1968.

Our school system has a reputation of being innovative. We have attempted to give schools a lot of autonomy. To this end we have developed a decentralized organization whereby the county is divided up into twelve areas with an area director, or in some places it might be called a district superintendent, in charge of each area. We have made extensive provisions for a great deal of teacher involvement in the decision-making processes in the school system. Schools have been provided a lot of freedom in curriculum, in teaching methods, and in organization. You will find examples of every kind of school organization among the schools in Montgomery County.

We have had to recruit teachers extensively since our school enrollment has been growing about 5,000 pupils per year. We recruit nationally and, over a period of time, have sought people who are independent thinkers—who speak out and express their views. In Montgomery County, we have had a good financial base for education. Our cost per pupil has gone up in the past ten years from $340 to $840, or about two and one-half times.

The largest teacher organization in Montgomery County is the Montgomery County Education Association (MCEA). This has been a

Reprinted from Harold I. Goodwin and Patrick W. Carlton, *Above The Salt: Militancy in Education* (Morgantown: West Virginia University Press. 1968.) Dr. Elseroad is Superintendent of Schools in Montgomery County, Maryland.

very progressive organization. Up until five or six years ago, it enrolled over 90 per cent of the professional personnel in the school system. The membership has dropped off during recent years until now it enrolls a little under 70 per cent. It has been attacked by teachers in recent years on a number of points, one of which is that it is administration and supervisor dominated. I do not think this is a valid criticism, but from a teacher point of view, there is some evidence that might make it look that way. For example, of the five elected officers of the organization, more than half each year have been administrative or supervisory people.

In 1963, a new organization was formed in Montgomery County called the Classroom Teachers Association. It attempted to affiliate with NEA, but MCEA was successful in blocking that affiliation. The Classroom Teachers Association has never become very strong, but it has been an irritant to MCEA since its formation.

In 1966, a local affiliate of the American Federation of Teachers was organized in the county. Again, the reason given for the birth of the Union was that MCEA did not really represent the classroom teachers. The Union has grown slowly and probably has about 400 members at the present time. It has been given a lot of visibility, gets a great deal of publicity, and constantly harrasses the MCEA, criticizing it for the things it does do, and chiding it for the things it does not do.

Professional negotiations in Montgomery County has evolved from discussions on this topic dating back to the beginning of 1964. During that year, MCEA and the superintendent attempted to develop a procedure for beginning professional negotiations. We did not have a law in Maryland that authorized or established procedures for doing this, and we had a great deal of difficulty getting the Board of Education to recognize MCEA for consultation or negotiations purposes. After about a year and a half of discussion and maneuvering of various kinds, the Board of Education adopted, in June 1965, a resolution recognizing MCEA as the professional association that would be spokesman for professional personnel in the county.

The Classroom Teachers Association continued to attack the Board of Education and MCEA and was instrumental in getting a ruling from the Attorney General that the procedure was irregular because MCEA could only be the spokesman for its members.

In July 1966, the State Board of Education adopted a by-law which established procedures for granting recognition to a teachers organization for consultation purposes. The Board of Education recognized MCEA in accordance with this by-law, and since September 1966, we have been carrying on first consultations, and more recently, we have changed the procedures and terminology so that we now call it negotiations. At any rate, we have been carrying these activities on very successfully since the fall of 1966.

The procedures provide that MCEA and the superintendent will each appoint a team. MCEA's team was made up of the president, vice-president, and the executive secretary. The superintendent's team has been made up of the assistant superintendent for personnel services, the director of professional personnel, and an area director. These teams met about 30 times in the year-and-a-half prior to the strike. They dealt with virtually all of the subjects on which we had Board action or on which we were promulgating procedures that would affect teachers.

I can give you a few examples: The staffing standards for library aides; the revision of a number of personnel policies; a revision of standards for secondary counselors; the school calendar for FY 68; a new retirement plan—a county retirement plan to supplement the state retirement plan; a new conflict of interest policy. These are just a few examples of dozens of policy items that we developed with the teachers through their professional organization.

Through these two teams we worked out a very successful salary plan for the current year. It has proved to be an excellent salary schedule. A couple of weeks before the strike in Montgomery County, NEA put out a publication crediting us with the best salary structure of any large school system in the United States.

In preparing the budget for the next year, we entered into extensive negotiations with MCEA and successfully negotiated the calendar for the new school year, and a salary agreement. We started in mid-October and carried on daily meetings of the negotiating teams to arrive at an agreement on a salary program by November 15. The members of the two negotiating teams signed the agreement. It provided for a base salary of $610 per month for a 10-month teacher and had four or five other elements affecting salaries.

At the same time we worked out a calendar for ratifying the negotiated agreement. This calendar provided, at the request of MCEA, that the agreement would first be presented to MCEA, and after it had been ratified by them, it would be presented to the MCEA delegate assembly and ratified by them as provided for in their constitution. Our calendar called for the Board of Education to act on the salary package on December 20. At another meeting of the delegate assembly two days later, they voted to rescind their action on the agreement and so informed the superintendent by letter.

These actions produced great upheaval in MCEA. The president resigned in protest, as well as the other members of the negotiating team. The vice-president, a social studies teacher in one of the schools, moved up to the presidency, and he appointed a new negotiating team made up exclusively of classroom teachers. We took the position than an agreement was an agreement, that it could not be rescinded, and we continued to ratify the agreement according to our calendar. The Board of Education did, however, meet with the executive board of MCEA in a private session and again in a public session prior to taking its action on December 20. At neither of these meetings did MCEA indicate in what ways it wanted the salary program improved. Thus, on December 20, the Board adopted this originally-ratified salary package.

On December 21, the superintendent wrote to the president of MCEA suggesting a meeting to determine whether or not there were elements of the salary package on which there should be further discussions. A little more than a month later, on January 26, we finally got the negotiating teams together to begin discussing possible changes in the $610 base. During this intervening month, however, MCEA had a mass meeting of teachers to which the President of NEA had come and spoken. He in effect told them, "If you do not strike, you ought to be ashamed of yourselves." I believe this meeting had a great deal to do with creating a psychological and emotional climate for the strike which came along a little later.

On the 26th of January, we convened the negotiating teams to attempt to negotiate a better salary base. They worked from Monday morning through Thursday noon and could not reach an agreement. I met with the two teams and explained to them that, as they quite well knew, according to our procedures, if they were unable to reach an agreement, the two points of view were to be presented to the Board of Education. I asked if they would like to do this. They indicated that they would, and we called a meeting of the Board of Education that afternoon.

The Board met at 2 p.m. The superintendent presented the position of his negotiating team that provided for increasing the base to $6,200 with an additional $50 at the beginning step. The president of MCEA was invited to present the position of his association. He said that they believed an impasse existed and that the Board should invite mediators to come in and resolve it.

Our procedures had made no provision for impasse. The President of the board explained that the board was, in effect, attempting to resolve the impasse; that they were meeting to hear the two positions and would attempt to find a resolution after hearing the arguments for each of those positions.

The president of MCEA said that he felt he should present the position of the association to a delegate assembly meeting scheduled later that afternoon, before presenting it to the Board of Education. After about 45 minutes of general discussion which was not fruitful, the MCEA representatives asked to be excused and left about 3:45 p.m. to go to their delegate assembly meeting. At that meeting they voted to go on strike (withdraw their services).

At the time the strike was called, MCEA had not placed its salary demands before the Board of Education. It was not until after the strike was called that the Board learned that MCEA's position was a base salary of $6,400 plus $200 on the first step, or beginning salary of $6,600.

On Friday, February 2, we decided to hold school, and we urged teachers to report to their schools by radio and television. About half of the teachers, however, did not report for work, and so we closed schools on Monday, February 5.

The negotiating teams resumed meeting on Monday, the 5th, and decided to work around-the-clock until an agreement was reached. Late in the evening of February 6, the negotiating teams did reach an agreement at a starting figure of $6,325. In the meantime, that afternoon, we had gone before the Circuit Court and asked for an order to enjoin teachers from striking. The Court granted that injunction and ordered the MCEA to appear on Thursday to respond to the order. With the agreement of the negotiating teams at $6,325 and the order of the Court enjoining teachers not to strike, the superintendent announced on radio and television that teachers should report to their schools for a professional day on Wednesday and to receive students on Thursday. During the strike we had had professional days for about half of the teachers who were reporting to schools every day.

MCEA called a meeting of its delegate assembly at midnight on Tuesday to ratify the $6,325 salary agreement. Much to our surprise, they did not ratify the agreement. They got caught up in a discussion about a no-strike clause, which was relatively meaningless from our point of view, and talked as if they did not really want to end the strike yet. MCEA held two mass meetings on February 7 to present the agreement to teachers, but it was presented in such a way that teachers did not understand it, and they were not encouraged to support it.

Hence, the strike continued. On Thursday, Feburary 8, the Court granted an interlocutory injunction ordering the strike to stop, but did not order teachers back to work. The court order said that all picketing must stop and that no meetings or activities could be carried on to promote the strike. Thus, on Friday, we reopened schools and expected teachers to be back under court order.

Much to our surprise, Dr. Gary Watts, Director of Urban Services for the NEA, called a mass meeting of teachers in Montgomery County and about 1,800 of them attended. Dr. Watts and several others in MCEA who were instrumental in carrying on this meeting were cited in contempt of court. Subsequently, he and one other person were found guilty of contempt but had their sentences suspended.

Many of our teachers did return to work on Friday, and all but six of our schools operated fairly successfully that day. We were prepared to operate schools again on Monday, and I believe that most of our teachers would have been back on the job at that time.

We carried on negotiations over the weekend and reached an agreement at a $6,340 base, $15 higher than the figure that had been agreed upon four days earlier. The MCEA delegate assembly met on Sunday to consider the agreement reached by the negotiating teams. All schools opened on Monday, and all teachers reported. The teachers discussed and then voted on the salary agreement by secret ballot in their schools on Monday and approved it. The delegate assembly met Monday evening and ratified the agreement. The Board of Education met on Tuesday and also ratified it so that the base figure in the salary package during this period of time had been changed from $6,100 to $6,340.

Now a little bit about what has happened since the strike ended. All teachers reported to work on the Monday after the court order, and they have been at work regularly since. There were hard feelings in some schools because about half of the teachers were working throughout the strike, and they were getting paid. The other half who were on strike did not get paid. We delayed the opening of schools for pupils on Monday by one and one-half hours so that principals would have a chance to meet with their teachers to get reorganized. Generally, the attitude was very good. It appeared that teachers were relieved and anxious to get back to work.

In an attempt to have the superintendent and other top administrative persons in the school system have first-hand discussions with teachers about their concerns, we have offered to all schools to have the superintendent, deputy superintendent, and four assistant superintendents clear their calendars for Wednesday afternoons. Any one of them will be glad to go to any school in the county to meet with small groups of teachers, or the whole faculty, to discuss whatever topics are on their minds. As a result of this, I have scheduled meetings on Wednesday afternoons for most of the rest of the year to meet with faculties, and other members of our staff have done the same. In the meetings we have had to date, we find that there is genuine interest and desire on the part of teachers to express and exchange their views and concerns about the school system.

What were the causes of the strike? As I have told you, according to the NEA, we have the best pay structure of any large school system in the United States; we have excellent facilities; we have a challenging community in which to teach. Why the strike? I think there are many facets to the answer to this question. We are living in a protest era. I predict we will have a great many teacher strikes across the country, and we will have strikes or work stoppages of one kind or another in many areas of employment where it has not been true in the past.

Another important facet was the NEA urging. President Alonzo[1] said to our teachers, "You ought to be ashamed of yourselves if you do not strike." He came to Montgomery County, walked the picket line, and helped to fan the fire for a strike. Some of us believe that NEA wanted a strike in Montgomery County so they could go to a lot of other places in the country and say, even with a good salary structure, Montgomery County teachers went on strike; you can do no less.

A third contributing factor was internal problems in the way business was conducted by MCEA. There has been a conflict within MCEA as to whether or not the leadership really represented the classroom teachers. Also, for more than a year MCEA has continued to publicize in all of its literature that it was demanding an $8,000 starting salary for teachers. They had so built up this expectation in the minds of young teachers that they were in a very difficult position in negotiating for a reasonable starting salary.

A fourth and major reason is or was the challenge of the Classroom Teachers Association and the challenge of the union. The union was breathing down the neck of MCEA and in a sense, I believe, many of the people in MCEA felt they had to out-union the union. And then, of course, the membership of the MCEA had dropped from over 90 per cent to under 70 per cent.

---

[1] Braulio Alonzo was President of NEA in 1967-68.

Montgomery County is situated between Washington and Baltimore. You must remember that within the last year both Washington and Baltimore have held teacher elections. In both cases these cities had small union organizations and large NEA organizations, but in both cases, the union won the election. Some people felt that the union was concentrating on Montgomery County to make this the place for a breakthrough in a suburban school district and that MCEA needed to make a show of strength in order to be sure of winning a likely teacher election in June.

Then, too, the $6,100 base was low. We had six elements in our salary package this year. In preparing for our original negotiations, we agreed to concentrate on the other five areas and not to put a lot more money into the base. In Montgomery County we negotiate and adopt our salary plan earlier than any of the surrounding jurisdictions. After the adoption of the $6,100 base in Montgomery County, comparable school districts in surrounding areas adopted starting salaries of $6,200 and $6,300, and it became apparent that the $6,100 figure was too low.

By way of conclusion, a couple of summary observations. Although I deplore a strike which closes the schools down as a way of settling disputes, I believe the use of the strike by teachers is here to stay, and it may be that we can minimize the rush to use the strike if we do not get too exercised about a few days lost from school because of them. I think, too, we have got a lot of fuzzy thinking about the role of administrative and supervisory personnel in teacher negotiations. This is an area that needs to be given a great deal of attention to resolve the role of middle administration personnel in handling disputes and resolving differences, and particularly the role of these people if a strike is called.

It has been perfectly obvious to us in school administration for many years that teachers must have an important role in decision making. Teachers have had some experience in this in recent years, and they are determined to play an increasingly important part. To some extent, we have a power struggle between the organization representing teachers, and the Board of Education representing the public. This power struggle is going to have to be resolved by teachers, too, and they will have to give on some things to have a bigger voice in the decisions that affect the operation of the schools.

I think there is a danger of going overboard in looking to professional negotiations or collective bargaining as the forum for settling all disputes. It seems to me that professional negotiations or collective bargaining is an appropriate procedure where you have two positions and you are trying to find a middle ground or compromise between them. But many problems in education do not fall into this category, and we ought to think clearly through what kinds of problems lend themselves to solution through the negotiations or bargaining technique, using this procedure for those problems, but not extending its use to problems which can better be resolved through a group process or a research study approach.

Lastly, we need to continue to struggle to have teachers recognized as professional people who are doing a tremendously important job in society, and we need to keep struggling to get teacher pay up. With this, however, must go a demand for better performance. It has been my observation that most of our teachers do an excellent job, are highly dedicated people, and are devoting their talents, training, and energy to helping young people grow and develop. They are truly competent professionals. We do, however, have pupils in our schools who are not challenged, pupils for whom the school is not really a meaningful place, problems in curriculum which are not relieved for those particular pupils. We have to find solutions for these problems. We have to make greater strides to be sure that the educational experience is vital for every person in our schools.

And so, I believe if we are to move forward on this problem, and we are to push ahead on getting salaries up, we will attract more competent people into teaching, society will be better served, and these two movements will go forward hand in hand.

New York City—Workshop for Teacher Militancy

Bernard Donovan

Today's problem in New York is yours, wherever you are, in one shape or another. The background of this situation in New York City has to be explained in terms of the strength of our teachers' organization. Ten years ago in New York City we had about 117

Revised from an article in Harold I. Goodwin and Patrick W. Carlton, *Above The Salt: Militancy in Education* (Morgantown: West Virginia University Press, 1968). Dr. Donovan is Superintendent of Schools in New York City.

teacher organizations. No one of them was strong enough to do anything, so we had a real vacuum. As far as the Board was concerned, it could play one teacher group off against the other. No teacher group could really be successful. We had kinds of organizations you've never heard of. We had 7th and 8th grade women teachers. We had history teachers in the junior high schools, history teachers in the senior high schools, Protestant teachers, Jewish teachers, Catholic teachers, Brooklyn Catholic teachers. That made for weakness as far as teachers were concerned.

A second factor about New York City is its size. Today we have 55,000 classroom teachers teaching 1,100,000 children in the public schools. The very size of the system is a problem both to teacher organizations and to communication between teacher, superintendent, and board. Thus, the organization of teachers in New York City was a difficult one for the teacher organizations.

A third point is that in a system of that size there is an impersonality about teaching that leads teachers to feel, "Well, I'm number 99,429 on the payroll but nobody else recognizes me." A strong teacher organization gives a teacher a feeling of security, a feeling that somebody cares. We are a union city. Everything is unionized in New York City.

We had another reason for teachers organizing in New York City. We did have some autocratic administrators. Teachers resent autocratic administration—administration that does not carry with it a reason for doing things. There have been autocratic administrators, and unfortunately, there still are quite a few. We had an apathetic staff. We had good salaries, relatively, some years ago, and good pensions. We had these things before other school districts had them. But all of a sudden the other school districts began to come up, began to surpass us. The teachers got a little excited and the organizers of the teachers had more with which to work.

We had a no-strike law in New York State. In fact, it was the second one we had had. The first one was ignored frequently enough to get it changed. Now the second one is being ignored frequently enough that it is sure to be modified.[1] Under this law, for the first time, striking teachers were punished by a fine against the union and by jailing of the leader of the teachers. We did *not* ask that this happen. The law makes it happen automatically. The issue goes to

---

[1] Since this writing the Taylor Law has been amended. The Rockefeller Amendments to the Taylor Law, (or RAT law as Albert Shanker called it in 1969), contains punitive anti-strike clauses.

court, and the court makes its own decisions. In spite of that, we have had strikes.

The Board of Education of the City of New York is financially dependent upon the city and does not raise its own funds. That creates a special problem. When the union is through negotiating with us, they move on to negotiate with the Mayor, He is the man that has the funds. We do not raise taxes. That is true of the six big cities in New York State. All of the school districts in New York State raise their own taxes except the six biggest cities: Buffalo, New York, Rochester, Syracuse, Albany, and Yonkers. This creates a problem in militancy because the militant teachers organizations know that they can wring us for as much as possible, then move on and squeeze a little harder elsewhere. It is a tactic of negotiations. We also know that one of the reasons for militancy was a very sympathetic Mayor Wagner, a labor-minded mayor. I do not say sympathetic in that he failed to negotiate ethically, but that he had a sympathy for unionism that helped our teachers' union to grow.

Now, what is it the union wants that makes them militant. I'm not going to talk to you about salaries and pensions and sick leave and welfare. That is a normal goal of a union. It is after that that we come into the "gray area," the area of working conditions. We have no court decisions in New York State to tell us what "working conditions" encompass. We have determined this by the back-and-forth of negotiations. Every year they become broader.

The first working condition we talked about in education, beyond salaries and so forth, was class size. Class size is a working condition. It also happens to be a matter of educational policy. Class size is something you create in terms of the kind of student, the nature of the program, the kind of class it is, and a lot of other educational matters. But class size is a burden on the teacher's back, belonging to that "gray area" of policy *and* working conditions; therefore, our Board has resisted the average class size but has acceded to what we call the intolerable maximum. In other words, we will not say a class of slow English learners should be 25. We do say that no high school class shall exceed 35. There are exceptions like physical education, choral music, and so forth. This has been agreed to by the union. This is one of the areas that is under more and more discussion.

The second matter is something very hard to describe unless one understands that New York City is an examination city; nobody gets a job in New York City unless he passes an open competitive examination. That applies to teacher, chairman of department, assistant principal, and principal. I choose nobody. I have to take a principal off a list after he has completed an examination by a fully independent board. The only people I had any authority to choose are my assistant superintendents, and I lost that in decentralization. The community is going to choose them now. But the union says it wants objectivity in the selection of people. The union does not want favoritism; it will not stand for favoritism. It does not want a principal of a high school to pick out Miss Jones to be a guidance counselor because he likes Miss Jones. Let me take the teacher who supervises student publications. When that teacher's term of office is over, the union wants the job publicized to the faculty. Those who want the job apply for it, and the senior man gets it. The principals do not want that. Principals now say, "Wait a minute. Senior men may not be the kind of men who can run the student publications and get along with the children. He might be a fine teacher of Shakespeare, but he might not do well with the children. I want the man third down the line, and I want the right to pick that person." Each year the principal's authority is being narrowed.

The union is also arguing with us over supervision in general. In the last contract request they asked that no plan book be submitted to principals. They asked that after a teacher has received his tenure, which is at the end of the third year, he no longer be visited by a supervisor and that no official reports on the teacher be written. To none of these did we accede. If we were to accede to that we would generally give up any responsibility we had for seeing that teaching continued to be effective. I will grant you there are principals who do not use the plan book correctly. The principal who asks every teacher in the school to turn in a plan book every Friday afternoon and get it Monday morning is a bad example. He is not a principal; he is an inspector. But a principal has the right to find out, occasionally, if a teacher has planned. How can this principal be held responsible for the productivity of the school if he does not have that right? We do have a right to visit any teacher at any time to find out how effective his teaching is. But I do not believe that teachers on tenure should be overburdened with such observations.

Not all supervision is effective. I had a principal who walked in every morning about a quarter past nine, walked across the front of the room, looked out the windows, and walked out the back. That was all. He never said a word. I never knew if the windows were open enough, not open enough, what he saw, or what he did not. I do not like that kind of business at all—checking up on everybody every day. But I do think a person has a right, occasionally, to walk into my room, sit down, and listen to me teach for a while, see what I do, and write a report on me. I am being paid a salary to teach, not just to collect my check at the end of the month.

The other big difference of opinion we have with the union is the relief of what are called non-professional chores. We have hired thousands of school aides to watch the loading of buses, to patrol the halls, to help in the cafeterias, and to take away much of the non-professional work teachers used to do. We think that is right. If that leaves a teacher more time to prepare his lessons and do his teaching, fine. I must tell you now, and every time I say this it is recorded back in New York; I have not seen that this relief has improved teaching. I stand by that statement.

One of the unfortunate aspects of the teacher militancy in our city has been an estrangement from the community because of the militancy. A great part of our community is estranged from the teachers. The minority group communities, the Negro and Puerto Rican sections of our cities and their children, now make up 52% of our public school population. They have become embittered over the strikes by teachers and feel that the public schools do not teach their children well. In a recent strike people in the communities came in to man the classes. The Negro teachers, to a great measure, refused to walk out, and this created a cleavage here that is going to take a long time to heal. But we now have the community threatening teachers and pointing out teachers that are ineffective. We have teachers pointing out community leaders who are harrassing. We really have a confrontation, and we sit in the middle. When a member of the union struck a child and I preferred charges against him, the union wanted an impartial hearing for this teacher. They said to me, "You cannot do it because you cannot be impartial. Between the union on one side and an equally, if not more, militant community on the other side, you will bend with one pressure or the other." They indicated that neither the superintendent nor the Board could be strictly impartial; therefore, they wanted impartial arbitration by somebody outside the system. Two days ago I suspended two Negro teachers for taking their classes out of school to go to a Malcolm X Memorial. The union has indicated to me that it does not think their two teachers will get a fair shake. However you do it, there is one side that thinks you are going to do it the wrong way. So the question today is, do we need outside arbitration to insure objectivity?

Militancy in New York City has culminated in strike several times. There has been some harassment of principals. Harassment does not mean physical force. In certain schools the head of the union is a pretty rough guy, and he keeps after the principal—I want this done, I want that done. I must say, too, there are some schools where the principals are pretty rough. They keep after the union men and produce a little harassment, too. It is not all one way; except that, generally speaking, principals are not that strong. The union prints public advertisements in which it criticizes the school system in New York City. It makes public charges about things that we fail to do. It has the support of other labor groups, and it does seek legislation. There is nothing unusual about doing such things; these are the means of militancy for any organization. I am not being critical of any of them; I am merely stating a fact. What are the effects of it? First of all we have in New York City today much more aggressive teacher organization and teacher feeling than we've ever had. Five or six years ago the union had about 2,000 members. That was what the union had when it won the election. It now has 49,000, maybe more. We have a group of teachers who stand up and speak without an invitation—on anything. Despite the irritation, despite the annoyance and despite the pain and the aggravation, I think in the long run that it is going to be healthy. You will recall those books on school administration that talked about democratic administration. We should listen to the voice of the teachers; we should give him a part in decision-making. Well, that is what they are asking for. The teacher is beginning to believe that stuff. It has taken a long time for those ideas to come alive. Some of the administrators who have read them wish they could tear them out of the book.

Another thing is that we do have a somewhat divided staff for those *other people* who are not in the union. Those people who do not belong to the union are somewhat aggravated by union activity. I guess that is natural when you have one organization in the majority and a few others who are in the minority. There are today growing signs of antagonism between the union and the Negro teachers of our system—great signs of it.

We also have a group of embattled supervisors. This morning I heard talk about whether or not supervisors should organize. In New York City they have organized and been recognized by the Board. All of the supervisors in our city got together to defend themselves, as they said, from the effects of a union contract on them. Every union contract that gave more to the teachers took something away from the supervisor—either power, authority, a right of choice or something. Sometimes they were imagined more than real. Now we have an organization called The Council of Supervisory Associations made up of assistant principals, senior high school principals, and assistant superintendents. That is why I say that everybody is organized but the superintendent. The Council got together, went to the legislature, and got themselves an exceptionally good index. In our city when a teacher gets a raise, the assistant principal gets a raise, 1.45, and the elementary principal gets 1.7; junior high, 1.85; high school, 2.00, and assistant superintendents, 2.15. We are all together when it comes to the union's fighting for increases. How can we lose? Then on top of that we negotiate with that organization for further increases. We are now looking at this under the new law. We did this before the Taylor Law came in. We are looking to see whether all of these segments really have a right to be organized in *one*. The assistant superintendents of the city, who, theoretically, are carrying out the directions which I give within the policies of the Board, are in with organizations below them. It just doesn't seem to fit well. I agree sometimes with the gentlemen from Illinois that the superintendents *at least* belong to management. The principals in our city get there by competitive examination and not by our choice. We cannot fire them—they get tenure as principals; you can only fire a principal if he is totally ineffective, and who ever heard of a principal being totally ineffective—they may have some rights, and we are looking at them.

The other thing we have, as I indicated, is a very embittered, disadvantaged community. We have a number of disenchanted parents. This last time during the strike, the United Parents Association, which enrolls most of the parents in the city, came out against the union and actively manned classes in the schools. We also have a mayor who is angry at—well, he is angry at all unions right now. And we have a Board of Education which is very concerned about the future of these matters. Negotiations in our city have utilized so much of the funds available to us that there is nothing left for any other improvement in education. Because of our negotiations and other costs, we had to go to the mayor for 284 million dollars next year. The other day he told me we are not getting a cent.

I would like to raise a few questions about problems concerning militancy. What right do teachers really have to disrupt an instructional program when the program is already so short, and for the disadvantaged children of our community, the time is so short? If teachers do *not* have the right to disrupt, then how can they achieve their just demands in any other way? We just cannot go on interrupting programs every time somebody has a grievance. They cannot walk out and picket every time they do not get what they want. I don't think we can do that to children. But teachers do have a right to have *legitimate* demands settled by somebody.

Secondly, is it right to have supervisors unionized? If they are unionized, what are their roles? If they are unionized, should they be separate? I think supervisors have a right to *organize!* I don't know about *unionize.* I think they should be separate from classroom teachers. And I would venture to say that AASA does not belong in the NEA. It does not belong in the NEA anymore because the NEA is becoming, and maybe rightly so, a classroom teachers organization. If it is, *unfortunately,* the very nature of this makes it difficult for supervisors and teachers to be together in the same organization when negotiations is a big process. We are all in an educational business; we should be theoretically together. That is one of the reasons why I will not allow principals at the bargaining table. I sit at the bargaining table with my deputy superintendents. In another room I have the principals and others who advise me as to how far I can go and what it will do to their schools. They do not sit at the table because I do not want a confrontation between the men who are going to have to work out the problems in the schools and the teachers who are making the demands in that particular school.

What is the right of the public? After having the use of its funds decided through negotiations between the teachers and the board, with the public not having anything to say about it, what right does the public have to evaluate the performance of teachers? If teachers and the board are going to jointly make agreements, then is not the public going to say, "We had better have some objective proof of productivity?" This is what the public in New York is beginning to ask.

Fourth, I think that there are many elements in negotiations which strangle new ideas. We had to put a separate provision in ours this time—our union is interested in new ideas in New York City—for experimentation and demonstration. If you are going to hide-bind all of the assignments of teachers, the programming of teachers, the free time of teachers, what they can do and what they cannot do, how do you implement something new? How do you convey new ideas? How do you get to talk about a lengthened school year if you've negotiated the length of the year and nobody wants to go any further? When the cry is all less work, fewer days, and fewer hours, how do you talk about a longer school year? What are we going to do about the protection of mediocrity which occurs through many contracts? It does not say so, but to get rid of the mediocre person is next to impossible, especially with such protection.

And lastly, I want to say something *for* the union, if I may, because it looks as if I am against them. I am not. I have lived with this since 1961 and have done all the negotiating for the Board of Education—every minute of every contract, and this is our fourth one. I think the union has gained great things for the teachers in New York City which those teachers would *not* have gained, to the *extent* that they have gained, without the militancy of that organization. I think, though, that the union has helped to create a very unfortunate picture of the schools in New York City by constantly saying that it is a terrible school system, and then by constantly asking that more money be given to help continue it. I think that is damaging, and I think we are starting to work together to overcome that impression—to take a more positive look at it. I think the union is beginning to mature. After all, it is new in education. It took other unions a long time in many industries to mature. We are now working on a number of things. We are working on some experimental elementary school programs. We are working on new internships for training teachers. We are working on experimental all-year-round high school. I think the union will mature and be a powerful force in the education of New York City. I think we administrators have to learn that no progress has ever been made without stumbling a little bit along the way, and without making a few errors on the way, and without it being painful. So if New York City is a "Workshop for Teacher Militancy," it is all right with me; providing, the leaders of teacher militancy respect *their* public responsibility as well as *I* have to respect mine. We happen to be partners in the same business, and we will either rise or fall *together*, not separately, and as we do the city falls with us, or rises with us.

Teacher-Administrator-Board Salary Negotiations in Oregon— A Case Analysis

"The sleep of reason brings forth monsters."
F.J. de Goya (1746-1828)

Patrick W. Carlton

When man stops employing rational processes and turns to reaction or to political expediency, he becomes immediately liable to the imperfections and distorting influences that are inherent in these processes. This statement applies particularly well to the passage of legislation, in this case Oregon's teacher consultation law. This law was the product of compromises by powerful lobbying groups within the state, and as a result, bears only superficial resemblance to the bill originally introduced in the Oregon legislature during the 1965 session. The statute, ORS 342.450, popularly referred to as the teacher consultation law, grants to certificated personnel (teachers and all administrators except the superintendent) the right to "confer, consult and discuss on salaries and other economic policies" with local boards of education.[1]

The legislative history of this statute was stormy. Having been introduced by the State Education Association, the bill was strongly opposed by the School Board Association, which, under the leadership of its executive secretary, marshalled sufficient support among legislators to force substantive changes in the proposed bill. The bill was also opposed by teacher union advocates, who apparently felt that no law was preferable to a teacher association law.

Originally, the bill granted permission for "representatives of any organization or organizations" through use of established

Revised from an article in Harold I. Goodwin and Patrick W. Carlton, Eds., *Above the Salt: Militancy in Education* (Morgantown: West Virginia University Press, 1968). Dr. Carlton was formerly a Postdoctoral Research Associate at the Center for Advanced Study of Educational Administration, the University of Oregon. He is currently Associate Professor of Educational Administration, New York University.

[1] The material in this section is taken from Patrick W. Carlton, *Teacher Salary Negotiations: A Case Study and Analysis* (Portland: Oregon Education Association, 1968).

administrative channels, to meet, confer, and negotiate with their employing board of education... in an effort to reach agreement in the cooperative determination of salaries. ... Whenever it appears to the administrative officers of the State Board of Education that ... a persistent disagreement between the board of education of any school district and the certificated professional employees of the board (exists), the administrative officer of the State Board of Education may act to resolve the disagreement ...

The administrative officer may determine a reasonable basis for settlement of the dispute and recommend the same to each of the parties ... In the event that agreement is not reached, the administrative officer shall report his findings to the State Board of Education ..., to the parties involved and to the general public."[2]

The bill further proposed exemption of teachers from the prohibition against striking agencies of the state.

Under heavy pressure from the School Board Association, the representatives of the Oregon Education Association agreed to a revised version of the bill, which ultimately became law. In revised form, the bill provided for representation "individually or by a committee ... elected ... by a vote of a majority of the certificated staff personnel below the rank of superintendent .... " Thus, organizational representation was ruled out and a peculiar "teacher council" composed of "popularly elected" representatives, was provided for. Its disadvantages are readily apparent.

To begin with, the elected "conference committees," as they have come to be called, have no organizational ties, which means that no organizational funds are available to support their activities. This has left the school board with the responsibility for funding the activities of their bargaining opponents, a situation judged by many to be odd. Secondly, the committee has no formal organizational machinery designed to supply it with information on salaries and to communicate teacher desires to the group. Finally, the Conference Committee is accountable, in an immediate sense, to no organization, a fact which raises a question as to just how powerful such committees could and should be. True, the Conference Committee members can be recalled, and they have to stand for election to office, but, in a day-to-day sense, they are immediately accountable only to their collective consciences.

<hr />

[2] An analysis of ORS 342.450 to 342.470 Relating to Working Relations Between Boards of Education and Certificated Personnel (Eugene: Oregon School Boards Association, 1965), p. 1.

The revised bill excludes the term "negotiation," indicating that teachers "...shall have the right to confer, consult, and discuss in good faith with the district school board on matters of salaries...and related economic policies affecting professional services."[3] Apparently the exclusion of the words "negotiate" and "in an effort to reach agreement..." stem from the fact that negotiated settlements are generally thought by boards of education to involve a loss of legally delegated authority and to weaken their control in decisional matters. This appears, in fact, to be the case. As to the meaning of "confer, consult and discuss in good faith," labor relations provides little clue. It appears that this wording was inserted by teacher association personnel in the hope that the phrase would be accepted by boards as being synonymous with "negotiations." As seen later in this study, such has not been the case in Oregon.

The change in wording from "...salaries...and related personnel policies..." to "...salaries...and related economic policies..." was apparently an attempt on the part of board lobbyists to restrict the scope of consultation to salary matters, and to avoid consideration of other school policies. However, given the facts that most school matters are economically related, and that interpretations currently being given elsewhere as to what constitute bargainable areas in this regard, tend to enlarge the scope of such bargaining, this restrictive attempt seems doomed to failure.

An addition not found in the original bill deals with election and certification of the Conference Committee. This clause states that "the district school board shall establish election procedures and certify the committee which has been elected...." It can be seen that this situation could lead to domination of conference committees by boards of directors. The mere possibility that a statute might countenance control of a group's representatives by those with whom the representatives must deal, raises questions concerning the adequacy of the law.

The provision in the original bill calling for fact-finding by the State Superintendent of Public Instruction on his own initiative was deleted and a clause inserted dealing with the appointment of a board of "consultants," consisting of "...one member appointed by the board, one member appointed by the employees, and one member chosen by the other two members." This is a tried and true private sector bargaining practice. It appears that the major reason for this change involved fears on the part of school board personnel that

[3] *Ibid.*

interference by the state superintendent probably would not work to their benefit, since the state superintendent does not qualify as an unbiased party in such cases.

It is interesting to note that, while there is no requirement that *agreement* be reached under the law as finally passed, provision is made for the resolution of persistent *disagreement*. Such a state of affairs would very likely prove incomprehensible to one not familiar with the dynamics of the legislative situation in this case, in which two special interest groups, the Oregon Education Association and the School Board Association, lobbied vigorously in an attempt to gain organizational advantage.

The statute passed further omits the requirement that reports of settlement issued by the fact finders be made public. This was an attempt to avoid pressures that generally come to bear on the parties to a dispute in the event of public disclosures of this type. The prohibition against public employee strikes is continued under the new statute, those lines dealing with teacher exemption from this prohibition having been deleted. Significance here lies in the fact that the original Teacher Association sponsored bill sought to gain the right to strike for teachers within the state. Such an attempt indicates changing patterns of thought among the leadership of the traditionally conservative OEA which prior to this time consistently denounced the use of the strike as "infra dig" and unprofessional. It can be seen that there are difficulties involved in obtaining good legislation when powerful special interest groups are at work. In Oregon, the legislation passed does not qualify as outstanding.[4]

It satisfies neither of the interest groups involved, contains certain ambiguities, and seems destined to early amendment as a result. It is interesting to note that teacher groups and boards operated under the law in a relatively successful fashion during 1966-67, if the concept "success" can be operationized in terms of salary increases received by teachers. It appears that *de facto* negotiation is occurring and that the school boards, while fighting a "delaying action," are gradually moving toward negotiations with teachers in the traditional labor relations sense.

The specific object of research in oregon was a city of some 75,000 which I have chosen to call River City. River City has a school enrollment of almost 21,000, a 40% increase over the 1961

[4] Myron Lieberman indicated in 1967 that it was the worst law of this type that he had seen.

enrollment figures. All but 7 teachers hold the B.A. and 38% of all teachers employed by the district hold the masters degree. Teacher salaries have increased by 33% since 1957, from a starting salary of $3,768 for a B.A. and no experience in 1957 to $5,000 for the same qualifications in 1966. It should be noted, however, that the Cumulative Price Index rose 11.7% during the same period of time. After adjustment, one finds that the average salary increase from 1957 to 1966 averaged 2% per annum.

The School Board in River City is composed of middle to upper middle class professional people. Its ranks include a dentist, a lawyer, a minister's wife, the vice-president of a trucking firm, the director of a local charity, and two insurance agents. The board was expanded from 5 to 7 members in 1966, so that the 1966-67 negotiations were the first into which the board as presently constituted had entered. It soon became evident that the board was composed of two factions, a conservative group, composed of the more experienced members, and a liberal group composed of the three newly elected personnel. The single female board member, whom I shall call Mrs. Wrenn, stood somewhere between the factions, voting first with one side and then with the other. Her vote became a critical matter during the 1966-67 salary negotiations. The Teachers Conference Committee was duly elected in a school board conducted election in November, 1965. Normally composed of seven members, the committee had suffered a resignation and operated during the period of the study with only 6 members. The Committee had two factions which I have designated "liberal" and "moderate" because of their general approaches to negotiations. The group included two elementary school classroom teachers, a guidance counselor, a high school principal, a junior high school vice-principal, and a high school math teacher. The law required that the Committee bargain for both principals *and* teachers, and that the administrators be represented on the Committee.

The superintendent, Dr. Wright, was employed in the early 1960's as an "innovator." He followed a traditional "bricks and mortar" superintendent, and has earned River City Schools a state-wide reputation as "forward-looking" and "creative." Dr. Wright is adept at interpersonal processes, and moves quite well between the board and teachers, spreading "oil on the troubled waters" as necessary. The law omits the superintendent from formal negotiatory participation, a situation quite different from that which existed prior to passage of the consultation law. Previously, Superintendent Wright acted as the official spokesman for the board in salary matters and also represented teacher interests to the board. Suddenly, he was left "out in the cold," so to speak, a situation which he refused to accept, with interesting results. The negotiations that developed were carried on in an atmosphere of vagueness and uncertainty. At the first meeting of the season, the board's attorney, Mr. Ammons, stated in no uncertain terms that no negotiations would take place. Mr. Ammons was one of those responsible for the amendments to the law. He worked with the State School Board Association in lobbying for the changes. He was, consequently, vociferous in his claims that the board retained the right to make all decisions, and that the only obligation implied by the law was that the board must talk things over *with the teachers* before acting. He stated during an interview that "it's impossible to misinterpret the difference between the terms 'negotiate' and 'confer, consult, and discuss.' There *is* a difference—an intended difference."

It was apparent, also, that Mr. Ammons was quite ego-involved. He stated that ". . . it's annoying to beat them in the legislature and then have them beat us in the meetings." He said that the establishment of *de facto* negotiations is "hard on the old ego." In spite of Mr. Ammons' adamant opposition, however, a form of negotiations did develop.

The relationship that developed was a peculiar, "tri-partite" arrangement, in which teachers, board, and superintendent made proposals and counter-proposals, albeit in a highly informal manner. The board, throughout this period, claimed vociferously that it would not negotiate, then proceeded quietly to do so, much as the maiden who, "declaring she would n'eer consent, consented." This "tri-partite" bargaining gambit will be described in a few moments. The original teacher proposal called for a starting salary of $6,000 for a B.A. and no experience and a maximum of $11,262 for an M.A. plus 45 quarter hours and 15 years of experience. Current starting salary at that time, as mentioned previously, was $5,000. In a series of negotiatory moves, the board, teachers, and superintendent reached a negotiated settlement of $5,800 for a B.A. and no experience and a maximum of $10,556 for an M.A. plus 45 quarter hours and 15 years of experience. The maneuvers by which this agreement was finally reached are instructive.

Following the initial presentation by the teachers of their $6,000 proposal, the school board said little and opted for an early adjournment. At a meeting held several weeks later, the board, while vehemently denying that it was proposing anything, suggested a $5,500 salary schedule. There was no response from the teachers, who were honoring their "commitment tactic." One teacher negotiator indicated that they would "hang tough" on their proposal. At the same meeting, the superintendent proposed two salary plans, one based on a $5,700 starting salary and the other on $6,000. Neither the board nor the teachers responded to the superintendent's proposals.

Next, at a meeting some weeks later the board proposed a $5,500 starting salary with provisions for twelve-month contracts for some teachers. This was done casually and with great display of verbiage to the effect that the board would not negotiate. The teacher team did not respond to the board's proposal, either because they honestly did not recognize it as such or because they felt it desirable to continue the pursuit of their commitment tactic. The superintendent then suggested a starting salary of $5,700 with twelve-month contract provisions for part of the staff. The board failed to respond to this proposal, as did the teacher team, probably taking its cue from the board's actions.

At this point in negotiations, there was considerable confusion as to just what the board intended to do. Their constant declarations of non-negotiation and refusal to commit themselves to a position added to the vagueness of the situation. However, this vagueness also lent flexibility to the relationship, flexibility which was vitally needed by the negotiating parties.

In January, 1967, at a public meeting of the board, Superintendent Wright proposed a $5,800 base salary with provisions for summer employment for about one-third of the teaching staff. The Superintendent's proposal came after a series of bombastic remarks made by the mayor of River City, in which the mayor castigated the teachers for their financial anxieties and stated that "when it comes to paying (female teachers) $10,000 a year . . . then I think it's time to take a look at our whole card." These remarks aroused considerable ill-will among spectators, most of whom were local teachers or members of their families. Superintendent Wright chose this emotion-charged time to unveil his proposal. He, thus, appeared in the role of the "white knight" coming to the rescue at a propitious moment.

The teacher team returned at the next meeting with a proposal of their own. They had privately admitted that they could accept anything between $5,700 and $6,000 without engaging in militant acts. We can call this the teachers' aspiration range. The superintendent's proposal, then, was well within the teachers' aspiration range.

Their strategy at the meeting was to get the board to commit itself to the superintendent's $5,800 proposal. This the board declined to do. Had the board made such a commitment, the teacher team could then have returned to their constituents for a vote on the board offer. If the teachers turned it down, they could then have returned to bargain in the range of $5,800-$6,000. As an alternate tactic, the teacher committee proposed a $5,800 starting salary with provision for higher increments at the upper end of the schedule. This proposal would have cost some $100,000 more than the superintendent's proposal. It was later determined that this reduction in demands was intended as a signal to the board as to what the teachers would settle for.

There was some danger in this move, since it left the board free to offer any amount it chose. The board had not committed itself at this point. As a matter of fact, one board member did ask that a $5,700 proposal. be presented at the next board meeting by the Superintendent. This was done, but the liberal wing of the board immediately amended the $5,700 base salary to $5,800 and the board adopted it unanimously. Thus, the board avoided committing itself until it was certain what the teachers would settle for, then moved to fulfill its legal responsibilities by unilaterally adopting a $5,800 proposal. This fulfilled the "letter" of the legal precedent calling for unilaterality of decisional control, while winking at the "spirit." The teachers concurred in the matter through expressions of satisfaction and through lack of militant display in the weeks that followed. As it turned out, both board and teachers worked hard to get the budget passed. The taxpayers defeated the budget twice, and it passed on the third attempt by only a small margin.

The Role of Superintendent

The superintendent's lack of legally assigned function rendered his status ambiguous, to say the least. He was confronted with the classic role conflict situation, defined by Parsons as ". . . the exposure of the actor to conflicting sets of legitimized role expectations such that complete fulfillment of both is realistically impossible."[5] He was expected by the school board to press for economies, while on the other hand being expected by the teachers to join the fight for a large salary increase.

[5] Talcott Parsons, *The Social System* (Glencoe: The Free Press, 1951), p. 280.

The superintendent was, in a word, confronted with Gross' classic alternatives. He could either 1) maximize A, 2) maximize B, 3) compromise, or 4) practice avoidance.[6] That is, the superintendent could have conformed to the teachers' or board's expectations, performed some compromise behavior which satisfied neither group completely but which each side could "live with," or could simply have withdrawn from the process completely, thereby avoiding the necessity for making a decision.

After the first meeting between the board and teachers' conference committee, during which he practiced avoidance by taking virtually no part in the proceedings, the superintendent assumed a mediatory role, attempting to bring about compromise by negotiating with both groups and aligning himself with neither side completely. This meant, then, that there were three, not two, bargaining agents in the process, in a loose sense: that is, the superintendent, the school board, and the teachers' conference committee. Both the board and the teachers were, in essence, dealing with the superintendent, whose $5,800 proposal was adopted by the board and accepted by the conference committee. He had, in effect, bargained with both sides.

This article has described a microcosmic representation of the stressful, complex, often traumatic episodes that occur daily in the broad field of negotiations which can be defined as the movement of teachers, as a power bloc, to gain for themselves additional influence in the operation of the schools. It seems reasonable to predict an intensification of the drive by teachers for more control over their working conditions.[7] It behooves school board and administrative personnel alike to prepare themselves as well as possible to meet the needs of the future along this line.

To quote an old Chinese sage, "That individual who prepares himself for the exigencies of today, survives to reap the benefits of tomorrow."

[6] Neal Gross, et al., *Explorations in Role Analysis* (New York: John Wiley & Sons, 1958), p. 284.

[7] Patrick W. Carlton, "Labor Psychology and Educational Planning," *Educational Leadership,* XXV (February, 1968), p. 428.

Politics and Education in
the Sunshine State—
The Florida Story

James Cass

Last February, when half of all Florida's public schoolteachers resigned and walked out of the schools in the nation's first statewide teacher strike, it seemed that a new era in teacher militancy had arrived. And when, three weeks later, most of them drifted back to their classrooms after failing to win their stated objectives—or even to gain terms of honorable surrender for some of their members—it appeared equally clear that the strike had been broken and that the "new era" had come to an early and inglorious end. But it is doubtful whether either of these easy generalizations offers an accurate reading of the tangled events of last fall and winter in the Sunshine State.

Rather, it appears that what happened in Florida was just one more step in the sequence of events that has marked the growing militancy of teachers in recent years. In 1964 and 1965, statewide pressure by teachers forced administrative or legislative action in behalf of the schools in Utah and Oklahoma. Last September, a series of teacher strikes tied up the schools in a number of the nation's large cities and smaller communities, and even while Florida's teachers were walking out, their colleagues in New Mexico were prodding state authorities into reluctant action. It appears, therefore, that it was the special circumstances encountered in Florida in 1967-68 that converted the *threat* of statewide action into a full-fledged walkout.

It also seems unlikely that the Florida experience will deter either the National Education Association (NEA) or its rival for teacher allegiance, the American Federation of Teachers (AFT), from seeking future trials of strength with the forces they see as standing in the way of both professional and educational advancement. It may, in fact, harden their resolve to prove at an early date that the Florida defeat was due solely to local circumstances. But it is not

This article is reprinted from *Saturday Review*, April 20, 1968, Volume 51, pp. 63-65, and 76-79. By permission of the author and the publisher. Mr. Cass is Education Editor of the *Saturday Review*.

likely that teachers anywhere will ever again challenge with such innocence the established political, economic, and social structure of an entire state.

The future for Florida is less clear. Certainly its teachers, in the spring of 1968, lost much of their girlish laughter—and took a long step toward learning the hard realities of political action. But whether they will ever again feel that the struggle is worth the candle remains an unanswered question. The state itself demonstrated a striking ambivalence toward the economic and social necessities of a progressive, industrializing community. A business associate of the Governor, over cocktails in a posh Jacksonville club, can speak passionately and knowledgeably about the central role of education in attracting new industry to the state. But over the next cocktail, as the conversation turns to the then impending teacher strike, he can with equal ease say: "So we close the schools for a year. Two years from now you'll never be able to tell the difference!"

Many, it seems, have learned the words of commitment to the second half of the twentieth century, but too few have learned the tune. And it may be for this reason that the interdependence of education and politics was displayed there, in recent months, with such stark clarity. For the Florida story grows directly out of the involvement of education in the politics of the state, the resulting professional frustrations the teachers have suffered over the years, and their increasing willingness in the 1960's to employ means to influence education policy that were not considered appropriate for professionals even a few short years ago.

For many years Florida's politicians have employed the rhetoric of commitment to education, but with a few notable exceptions have failed to match their words with action. The governor, elected for a four-year term, and constitutionally forbidden to succeed himself, typically comes into office with a campaign pledge to improve the schools in one hand—and an even more compelling pledge to impose no new taxes in the other. The legislature, which meets biennially, has been dominated traditionally by representatives of the small rural counties of the northern and central areas of the state.

In part, then, events of the past year can be interpreted as a revolt of the state's increasingly urban, progressive teachers against the conservative, rural-oriented political and economic forces that have long dominated the state. It was, for instance, the teachers in Dade County (Miami), Pinellas County (St. Petersburg), Duval County (Jacksonville), and Broward County (Fort Lauderdale) who provided much of the early initiative for the walkout. But such simple analysis promptly runs afoul of the many contrasts and contradictions with which the state abounds. For early in 1967, court-ordered reapportionment gave more balanced representation in the legislature to the urban centers of the state—and a number of these areas promptly replaced education-oriented Democratic legislators with more conservative Republicans who ran on a platform of local tax relief. The growing population in a number of these metropolitan centers on both coasts of the state (Fort Lauderdale and Palm Beach on the east, for instance, and St. Petersburg and Fort Myers on the west) has consisted in substantial part of over-sixty-five, retired people—who now make up a higher percentage of Florida's population than that of any other state except Iowa, and therefore have become a major political and economic factor in the life of the state.

Emphasizing the urban orientation of the revolt also obscures the widespread discontent of teachers in the state. The NEA's strong state affiliate, the Florida Education Association (FEA), has a membership that includes 55,000 of the state's 60,000 teachers and principals. When the walkout came, despite a variety of personal and ethical issues that kept many teachers in the classroom, most of the state's sixty-seven counties were strongly represented. The reason is not far to seek. For many months, Florida's teachers had been looking forward to the 1967 session of the legislature, which, they had reason to believe, could be persuaded to fashion a new deal for education. In 1965, a number of county teachers associations had asked the NEA to make a study of education in the state. The resulting report—"Florida: A Study of Political Atmosphere as It Affects Public Education," released in March 1966—documented the short-comings of the schools and made detailed recommendations for reforming education policy and practice in the state. Armed with more hard information than ever before, the FEA developed its legislative program many months before election, and was convinced that the state's teachers would be able to persuade the Governor and state legislators, who would be elected in the fall of 1966, to give education a priority spot on the legislative agenda.

Since the Democratic nomination for governor was tantamount to election in this Southern state, special interest centered on the bitter primary battle that resulted in the nomination of the mayor of Miami, the late Robert King High, a man with some reputation for liberalism who had made political capital in South Florida by inveighing against the financial "power structure," based largely in the northern counties. His opponent in the election was a conservative businessman and financier from Jacksonville, Claude R. Kirk, Jr.—a political neophyte whose only experience in public life had been gained in a losing race for the U.S. Senate in 1964.

During the campaign, candidate Kirk issued a fifty-page position paper on education in which he promised "to make Florida first in education," But he also stated unequivocally that no new taxes would be required to finance his program. Mayor High's views on education were less clearly defined, but he did promise to support new taxes for education. Though far from satisfied with the education platform of either candidate, the FEA endorsed High.

But election day showed that the deep wounds inflicted during the Democratic primary had not healed, and candidate Kirk's conservative program proved to be attractive not only to Florida's growing number of Republicans, but to the traditionally Democratic business and financial interests of the state as well. High was soundly defeated, and Florida elected its first Republican governor since Reconstruction.

Even before he assumed office in January 1967, the new governor displayed many of the qualities that were to characterize his first year in office. A large—6 feet 2 inches, 200-plus pounds—impressive man, he early exhibited a flamboyant affinity for newspaper headlines, an impressive skill in political polemics (a troublesome questioner will find himself aggressively cross-examined on a related but irrelevant question), and a remarkable talent for colorful invective (education leaders who are referred to as "educrats" or wielders of "blackboard power").

For an ambitious and dynamic man with a taste for power, however, the Florida governorship offers serious limitations. Administrative responsibility is divided among the governor and the members of his cabinet—composed of the Secretary of State, Attorney General, Treasurer, Superintendent of Public Instruction, Comptroller, and Commissioner of Agriculture. All members of the cabinet are elected officials, making them independent of the governor, and all are Democrats. (The first four, above, along with the governor, comprise the State Board of Education.)

It is hardly surprising, therefore, that shortly after the new administration took office, a political cold war developed between the Republican Governor and the Democratic members of his cabinet—and that the contest was extended to include the Democratic majority in the legislature when that body convened in April. It was with this three-way tug of war that the FEA had to contend as it mounted its aggressive campaign for increased state support for the schools.

To document the need for additional funds, the FEA pointed out that Florida was ninth in the nation in total population, ninth in public-school enrollment, and tenth in total personal income—but that it was twenty-sixth in average teacher salaries, thirty-fourth in per-pupil expenditures, and thirty-fifth in per-capita expenditures for local schools. These figures were also reflected in tangible shortcomings in the schools themselves: a shortage of classrooms that put substantial numbers of students on double sessions, textbooks that were often out-of-date and sometimes inadequate in number, a token kindergarten program that served only a tiny fraction of the state's children, and a special education program that had never come close to meeting the needs of the state. Even in affluent, education-conscious Dade County, there were gross inadequacies, some schools that had lost accreditation, and a threat of disaccreditation hanging over others. In Governor Kirk's home school district of Jacksonville—Duval County—regional accreditation of all high schools was withdrawn three years ago, after five years of warnings. And when the Governor's own children reached school age, he found the elementary schools in Jacksonville so inadequate that he joined with eighty-odd other parents to found the South Side Day School.

Other factors, too, complicated the Florida education picture. The fastest growing state in the nation during the 1950's, Florida remained among the leaders in population growth during the 1960's—and the most rapid increases were among those of school age (five to seventeen years) and those over sixty-five. One partial result was the necessity for recruiting 11,000 new teachers each year to meet rising enrollments and to replace those who retired or moved elsewhere. Many of these new teachers had to be found in other states, and for a number of years, Florida had fared well in attracting some of the best of its neighbors' annual crop of new teachers. Although Florida's average salaries are relatively low when measured on the national scale, they compared favorably with those in other Southern states. But last year Georgia and Alabama raised teachers' salaries $1,200 and $1,000 respectively, and recruitment promised to be more difficult in the future.

The impact of population growth and escalating school problems was multiplied by a narrowly based tax structure that left untouched major potential sources of revenue in the state. Depending largely on an ad valorem real estate tax at the county level, and a sales tax and other consumer taxes (on beverages, cigarettes, and gasoline, for instance) at the state level, Florida is constitutionally forbidden from levying an income tax on either individual or corporate income. According to the Florida Development Commission, business and industry pay just 7.87 per cent of the total taxes collected in the state, in contrast to an average of 15.69 per cent for the states of the Southeast, and an average of 18.17 per cent for the entire United States. The Development Commission views the situation as ideal for enticing new industry to Florida that will contribute to an increase in the state's total wealth. It was this assumption—that new industry feeding an expanding economy would provide adequate revenues to meet the needs of government—that provided the basis for the Governor's no-new-tax pledge.

But informed students of the state's economy hold other views. Until the tax base is broadened to obtain reasonable revenues from business and industry, they say, education can never be financed adequately. They hasten to add that it isn't that the financial and industrial interests of the state are "deaf to the needs of education"; it is just that other matters are more important to them. As teachers have observed major sectors of wealth in the state paying only a minor share of the costs of government, their frustration has grown.

As the spring of 1967 advanced, the political debate grew more acrimonious. The Governor remained irrevocably committed to his no-new-tax pledge—and was giving increasing evidence of interest in the national political scene. As his speech-making travels to other states multiplied, it became clear that he was attempting to establish himself as a conservative Republican alternative to former Governor George Wallace of Alabama, and, thus, as a Vice-Presidential possibility.

The legislature found itself unable to agree on education legislation—with the ever-present threat of veto—and the regular session ended with no action taken. During an extended thirty-day session, a succession of education acts was passed, only to be vetoed by the Governor. The FEA, meanwhile, was aggressively demanding massive new funds for education, including $300 million for teacher pay raises. When the regular session ended with no action, the FEA followed through on a long-standing threat to impose sanctions (a form of professional blacklisting) on the state, which included: censure of the Governor, nationwide notice to business and industry of educational "conditions in the state," and warning to teachers in other states, as well as to Florida teachers not under contract, that if they took jobs in the state they would be subject to charges of violation of the Code of Ethics of the Education Profession.

Finally, on June 29, the Governor used his constitutional power of line-item veto to write his own budget, eliminating $103 million from the education program passed by the legislature, and leaving just $77,000,000 for teacher pay increases.

The FEA immediately demanded that a special session of the legislature be called to meet its demands—and talk of mass resignations and a statewide walkout in the fall became more common. The possibility received added impetus early in July when the NEA, at its annual convention in Milwaukee, redefined its position on teacher strikes. In a complete reversal of its traditional posture, the association asserted that when good-faith attempts at resolution of conflicts have failed and strikes occur, "the NEA will offer all of the services at its command to the affiliate concerned to help resolve the impasse." The FEA's hand was substantially strengthened.

But the Governor had seized the initiative. He had kept his pledge, and had an education bill with no increase in taxes. The teachers' high hopes for making 1967 a banner year for education in Florida seemed doomed. The months of preparation and struggle, however, had given the teachers a sense of professional purpose that they had never had before. "One thing the Governor has accomplished for education," FEA leaders were fond of repeating, "is to unite the teachers—something they were never able to do for themselves." But the issue went deeper than that. What the teachers had developed was a sense of professional group solidarity that made them a formidable political force—more potent, events later proved, than they themselves realized. With only fragmentary support from their communities, a legislature that was unable to override a veto, and an administration adamantly set against their demands, they turned in upon themselves for mutual support within the group.

At a statewide teachers rally in August, 1967, at the Tangerine Bowl in Orlando in the center of the state, more than 30,000 wildly cheering teachers, gathered from all corners of the state, greeted with tumultuous approval their leaders' request that they resign in a body if the state refused to provide additional funds for the schools. FEA began to collect signed but undated resignations in earnest.

The Governor dismissed the Orlando rally as a "voodoo meeting" and, over a statewide television and radio network on September 5, 1967, presented his own plans for making "Florida first in education"—by 1975. Outlining a broad program of reform for the schools, he made it clear that he would not approve additional funds for education until a long-term program for the restructuring of the schools had been developed. To create such a master plan, he proposed to appoint a thirty-man, blue-ribbon Commission for Quality Education in Florida that would be instructed to bring in its report by a year from the following December. He had nothing to say about the current crisis, but in his closing peroration, he admonished the state's restive teachers to "ask not what the state can do you you—rather ask what can the state do for education and what can you, as a teacher, do to make education do more for our children."

During late August and early September, 1967, a number of local teachers' associations had been negotiating with their county school boards, and in several cases more than half of the school system's teachers had resigned after the boards refused to raise the local funds necessary to make the improvements they demanded. Late in September, the FEA scheduled another statewide rally for a final showdown—if a special session was not called for November.

But, behind the scenes, active negotiations had been under way among members of a joint legislative committee, representatives of the Governor's office, the state superintendent, and the FEA. On October 5, 1967, in a dramatic about-face, the Governor announced that a special session would take place shortly after the first of the year. "It has never been a question of whether there would be a session on education," he asserted. "It was a question of when." Arrangements were made for the Commission on Quality Education to complete its fifteen-month study in two-and-a-half months to provide the basis for legislation by the ten-day special session, scheduled for January 29, 1967, and to be devoted to education.

When the legislature convened, it replayed in miniature the drama of the regular session in the spring. No agreement was reached on legislation during the allotted ten days, and a compromise was found only during the closing hours of a week-long extension. The result was a $350-million package, of which some $70,000,000 was for noneducational purposes, and about $66,000,000 was slated for local tax relief. A total of $158 million was allocated to the state's elementary and secondary school programs, including $58,000,000 for increased teacher salaries. Predictably, new revenues required were derived from an increase in the sales tax and other consumer taxes.

Both the FEA and the Governor promptly labeled the legislation uacceptable. The teachers objected because it provided major funds for noneducational purposes, and therefore, education was saddled with the onus of new taxes from which it would not benefit. The Governor rejected the package—and threatened a veto—because the legislature had not agreed to his demand that any new taxes be submitted to popular referendum, which would bypass his no-new-tax pledge. (He had long said that he was willing to support any new taxes that the people voted on themselves.)

Without waiting to discover what action the Governor would take, the FEA went ahead with plans for the long-threatened walkout. On Friday, February 16, the day the legislature adjourned, the state's teachers were notified that their resignations (a reported 35,000) had been "activated" by the FEA and that they were not to return to their classrooms on Monday. When that day came, some 30,000 of the state's 60,000 teachers stayed home—and at long last the strike was on.

From the beginning, it was clear that salaries were no longer an issue, at least for the majority. Substantial increases from both the regular and special sessions acts had raised average salaries in the state to an estimated twelfth place in the nation. Too, many of the educational programs the teachers had been supporting received substantial funding. Therefore, the inevitable question is why they walked out. The teachers claimed that the acts passed were still inadequate, and that the special session called solely to act on education issues voted funds for noneducation programs. But the reasons go deeper.

It seems clear one factor was that this past spring Florida reaped the fruits of its success in attracting many of the better young teachers from other parts of the country. It is often the more vital, the more adventurous—the more committed—teachers who leave the safe confines of home to try their fortunes elsewhere. Some of them found more limited facilities for effective teaching in Florida than they had known before—or than they had anticipated. All suffered as their expectations for dramatic improvements in the schools in 1967 were progressively frustrated.

It is clear, too, that concessions won by force from a reluctant donor can lead only to a sense of alienation and a feeling that more force might have garnered greater rewards. By the exercise of group power, Florida's teachers had bent an unsympathetic governor to their will and forced him to call a special session of the legislature. In the process, they had developed a feeling of group solidarity that gave them an unaccustomed feeling of power. They found it difficult not to exercise it—in a situation in which a more sophisticated group might well have hesitated.

The strike itself was a triumph and a disaster. Starting with half the teachers in the state—and with many others in strong sympathy with the movement but unable or unwilling to make the personal sacrifice—the number dwindled to less than a third by the time the settlement came. One reason for the attrition was the complex issues posed by the walkout. State law forbids strikes by public employees, and those convicted of striking are forbidden to seek public re-employment for a period of one year. There was some confusion over whether the presentation of signed resignations successfully circumvented the provisions of the law, but in any case, a provision in the contracts calling for thirty-day notice was not observed. Therefore, the teachers were clearly in violation either of the law, or of their signed contracts, or both. But with the number of teachers who walked out varying from a handful in some small counties to 6,000 of Dade County's 9,000 teachers, both school and state officials tended to concentrate on means for enticing the teachers back to the classroom rather than on retaliation.

More important—and more interesting—however, were the many ways in which the established society marshaled its forces to contain and control the alien force. The first state in the country to pass a right-to-work law, Florida has never been hospitable to anything smacking of union activity. But no one knew, in the beginning, exactly how much power the teachers had—including the teachers themselves. Therefore, the initial effort was to find ways to keep the schools open—and so to dilute the impact of the walkout.

State regulations were modified to allow anyone with two years of college to teach in the schools as a "qualified" substitute, and to allow those who could not even meet this requirement to man the classrooms if enough "qualified" people could not be found. Retired teachers, parents, and others with some higher education were urged to serve in the emergency—and some business corporations offered employees the opportunity to continue on full pay while serving as teachers, and enjoy their substitute's pay as well. Newspapers published daily lists of the schools that were "open," even though some of them were maintaining only a token number of classes and little instruction took place. (As State Superintendent Floyd Christian told the state board of education, "We are keeping school, but we are not teaching school.") In some cases it was the students who finally rebelled at classes that provided only custodial care.

When the teachers' resignations were presented en masse by leaders of the movement, they were told that they could not be accepted. Each teacher had to write out a separate resignation and send or deliver it individually to the local board. Selective acceptances of resignations also served to remind the teachers again that they were playing with professional fire. Meanwhile, in some counties court orders forced the teachers back to the classroom—or forbade them to leave in the first place. And the weight of public opinion was brought to bear in an infinite number of ways that ranged from indirect moral suasion (fulsome public appreciation of the teachers who did not strike and the substitutes who took the places of those who did) to petty harrassments of many kinds (installment loan payments collected with excessive promptness, members of teachers' families warned that they would suffer if the teacher did not return to the classroom). In addition, county teacher associations found repeatedly that the attorney they had hired was no longer free to keep them as clients, and the hall they had hired for a teachers' meeting had suddenly became unavailable.

But the ambivalence with which the state approached the crisis is, perhaps, best demonstrated by the contrasting actions and attitudes of the Dade County school board, and the Associated Industries of Florida, an association of all the major business, financial, and industrial interests in the state. In the second week of the strike, the executive vice president of the Associated Industries directed a letter to members of the state board of education urging them to use their power to see that all resignations submitted to county school boards be made effective immediately. "It is far better to endure pain briefly now while effecting a cure," the letter said, "than to allow a cancerous growth to erode our basic system of government." Since more than a third of the state's teachers were still out of their classrooms, and Florida has to recruit 11,000 new teachers each year under ordinary conditions, the Associated Industries was, in effect, proposing that the state put itself in the position of having to replace more than half of its teachers by the time school opened in the fall.

A few days later, the Dade County school board took a very different position when negotiating the return of its teachers at the conclusion of the strike. By no means in sympathy with the strike, the board was primarily concerned with the welfare of the schools. Therefore, when the FEA demanded that all striking teachers in the state be taken back by their local school boards before any would go back—and it was clear that some "hard line" boards would not allow all striking teachers to return—the Dade County board not only accepted back all of its own teachers who wanted to return, but also offered to hire as many as possible of the teachers who were rejected in other counties.

When the teachers walked out, the Governor played it cool—and continued to pursue the Vice-Presidential nomination. By striking, the teachers had handed him all the options: to veto (as he had threatened), to sign (as a friend of education), or to allow the bills to become law without his signature (which, in fact, he did). Meanwhile, away from home he was able to appear as the strong man who "stood up to the strikers," and at home he could afford to wait to make a decision until he discovered how strong the teachers proved to be.

After the Governor allowed the bills to become law, on March 8 (a veto, he said, "would be yielding to the demands of the militant education associations"), all that remained was to find a face-saving formula for the teachers' return. (The teachers claimed that to hold out longer would allow the anti-education forces to destroy the schools.) A crucial element of that formula was agreement that no teachers would go back until all could go back. On Saturday, March 9, the FEA sent word to county teacher associations that their members were free to return to their classrooms on Monday. Almost immediately it became clear that some counties would not honor the agreement reached at the state level, and that a substantial number of teachers would lose their jobs. A frantic effort was made to reverse the back-to-the-classroom directive. But it was too late. The group solidarity that had held firm in the face of external forces had been shattered by an internal snafu.

As the strike ended and the teachers returned to their classrooms, there was no doubt that the events of that period will have profound and lasting effects on the teachers and the schools in Florida. It is still too early to draw up any balance sheet of what was gained and lost, but some preliminary judgments can be made.

It seems clear, for instance, that, of the teachers who walked out of their classrooms, a substantial proportion (though by no means all) were among the better teachers in the schools—the ones who felt most keenly the inadequacies of time and facilities for teaching. (The deadwood and marginal performers are less likely to be moved by professional frustrations to risk their careers in seeking reform.) In some of the "hard line" counties it is against these teachers—often leaders within the local group—that local resentment is most intense. The schools and their students will, in such cases, be the losers.

It seems equally clear that numbers of teachers have already left Florida to teach in other states—and that many more will follow them before the effects of recent events have faded into the past. During the walkout, recruiters from a number of cities and states were busy interviewing teachers—as well as prospective teachers at the state's universities. Even among those who remained in their classrooms, there are numbers who have stated their firm intention to leave the profession or to pursue teaching elsewhere. The magic name "Florida" will continue to attract recruits from other parts of the country, and the higher salary schedules made possible by the new legislation of 1967 and 1968 will facilitate the process. But not all the teachers who leave will be easily replaced—even though their positions may be filled.

The schools in the state made substantial gains in the support they will receive—and educational programs of many kinds should be strengthened. But a high price may have been paid. In a period of rapidly increasing professionalism among teachers, Florida's schools, through the employment of untrained laymen to man the classrooms, told the public, in effect, that anyone can teach. The long-term effect on public attitudes toward the schools and their support cannot yet be assessed, but it is hardly likely to be positive.

But most important of all, it seems certain, is the effect of the strike and its aftermath on the teachers themselves. The motivations that prompted 30,000 professional teachers to abandon their classrooms inevitably were mixed and varied. Some no doubt were moved solely by the desire for higher pay. Others went along with the crowd. But many teachers in affluent school districts where they had little or nothing to gain personally in salaries or working conditions proved to be among the most militant, often at great personal sacrifice. It seems clear, then, that these teachers acted (whether rightly or wrongly) out of a strong personal commitment to the improvement of education in Florida. They believed that an opportunity was offered to make a major breakthrough in support for the schools of the state—with the ultimate beneficiary the child in the classroom.

But when they returned to their classrooms, overwhelmingly they were not only defeated, but disillusioned. No one cares, they said, except us. The state responds only to power, the local school boards are more interested in retaliation than in education, and even the parents remain unconcerned. So why should we continue to care? Perhaps this is the most destructive legacy of all.

The Academicians

The model now emerging in collective negotiations in education is patterned closely after the general model employed by organizations more experienced in the bargaining process, particularly labor unions. This is hardly surprising. The collective efforts of the National Education Association, expressed through professional sanctions, were fairly unproductive. The sanctions model simply lacked sufficient power options to overcome the resistance of management. But the acceptance of an alternative negotiations model was, for the Association, very difficult. Long accustomed to the avoidance of "blue collar" tactics, the Association viewed as unprofessional the negotiations developing within the American Federation of Teachers. However, following the gains obtained by the Federation through a series of strikes, the Association altered its stand on the strike as a power tool. It is evident that the standard private sector negotiations model is rapidly becoming the norm in educational bargaining.

The lesson learned by the Association from the bargaining tactics and strategies oriented toward the private sector is part of the general movement within education toward a more militant posture aiming at a greater share in economic resources, in determining welfare conditions, and in the making of major policy decisions. This changing state of affairs has been analyzed by a number of scholars. Part Three attends to four dimensions of that analysis. Section A is concerned with the relationships between private sector and public sector bargaining. Section B centers upon more theoretical considerations in the negotiations model and devotes some attention to the strategies and tactics of negotiations. Section C focuses on the trend toward collective negotiations in higher education.

*Collective Negotiations and
Public Sector Bargaining*

According to Warner, the phenomenon of collective bargaining in the public sector has developed so rapidly in recent years that little organized and scholarly attention has been devoted to its study. He proceeds with a discussion of characteristics and problems arising as a result of collective bargaining, focusing particularly upon the impact of the process upon public finance and governmental authority. Doherty explicates a number of the basic questions concerned in the application of the labor model of collective bargaining from the private sector to collective negotiations in the public sector. His analysis includes consideration of the strike question, the composition of bargaining units, and various cost considerations involved in bargaining.

The issue of negotiation costs is also treated by Moskow and McLennan as a tactic of negotiations. They point up several mechanisms employed in negotiations, such as the use of fact-finding and arbitration. Using the Tennessee Valley Authority as a backdrop, Massey draws specific parallels between the phases and steps in grievance procedures in the private sector and developing practices in education. Doherty returns with the results of a study of school superintendents involved with the Taylor Act in New York and the impact of the act on collective bargaining. Doherty covers problems involved in the application of the labor model to education in terms of the differing reasons for the existence of public and private sector organizations.

What Does Public Management Think About Collective Bargaining in the Public Service?

Kenneth O. Warner

In response to the question, "What does public management think about collective bargaining?", a friend of mine who is an expert in public administration recently said: "That's a good question. Do you have another?"

His reply was not intended to be flippant. It implied that the question is tough ... that it's hard to answer simply ... that solid facts about the query are lacking ... that it involves a complicated subject ... that public management holds widely varying views on the question.

The Purpose and Problem

The primary purpose of this paper is to set down the ideas of public management about public sector bargaining. In this approach public school administrators and boards of education are regarded as being on the public management side of the bargaining table.

The major problem presented in attempting to answer the question is the limited amount of systematic study that has been given to this particular subject. The phenomenon of wide-scale collective bargaining in the public sector is of such recent origin that scholars have not yet researched it in depth. In fact I know of only one unpublished study that deals systematically with the topic. Winston W. Crouch, of the University of California at Los Angeles, recently completed a study of "Employer–Employee Relations in Council–Manager Cities," which sheds some light on what one group of public administrators thinks.[1]

Revised from *Collective Bargaining in the Public Sector,* A Conference Report from the 5th Annual Orvil E. Dryfoos Conference on Public Affairs, Public Affairs Center, Dartmouth College, Hanover, N.H., 1968. Mr. Warner is Executive Director of the Public Personnel Association.

[1] Winston W. Crouch, "Employer-Employee Relations in Council-Manager Cities," unpublished study.

Where Can the
Answers Be Found?

Answers to the question posed in this paper must be sought from three sources:

1.   The issues raised by public officials who are now taking stock of their role in the bargaining process and who are puzzled by the problems that now confront them as they approach the bargaining table.
2.   The relatively limited experience of educators and public officials in negotiating contracts with public employees;
3.   The obvious changes in administrative practices that result directly from collective bargaining.

Aids to Crystallization
of Views

A number of developments during the past few years have contributed to the awakening of public management and to a crystallization of its views on collective bargaining. Included are the following:

Laws and Agreements. Union-sponsored comprehensive bargaining laws in a dozen states, and piece-meal arrangements in a score of others, have forced public officials to take stock. Several thousand agreements in all levels of government brought public officials face-to-face with a new set of problems calling for solution.

Inquiries. For the past six or seven years personnel officials in this country and Canada have peppered the Public Personnel Association with sticky questions confronting them in their day-to-day relations with organized employees. These questions in themselves give some rather definite clues to the thinking of the personnel fraternity.

Seminars and Conferences. During the past five years the Public Personnel Association has sponsored more than a dozen seminars attended by 1,000 public officials from the United States and Canada. These seminars have widespread support; many were cosponsored by other organizations of public officials such as the

National League of Cities, the International City Managers' Association, the National Association of Counties, several state leagues of municipalities, local associations of school boards and county officers. At the same time seminars and conferences were being sponsored all over the country by colleges and universities and many other associations of public officials and school officials. These seminars and conferences contributed measurably to expression of ideas on bargaining and crystallization of thinking.

Official Studies. A dozen official studies of public employee relations conducted between 1961 and 1968 also gave public officials a better understanding of issues at stake. (These studies include the following: 1961 Task Force Report initiated by President Kennedy; the 1967 Committee appointed by President Johnson to review the effectiveness of Executive Order 10988; the 1967 Report of the Task Force on State and Local Government Labor Relations, undertaken by the National Governors' Conference; reports from New York City, 1966; Connecticut, 1965; Illinois, 1967; Michigan, 1967; Minnesota, 1965; New York State, 1966; Rhode Island, 1966; Maine, 1968; New Jersey, 1968.)

Trauma and Frustration

In my judgment the general reaction of public administrators to collective bargaining is one of frustration. Felix Nigro matter-of-factly says that bargaining has brought significant change to public administration both in doctrine and in practice.[2] I put the proposition in somewhat more challenging terms by saying that we are now going through a period when much of the content of public administration is being repackaged to fit the collective bargaining container. In essence this amounts to a revolution in public administration. When I speak of repackaging and a revolution, these are not just catch words. Witness the result in Canada of the decision by Parliament to install a genuine collective bargaining program for its federal employees, including (with some exceptions) the right to strike. This decision entailed a large-scale restructuring of the Civil Service Commission, the Treasury Board, and such areas as classification, pay, fringe benefits, etc. It is the extent of this repackaging process that frustrates public management. This frustration is brought about chiefly for two reasons:

[2] Felix A. Nigro, "Collective Negotiation in the Public Service," *Public Administration Review,* March-April, 1968.

1. It poses a serious threat to long-held management concepts, and
2. It plunges public managers into a strange, new, and to them untried system of public employee relations.

The severe shock induced by these developments has shaken public management into a state of trauma. As a result, for a decade or so, policy and administrative officials may be forced to the couch to ease their labor pains. They may become good subjects for group therapy which will bring them back to normal by letting them talk out their problems in the light of a better understanding of the bargaining process.

Support of Assertions

Standing alone these dramatic assertions may not be very convincing. But they can be supported, or at least explained more fully by citing opinion, fears, and facts. For example:

1. *Bargaining discards the traditional public management method of dealing with public employees.* Despite their preachments regarding cooperative and joint decision making, public management in this country traditionally has the last word in setting employee relations policy. That's why the method is called unilateral. The idea of sharing management authority has been and continues to be anathema to many public managers.

2. *Bargaining involves "gamesmanship."* The idea of give and take, trading, haggling, withholding, and all the other typical rituals of private sector bargaining frustrates the average public official. As stated by Eugene F. Berrodin, "By definition, a game implies some degree of nonsense activity, or at least non-productive activity."[3] On many occasions in our seminars public officials have said, "Why do we have to degrade ourselves and stoop to all of the hocus-pocus involved in bargaining? Can't we do this more intelligently?" The implication is "If you do it my way, that's intelligent."

3. *Bargaining thrusts public officials into a strange new world.* The terrain is unfamiliar; there are no guideposts to follow. The language of the new land is foreign. It may come as a surprise to some who are experienced in labor relations on

---

[3] Eugene F. Berrodin, "Cross Currents in Public Employee Bargaining," unpublished paper.

either side of the bargaining table that relatively few public officials know the terminology of bargaining. Many lack understanding of elementary terms like union shop, arbitration, and exclusive representation. This was brought home to me most forcefully a few weeks ago when I attended a labor relations seminar for municipal attorneys. Many times they demonstrated the truth of my observation. It is quite clear that few in the public sector have a background in the philosophy and lore of private sector labor relations. As noted by one observer, "To many public officials, particularly those who hade made public service a career and have no private business experience to draw upon, the collective bargaining process is a dark and uncharted area that they approach with much anxiety. To some extent, of course, many public officials are demonstrating an inborn resistance to change—but to a great extent their resistance to the adoption of the collective bargaining process is based on a genuine fear of the unknown."[4]

4. *Bargaining contravenes representative government.* Persons who have been immersed in private sector bargaining may scoff at this notion, held by many public officials.[5,6,7] The essence of the idea is simply this: we elect public officials to make laws, provide services, and administer them for the general good. Bargaining interferes with the concept of representative government because it delegates authority of legislative bodies to administrative officials and in some cases permits major public policies to be "negotiated" rather than determined by elected representatives. As has been stated in support of this position, "The extension of collective bargaining into the establishment of public policy (that is public policy questions which go beyond the traditional subjects of wages, hours, and other terms and conditions of employment) poses a possible threat to our system of representative government."[8] Bargaining as a method of

---

[4] M. D. Tarshes, "Developments in Employee-Employer Relations in the Public Sector," *Government Employee Relations Report,* No. 238, April 1, 1968.

[5] Fredrick C. Mosher, *Democracy and the Public Service,* Oxford University Press, 1968.

[6] Tarshes, *op. cit.*

[7] Kenneth O. Warner, (ed.) *Developments in Public Employee Relations,* Public Personnel Association, 1965.

[8] Tarshes, *op. cit.*

determining basic government policy, in contrast with determination by the legislative process, this observer notes " is an approach which is completely inconsistent with our system of government." The extreme view on this subject is that collective bargaining can lead to political anarchy.

5. *Bargaining denies management the right to manage.* This position rests chiefly on the notion that the prerogatives of management to direct the public enterprise are curtailed or denied to the extent that matters are negotiated instead of determined by the bilateral process implicit in bargaining.

The Specifics

It is my firm belief that little progress can be made in solving the problems of employee-management relations until the issues now being threshed out are recognized and conflicting positions clearly stated. Whether the views of management and unions are sound matters less than that they be declared.

What follows next is a quick survey of the impact of collective bargaining on public administration. It attempts to show the breadth and depth of the impact and particularly to spell out implications for personnel administration.

Broad Areas of Impact

Management, both in education and the public service, is awed by the scope of impact bargaining is making on administration. That is most notable in the broad field of public finance and organization.

Public Finance. There are obvious relationships between bargaining and fiscal processes in all public agencies. Where wages and benefits are subject to bargaining, the size of the budget and corresponding appropriations are affected. Budgeting procedures, tax arrangements, and sources of revenue are similarly affected.

Impact on Budget. As pointed out by Arvid Anderson, the budget-making process affects the scope of negotiation, the bargaining timetable, and the period through which a bargaining arrangement may run.[9]

[9] Arvid Anderson, "Current Trends, Recent and Predicted Developments," (unpublished paper from Public Personnel Association Seminar, Albany, N. Y., April, 1968).

In developing a workable timetable public officials must dovetail several considerations: the time for starting and stopping negotiations; the length of the contract period; the relation of the contract period to fiscal years; state legislation governing budget procedures of local governments; and state legislation or constitutional arrangements that regulate sources and distribution of revenue.[10]

For example, unless a contract or agreement is reached before the budget is approved, a government agency faces a dilemma. It must set up a contingency fund to meet expected increases as a result of future bargaining, maintain an open-ended budget, or not make pay adjustments until the next budget period. None of these methods of dealing with the problem is completely satisfactory, although some governments have been forced to use contingency or reserve funds. One observer of the process told me, "This destroys much of effective budget projection."

Unquestionably the budget process will be subjected to strains and stresses as a result of bargaining. In some jurisdictions under statutory bargaining distinct trends are already apparent. They include: a threat to legal restrictions that control the integrity of appropriations and tax limitations; demand for a municipal budget that is simple, understandable, and open for study by unions and the public; severe pressures on traditional budget and personnel techniques such as step increments; package deals in wages and benefits instead of cent-per-hour rates for given job classifications.

Impact on Amounts of Expenditures. It is difficult to decide whether expenditures for personal services increase more under bargaining than without it. A rise in the cost of living and general inflation unquestionably increase the cost of doing public business. But on the basis of a sampling of finance officers in the United States, I believe the most commonly held view is that bargaining does increase expenditures. This is true when fringe benefits are reduced to a dollar and cents cost.

Here are a few ingredients of the more bountiful benefit package, as envisioned by finance officers. Additional paid holidays, premium pay for certain specific holidays, new versions of stand-by pay, increased clothing allowances, increased vacation and sick leave, payment for unused sick leave on retirement or termination, lower or no public contributions to insurance and health programs, educational aids, more liberal pensions, increase in shift premiums, hazard pay,

---

[10] Kenneth O. Warner, "Financial Implications of Employee Bargaining in the Public Service," *Municipal Finance,* August, 1967.

special compensation for such things as carrying guns and working weekends. As one official expressed it, "Under collective bargaining, fringe benefits may be limited only by the capacity of employee representatives to devise them."

Impact on Taxes. So far as I can learn there has been no systematic study in this area. But on the basis of work done by the National League of Cities, it is clear that municipalities in this country are in poor financial shape. Part of the problem is inadequate revenue, which may be another way of saying municipalities do not get a fair share of the revenue pie. Educational people would also probably say they are in a similar position. If this is accurate, and bargaining pushes up the cost of personal service, as implied above, it follows that the quest for shared taxes or new tax sources for schools and local government will become acute and impose another knotty problem on local officials. As one observer said "... (My) city has little power to initiate new tax sources. Thus we are caught between mill limitations set by the state for property taxes and an inability to raise revenues from either a local sales or income tax. Should the economy falter, a cutback in services seems inevitable."

In a dispute between the City of Detroit and its police officers, a fact-finding panel recommended that the *maximum* salary of Detroit patrolmen with four years of service be increased from the present $8,335 to $10,000 a year. The panel's recommendations are non-binding. The panel declared that the "Detroit Police Department faces a manpower crisis," a major cause of which is a wage structure far below the level required by market forces. Referring to recent riots, the panel said, "the police force is the first line of defense against civil disorder ... but the present manpower crisis in the Detroit Police Department measurably heightens the dangers of uncontrollable disorder in the community. An immediate wage increase for Detroit policemen is *a matter of greatest urgency for the public welfare.*" Although the city contended it lacked necessary funds to pay the increase, the panel found that the city failed to establish that there are purely legal barriers, and that city has the legal authority to raise property taxes. The city has unused taxing powers.

According to the fact finders, *"The first order of business must be* the adjustment of police salaries that is now urgently required. *The second order of business must be* to make those budgetary adjustments that are necessary, including the seeking of new revenue sources." ·

In short, the panel recommended that because of the importance of a fully manned police force to the public welfare of Detroit residents, the city must place top priority on higher salaries and then increase taxes to provide funds.[11]

Impact on Municipal Bonding Authority. The extent of municipal bonding power generally rests on state statutes. There are instances over the country where voters have approved increased tax levies for policemen and firemen through referendums. It is conceivable that in some instances the quest for more income could lead to an expansion of bonding authority. In any event this is a specter which particularly bothers municipal officials.

Impact on Capital Improvements. Here again, I have found no studies which try to show that bargaining has curtailed expenditures for capital improvements. In a few isolated cases officials may believe this has occurred. One official reported to me last year that an employee group made some headway in giving priority to pay and benefits over capital improvements. He views this as short sighted, and states, "Benefits gained at the expense of capital improvements may come back to haunt employees as well as the public, for erosion of the physical plant makes what remains expensive and difficult to maintain."

Subcontracting Government Services. This practice now involves millions of dollars of expenditure in the federal service, and state and local governments have executed more than a thousand contracts. Already, when management has tried to effect economy by subcontracting services, unions have raised objections on a number on grounds.

Organizational Arrangements

Another important area to feel the bargaining impact is that of organizational arrangements. These include the manner of organizing the agency, regional arrangements, and even intergovernmental relations.

Internal Organization. Here the major problem is: who bargains for the public employer. Because of the diffusion of responsibility in the public service, resolution of this question is much more difficult in the public than in the private sector.

---

[11] *Government Employee Relations Report,* No. 234, March 11, 1968.

This determination of who represents management is a very serious problem. Management should bring the power to negotiate to the bargaining table. Union officials say, "Don't send a messenger boy or bargaining will be a sham." Bargaining responsibility should be given to a management negotiator who has sufficient authority to make or to effectively recommend agreements, within limits of the authority conferred upon him.

The chief problem arises when decision-making responsibility is divided. In government, decision-making may be divided between the executive and legislative branches. Another aspect of the problem is encountered when agencies are funded by several sources. For example, a welfare agency may obtain funds from the county it serves, from a state department of welfare, and from a federal agency. Receipt of these funds may entail certain restrictions on how they are used. Such a county welfare agency may be unable to raise money to increase salaries determined through a bargaining agreement because it does not have the power to tax and is dependent upon these other sources for revenue.

A further factor to consider is that decision-making in the public service is heavily weighted by political considerations.

There is no one answer as to who speaks for public management because the public employer is not a single type. The answer varies depending upon the type of governmental units which have different legal and structural forms.[12,13]

Today the practice follows a crazy quilt pattern. There is no agreement about who should conduct negotiations. Should it be someone in the personnel department, a separate labor relations officer in the office of the executive, an independent agency—or the governing board, as a whole or through a committee? This latter query applies to a school board, city council, or even a state legislature. Should the final negotiating authority be the political leader of a given jurisdiction—a mayor, a governor—or a school board president?

In actual practice, in one place or another, all of the foregoing individuals or agencies have engaged in negotiations—some within the law; some outside the law. And while this may appear to involve an

[12] Milton Derber, "Who Negotiates for the Public Employer?" (unpublished paper from Public Personnel Association Seminar, Albany, N.Y., April, 1968).

[13] *Report of Task Force on State and Local Government Labor Relations* to the 1967 Executive Committee of the National Governors' Conference, Public Personnel Association.

elementary situation that could be easily solved, it accounts for continuing frustration among public administrators and educators.

Another facet of the "who does what" is the problem of what agency should administer the labor relations law or program. This is the agency that determines bargaining units, conducts representation elections, hears complaints, and provides services for resolving disputes.

The value of such an agency has been demonstrated in the private sector. It is equally valuable and necessary in the public sector. Recent testimony by a number of union and agency people before the President's Review Committee of Executive Order 10988 called for establishment of an independent board to administer federal labor relations. An Army spokesman urged that the proposed board should determine appropriate bargaining units, supervise elections, determine majority status, and adjudicate complaints under the Code of Fair Labor Practices.[14]

To date no common organizational pattern has emerged. Already existing agencies are used in a number of places. They include departments of labor, civil service commissions, state boards of education and local school boards, independent employee relations boards that serve both private and public sectors, and in at least one instance, the executive office of administration. New independent agencies to deal exclusively with public employee labor relations have been proposed—and have been established in New York City and State.

The proper administrative agency remains a moot issue at all levels of government. For states, the recent Task Force on State and Local Government Labor Relations of the National Governors' Conference did not make a clearcut recommendation. This group urged that final determination be made on the basis of availability of existing machinery, anticipated volume of cases, and reputation of existing agencies. I personally favor an agency that deals exclusively with the public sector, although I recognize that in some circumstances a single agency might appropriately administer public and private sector arrangements.

Consolidation of Governments. Turning to another impact, it is quite conceivable that consolidation of local governments in metropolitan areas will be hastened by collective bargaining. So far

---

[14] *Government Employee Relations Report,* No. 216, October 30, 1967.

the notion of a full-fledged, completely consolidated metropolitan government has made little headway. But the need for concerted action among metropolitan governments in gathering data, determining strategy, dealing with the state legislatures to gain new sources of revenue, and developing a united front for purposes of negotiation—all these factors could encourage basic organizational changes.

Regardless of whether government consolidation becomes a reality, impetus may very well be given to more intensive cooperation among government units in given geographical areas.

Regional Organizations. Regional cooperation has actually developed into regional government organizations for specific purposes. In the province of British Columbia—in the Vancouver metropolitan area—three municipalities have joined forces to pool bargaining research efforts, discuss common strategy, and in some cases to conduct joint negotiations. The goals are to compete with strong unions and to prevent leapfrogging practices of unions in the individual cities. The provincial organization of British Columbia municipalities also conducts bargaining research and services for smaller cities throughout the province.

Close collaboration, approximating a special purpose regional organization, also exists in the United States. In Wisconsin, cities and counties formed a voluntary nonprofit corporation to provide in that state cooperative services in county and municipal employee-management relations.

Suffice to say, even though embryonic in nature, the organizational considerations mentioned here are vexing to public administrators. They add a new dimension to certain aspects of bargaining.

Threats to Long-held Concepts

Public management has found it difficult to adjust quickly to a series of threats to long-held basic notions. These include the concept of sovereignty; third-party decisions on the content of negotiated agreements, that is, arbitration; public service strikes as a method of settling impasses, and the invasion of management prerogatives. Each of these subjects has been treated quite fully by unions and management; their respective positions are well known. For the purposes of this paper I believe it is sufficient to cite them as additional examples of frustration creators in the minds of public management. Beyond that, however, I believe it appropriate to pin-point the major issues in each area and to note the changing attitude of some segments of public management toward these concepts.

Sovereignty. The notion of sovereignty, in the sense that all legal authority resides in the governing body, has been cited by some lawyers and administrators as ample grounds for not setting salaries, wages and other conditions of employment through the process of collective bargaining; in short, a defense of unilateral decision-making. There has been so much erosion of this thread-bare legal concept in actual practice that it no longer stands as the bogey-man in government labor relations. The very fact that a number of states now have collective bargaining laws negates the original view of "sovereignty" and gives credence to Felix Nigro's view that this notion has undergone redefinition. [15] The question is no longer whether a public agency is "sovereign" but rather in what way it will choose to exercise its sovereign power. This emerging view is gradually gaining acceptance, but not without some intellectual pain to those who once held it immutable.

Public Service Strikes. In the light of recent developments, the emotional balance of anyone who would try to deal with this subject in a few hundred words might well be questioned. But under the circumstances I risk accusation.

To put it mildly, the subject of public service strikes is one that calls for most intensive reappraisal. Increased unionization and a mounting strike incidence heighten the interest of public officials in how to prevent or shorten strikes. While many public employee organizations, especially fire and police groups, have no-strike clauses in their constitutions, other public employee unions talk strongly of the right to strike as if it were a civil right. Despite prohibitive legislation, strikes in public agencies continue to occur. Although the number of government work stoppages—in relation to the total work force—in years past has not been large, and work time lost has been far less than the corresponding ratio for private industry, the well-publicized strikes across North America during the past two years cause increased concern to public management.

[15] Nigro, *op. cit.*

Elsewhere[16] I listed the critical issues confronting public officials in this area of public administration as follows:

1. Can strikes be prevented by no-strike laws?
2. Should public service strikes be legalized, and if so, what public policies should govern them?
3. Can strikes be deterred by formal recognition of employee groups and true collective bargaining?
4. From the employee's point of view, will collective bargaining be realistic and complete without the right to strike?
5. Can public service strikes be avoided through compulsory arbitration? Or through other procedures for the resolution of impasses, such as mediation or fact-finding?

Few subjects in public labor relations elicit greater emotion and more heat than the strike issue. Panaceas and solutions have been brought forth by industrial relations experts, private organizations and unions, but to date none has proved to be effective.

At least four alternatives for dealing with the problem have been suggested:

1. Absolute prohibition of public service strikes. Experience indicates that this has not worked.
2. Establishment of detailed procedural safeguards providing for persuasion and settlement of conflicts through a political process rather than by force.[17]
3. Establishment of essential and non-essential services, permitting strikes in the latter but prohibiting them in the former.[18] This would involve, as suggested almost twenty years ago by Leonard White, distinguishing between *primary interests* and *secondary functions* wherein the former constitute an immediate danger to the public health and safety, and the latter do not.[19]
4. Permission for some sort of semi-strike or non-stoppage-of-work strike. This proposal involves a fairly complicated arrangement whereby, under certain

[16] Kenneth O. Warner and Mary L. Hennessy, *Public Management at the Bargaining Table,* Public Personnel Association, 1967.

[17] George W. Taylor, "Public Employment: Strikes or Procedures?" *Industrial and Labor Relations Review,* July 1967.

[18] Jack Stieber, "A New Approach to Strikes in Public Employment," *MSU Business Topics,* Autumn, 1967.

[19] Leonard D. White, "Strikes in the Public Service," *Public Personnel Review,* January, 1949.

circumstances, management and unions would bear economic damage by withholding of wages of both management and workers in cases of strikes in primary functions.[20]

It goes without saying that this entire subject is shot through with public policy issues that far transcend the immediate interests of public administrators. But again, the strike issue illustrates the heavy pressures on top level administrators.

If strikes are banned then a question arises, "Will the public trade a provision for voluntary or compulsory arbitration of the issues involved?" This question also concerns public management.

Arbitration. In the private sector, arbitration has been used in two separate, distinct situations. The first situation is "Voluntary binding grievance arbitration as a terminal mechanism for resolving disputes over the interpretation and application of labor contracts. This practice which now prevails in more than 90 per cent of collective bargaining agreements in private industry is generally accepted as a more equitable and less costly way of settling disputes than the strike and has proved advantageous to both employers and unions."[21] The use of voluntary binding grievance arbitration is slowly increasing in the public sector, and seems to be fairly acceptable to both management and labor.

The second situation is use of arbitration over terms of new agreements, over bargaining disputes. In the remarks that follow I refer to arbitration as used in settlement of bargaining disputes.

Consent to arbitrate challenges another long-held public management concept. In essence, compulsory arbitration involves an arrangement whereby parties to a labor dispute who cannot agree must submit the matter to a third party for study, recommendation, and in some cases, final determination. A variety of practices may govern the composition of the "third party," the type of matters that can or must be referred to arbitration, and the status of decisions reached by the arbiter or arbitral tribunal.

In the public service the third party may be an individual selected by and acceptable to both parties to a dispute. Or,

---

[20] H. L. Fusilier and Lawrence L. Steinmetz, "Public Employee Strikes: An Operational Solution," *Quarterly Review of Economics and Business,* Autumn, 1967.

[21] Crouch, *op. cit.*

arbitration may be conducted by a permanent tribunal appointed by the legally constituted governing authority and composed of persons who represent interests of the public agency and organized employees. It is also possible to set up a so-called neutral group designed to represent all interests in the proceedings: public, employer, and employee. The neutral group might be constituted on an *ad hoc* basis to deal with individual disputes as they arise, or drawn as needed from a panel agreed to in advance.

The method of rendering decisions varies. Decisions may be confidential (that is, not a matter of public record), advisory recommendations, or binding decisions.

Members from the ranks of both management and labor join intellectual hands in expressing suspicion about compulsory arbitration of contract provisions. Management sees it as an infringement of its right to manage. Labor sees it as taking away its prerogative to accept or reject management proposals. Both sides believe another party may lack the background, knowledge, and understanding of complicated issues often involved in a dispute. They also think it decreases the effectiveness of the bargaining process, and that bargaining teams may rest on their oars if a third party can step in and make a final, binding decision.

At a recent press conference, AFL-CIO President George Meany suggested that voluntary arbitration might prove to be an equitable means for resolving major public employee disputes. Admitting that he did not know how unions of public employees would feel about this voluntary arbitration, Meany added that " There is one thing for sure, and that is that they are all completely opposed to compulsory arbitration. That they are unanimous on it I am sure."[22]

The foregoing brief summary is admittedly incomplete. Perhaps enough has been said to demonstrate that compulsory arbitration can and does affect the freedom of the bargaining process. In plain language, when compulsory arbitration is involved, management and employee groups must be prepared to give. The central issue is whether it is better to give in some measure, if necessary, or to cap the bargaining process with a strike or deadlock when bargaining fails and arbitration is denied.

Such are the problems faced by public management in deciding what to do about arbitration.

[22] *Government Employee Relations Report,* No. 233, February 26, 1968.

Management Rights

This subject of management rights is necessarily a matter of prime concern to public administrators—and to employee groups. A loose definition of management rights is those matters on which management can make completely unilateral decisions. A management representative from industry lists private sector management rights in four categories:

1. Purely unilateral rights which must not be delegated or assigned to nonmanagement groups. Included are such matters as product pricing, accounting methods, plant location, assignment of employees, schedule of manufacturing, etc.

2. Management rights which should be shared with employees in some degree. These include activities designed to keep employees informed about what's happening, such as changes in management personnel, notice of production schedules, information about upcoming products.

3. Management's right to listen to employees, without necessarily having to agree to change. An example is communications from employees about the option of scheduling two half-days, one before Christmas and one before New Year's versus one full day on and one full day off.

4. Management's right to share responsibility with employees. This right involves gaining employee participation in company affairs. A specific example might be the joint planning activities of a union and a company in preparation for automation involving job design, training, and reassignment of employees.[23]

In the public sector there is considerable agreement by management on several types of management rights, although these types are not everywhere acceptable to employee organizations.

1. Basic or fundamental rights. These stem from the concept of sovereignty and how far the sovereign government will or can go in delegation of, or sharing the responsibility for, governing.

2. The right to determine the agency's mission, assignment of personnel, governmental services, and functions to be rendered.

[23] Kenneth O. Warner and Mary L. Hennessy, *Public Management at the Bargaining Table*, Public Personnel Association, 1967.

3. The right to prepare budgets, appropriate funds, levy taxes, and maintain a personnel system operating according to the merit principle.

Management rights can be protected through legislation and administrative orders. Federal Executive Order 10988 and certain bargaining laws for public employees, particularly the Wisconsin law covering state employees, contain strong management rights clauses and appreciably restrict the scope of bargaining. Management rights clauses can also be negotiated and placed in contracts.

Even a management rights clause may not prevent erosion of what management considers its prerogatives. For example, note Section 5(c) of Mayor Lindsay's Executive Order 52 which implements the New York City collective bargaining ordinance:

> It is the right of the City, acting through its agencies, to determine the standards of services to be offered by its agencies; determine the standards of selection for employment; direct its employees; take disciplinary action; relieve its employees from duty because of lack of work or for other legitimate reasons; maintain the efficiency of governmental operations; determine the methods, means, and personnel by which government operations are to be conducted; determine the content of job classifications; take all necessary actions to carry out its mission in emergencies; and exercise complete control and discretion over its organization and the technology over its organization and the technology of performing its work. *The City's decision on those matters are not within the scope of collective bargaining, but, notwithstanding the above, questions concerning the practical impact that decisions on the above matters have on employees, such as questions of workload or manning, are within the scope of collective bargaining.*

In short, if a management decision has an onerous impact on working conditions (and an arbitrator decides whether or not an impact is onerous) then management must negotiate the matter. The management decision itself is not judged or questioned, but the impact, if onerous, may be judged. In its practical effect, however, basic management decisions are being brought to the bargaining table.

From discussions around the country with knowledgeable persons in both public and private sector labor relations, there seems to be general agreement that in negotiating, public management because of its inexperience has unwittingly bargained away some management rights. The consequences may be great, since it is almost impossible to recoup management concessions once they are granted. This suggests again a point previously mentioned—the great need for expertise on the part of government negotiators.

Concluding Observations

Public management looks on collective bargaining with mixed views. The mix of ideas prevents a precise reading of how significant these views may be, hence a final evaluation must await scholarly research such as that recently undertaken by the Brookings Institution.

But it is clear that within the public management community collective bargaining has its ardent supporters, grudging acceptors, and vocal detractors. Whichever the group, all are deeply affected by a minor revolution in public administration—a revolution caused by repackaging the content of public administration to fit the collective bargaining container.

This minor revolution occurs particularly in state and local government. Although educational administration was treated here only slightly, in some respects it is most acutely affected. At the federal level, recommendations of a presidential review committee and actions to implement its findings will determine the severity of impact in that area of government.

In public management the most bruised individual is the personnel officer. He is being put on his mettle. His job will not disappear, but it will undergo tremendous change and assume entirely new proportions.

Where bargaining exists the merit principle of public employment will be seriously challenged. In my judgment it will be modified through continuing compromise and restatement. In the end its meaning will be notably narrowed. To the extent that this takes place we will enter a new era in the history of public personnel administration—the era of "negotiated merit."

It was not a purpose of this paper to resolve the ideological conflicts between employee organizations and public management. But this discussion identifies some points of agreement and disagreement which, if explored further, can lead to a less frenetic approach to labor relations in the public setting.

It seems obvious—even to one who reads and runs—that public sector collective bargaining is still embryonic. That means future events will shape its final form.

Teacher Bargaining:
The Relevance of Private Sector Experience

Robert E. Doherty

It is useful to look at the issues raised by teacher bargaining in the light of private sector experience. We do this not because everything that has happened in collective bargaining in industry is relevant or transferrable, but because public employee bargaining is an outgrowth of it. Moreover, most of the slogans, much of the rationale, and not a few of the techniques used by public employee organizations are borrowed directly from private sector unions. In other words, a great many public employee groups are persuaded that the private sector experience is almost entirely relevant.

Our over-all question, then, is to what degree it is appropriate to apply the private sector experience when we come to consider how best to deal with employee relations in the schools. It has been our national policy since the passage of the Wagner Act in 1935 that private employees working in industries engaged in interstate commerce have the right to form and join employee organizations and to engage in collective bargaining with their employers. Employers on the other hand have been required to bargain with organizations of their employees and to refrain from interferring with the rights of employees to join or support these organizations. Now we ask—should these same rights be extended to teachers and other categories of public employees? Is there sufficient similarity in the employment arrangements of teachers, and, say, automobile workers to grant them similar opportunities under law. Or is the teacher's position as a professional, employed in such a highly sensitive and important service as public education, so markedly different from that of the private sector employee that no real comparisons can be drawn?

In a way this question has already been answered. In ten of our states statutes have been enacted mandating some form of collective dealings for teachers. Procedures and mechanisms have been

Dr. Doherty is Professor of Industrial and Labor Relations, New York State School of Industrial and Labor Relations, Cornell University, Ithaca, New York.

developed to deal with representation and bargaining problems. In other states the parties are merely permitted to bargain, if both sides agree that this is the way to handle their differences, and no mechanisms or guidelines are provided.

But while some states have decided that the employment arrangements of teachers and private sector employees are roughly comparable, and that, therefore, teachers should be extended similar rights, other states remain to be convinced. Evidently feeling that collective bargaining violates the principle of governmental sovereignty, the legislatures, or the courts, or the attorneys general in these states have maintained that teacher bargaining is illegal. It is an interesting footnote to history that many of the arguments decrying teacher bargaining which one hears today are strongly reminiscent of those advanced against the Wagner Act in the 1930's on the grounds that it violated property rights. I don't wish to push this analogy very far: public employee bargaining does raise some serious problems for the conduct of representative government, problems that are quite different from those created in the operation of a business enterprise. But still the arguments are similar. And the relevance of one for the other, to put it in a rather backhanded way, is the futility of both. History long ago rendered the property rights argument obsolete; it is rapidly closing in on the idea that the rights of the sovereign are inviolate. We shall probably have an increasing amount of bargaining, with or without the benefit of statute, and certainly without ever deciding whether or not private sector experience provides suitable precedents.

So we leave that question unanswered to move on to a related one almost as difficult: should teachers be treated interchangeably with other categories of public employees? In other words, if teachers are granted the right to bargain, should they be covered by the same statute, their conduct regulated by the same administrative agency, their activities governed by the same rules and regulations, as toll takers and sanitation workers?

If we are to be guided by practices prevailing in the private sector, we should have to conclude that there are not sufficient grounds to provide for separate treatment. Although national labor policy treats railway and airline employees separately (they come under the 1926 Railway Labor Act), clearly the intent of our public policy is to cover all private employees with the same umbrella—engineers and hod carriers, opera singers and coal miners.

As for lumping teachers together with other public employees, the arguments can be summarized as follows: there are more similarities than differences between teachers and other public employees; it is more economical to deal with all public employees, utilizing the same machinery and regulations, than to establish separate mechanisms; and if teachers have a right to claim separate treatment, why not give the same right to public health doctors and nurses, social workers, and parole officers? These occupations can make similar claims of professional status as well as to the "uniqueness" of their employment conditions. Of the ten states granting bargaining rights to public employees, four have evidently been persuaded by the above arguments. In Massachusetts, Michigan, New York, and Wisconsin teachers are treated the same as everyone else.

The arguments against dealing with teachers in the same fashion as other public employees are less obvious but not without force. Public school teachers are by far the single largest occupation in public employment.[1] It does not necessarily follow that separate treatment for teachers would open the door to a frenzy of statute building. There is also a certain amount of force in the argument that teachers occupy a uniquely sensitive role in our society. As Walter Oberer and I observed at another time:

> Teaching has become recognized as a profession because of the acknowledged importance of education to a democratic society. One way such a society seeks to deal with particularly important, sophisticated, and sensitive occupational pursuits is to 'professionalize' these callings. This process of professionalization must be encouraged rather than eroded because of the increasingly complex character of modern society and the concomitantly increasing necessity for higher standards and self-policing of strategic callings. To the extent teachers are treated with other employees, are dealt with in the matter of collective negotiations by the same agencies, standards, and procedures, to that extent the professionalizing force will be dulled and perhaps ultimately lost. Typical *employee* goals and standards may replace typical *professional* goals and standards, with a stronger tendency to collective protection of mediocrity, even incompetence, as opposed to collective encouragement of aspiration toward excellence, of the seeking of prestige and personal satisfaction through service rather than mere material reward.[2]

[1] U. S. Department of Commerce, *Public Employment in 1966* (Washington: GPO, 1967), Series GE-No. 4, p. 9.

[2] Robert E. Doherty and Walter E. Oberer, *Teachers, School Boards and Collective Bargaining: A Changing of the Guard* (Ithaca: 1LR, Cornell, 1967), pp. 59-60.

So run the arguments for and against the relevance of private sector experience on coverage.

A similar question, though more narrow in scope, is the relevance of private sector experience concerning the composition of the bargaining unit. Which categories of employees shall be covered by the collective agreement? More specifically, should supervisors be included in the same unit as the supervised? If we were to take the National Labor Management Relations Act and the several state labor relations acts as our guide, we could easily answer the question in the negative and go on to the next issue. The LMRA not only excludes supervisory employees from the non-supervisory unit, it leaves supervisors outside its protection.

Four of the states with legislation covering teachers bargaining rights make similar exclusions, either by the statute itself or by subsequent court rulings. Presumedly, the legislatures in these states felt that the reasoning of the framers of the LMRA (supervisors are an integral part of management) is as appropriate to the public service as it is to industry.

The remaining states with teacher bargaining statutes apparently believe otherwise since in these instances all certificated personnel, with the exception of the chief school officer, are covered. In two states, Connecticut and New York, the question of including or excluding principals and other supervisory personnel is treated on a case-by-case basis.

It is one of the many ironies of teacher-school board negotiations that the argument over the exclusion of supervisory personnel has made ideological bedfellows of school boards and the affiliates of the American Federation of Teachers. Board members, if I might generalize from the modest experience I have had arbitrating representation disputes, seem to prefer exclusion believing, evidently, that the line officers cannot identify strongly with the sometimes obstreperous troops, and at the same time remain loyal to the top command. The Union employs much the same ideological argument, conceding that while there is a strong community of interest among all members of the educational enterprise, there are times when the interests between employers and employees diverge. Unit lines, their argument goes, should be drawn sharply enough to accommodate these conflicting views and interests. The fact that Federation affiliates don't have many members among supervisors anyway merely adds grist to their mill.

Local Associations, on the other hand, often seek bargaining units consisting of virtually all certificated staff members. This, of course, is largely because so many supervisors are Association members. But there is more to it than that. There *are* a great many differences between education and private employment in supervisor and non-supervisor relations. Education is more of a cooperative venture, calling for closer relationships and a higher degree of mutual respect than prevails in industry. Excluding supervisors from the unit could have a divisive effect on the conduct of the educational enterprise. It is also alleged that we do not yet know enough about public employee bargaining, certainly we don't know enough about teacher bargaining, to assume that private sector practices offer a suitable guide.

It is true, I think, that we don't know enough about this question to establish hard, fast, and inflexible rules and regulations. We need experimentation.

In the two states, Connecticut and New York, where experimentation on unit questions has been encouraged by statute, there seems to be a significant trend away from including supervisors in the bargaining unit.

Another experiment going on under the general rubric of representation issues is concerned with the *mode* of representation. Should we follow the private sector example and provide for exclusive representation, whereby a single employee organization with majority support is the sole bargaining agent for all employees, regardless of membership? Alternatively, should there be some multiple type of representation, for members only, proportional, or by a teachers' council elected at large? California and Minnesota are presently experimenting with proportional representation, and Oregon with the council. In New York the statute seems to allow for a variety of methods, although virtually all school boards and teacher organizations have to date opted for exclusivity.

I would hope that those of you from states where there is not as yet a statute will watch all these experiments closely. You might come up with the answer to the question that has been plaguing me: are the experiments now going on in Oregon, California, and Minnesota imaginative and constructive devices for resolving teacher-board differences or as the critics allege, merely techniques designed to divide the teachers and render impotent the considerable amount of potential power they now possess?

Although we might disagree over the amount of relevance private sector practices have for the previously discussed questions, I believe we shall have to conclude that experience under the LMRA is highly relevant to our next issue. I refer here to the controversy over the "scope" or "subject matter" of collective bargaining. The LMRA, like most of the teacher bargaining statutes, obliges the parties to negotiate over "wage, hours, and other terms and conditions of employment." It is the later phrase, terms and conditions of employment, that causes us trouble. What does it mean? Generally employers tend to interpret the phrase narrowly while employee organizations hold that no meaningful limits can be set on bargaining subject matter. Employers maintain that certain management prerogatives must be retained if the enterprise is to function efficiently; unions argue that managment prerogatives are merely a state of mind, not statements of immutable facts.

In the private sector this problem is dealt with by an unfair labor practice charge of a refusal to bargain. It is up to the administrative agency, and behind it the courts, to determine whether a given issue is a proper subject for bargaining. Over the years the NLRB and/or the courts have ruled that such issues as subcontracting, plant relocation, bonuses, merit plans, even the amount of rent a company can charge for company owned houses are an integral part of working conditions and are therefore negotiable. In other words, these issues have become mandated, the parties are free to bargain over them to impasse. Should there be a strike or lockout, such action would not be adjudged an unfair practice.

The parallel between the private sector and the public schools is apparent. Teachers and school boards have profound differences of opinion over which items are negotiable. *Indeed,* there are probably greater differences of opinion over the appropriate subject matter of negotiations in teacher bargaining than any other collective bargaining arrangement. Teachers sometimes argue that since virtually *all* board decisions have an effect on working conditions, few issues, if any at all, should be kept from the bargaining table. In Rochester the teachers are demanding that before the superintendent's contract can be renewed this decision must be reviewed by the teachers association. Presumedly the caliber of the man standing at the helm can influence the working conditions of the crew.

More to the point, the subject matter question in teacher bargaining has *already* become very analogous to private sector practices. A Wisconsin Circuit Court ruled recently that the makeup of the school calendar was closely related to working conditions and consequently was an appropriate issue for bargaining.[3] In Michigan

---

[3] *City of Madison v. Wisconsin Employment Relations Board,* Dane County Circuit Court, Case No. 121-135, April 26, 1967.

the Mediation Board decided not long ago that the parties may bargain to impasse over such issues as binding arbitration of grievances and the agency shop.[4] In short, private sector experience on the matter of bargaining scope is highly relevant. Some of us might not like the lessons it has to teach, but we would be wise to learn them anyway.

Important as the questions of coverage, representation, and bargaining scope might be, these are relatively insignificant issues when contrasted with the problem of resolving negotiating impasses. In the private sector the parties are free to use the ultimate weapons in their respective arsenals, the strike or the lockout, to induce a settlement. The motive power is essentially economic; both the employer and the union can weigh the cost of settlement against the cost of the strike in rather clear economic terms. The employer will attempt to calculate whether it would cost him more to accept a settlement close to the union's demands, or take a strike and perhaps settle closer to his own terms. He may calculate incorrectly, but he at least can make judgements that are grounded on some rather specific economic interests: his loss of profits in the event of a strike compared to the cost of the new wage bill without a strike. Union leaders also attempt some rather careful calculations. Acceptance of a settlement well below the union's final demand is a cost that must be weighed against the cost of a strike which would presumably bring the company's offer closer to the union's terms. In other words, workers usually get more if they strike, but the strike costs them something in the process.

Thus the private sector strike is essentially an economic matter, similar, in a way, to a situation whereby a potential buyer of a used car refuses to do business with the seller because the two of them cannot agree on the price. And since the strike is a private matter between two parties, we believe the public has no right to intervene, unless of course a continuation of the stoppage would jeopardize the health and safety of the wider community. Intervention is rare (there have been only 28 national "emergency" disputes since 1947) because we operate under the assumption in the private sector that when a strike does interupt a service or prevents the distribution of a commodity, alternative services and commodities are still available. If Ford is on strike, we can always buy a Chevrolet: if the airline

---

[4] *Government Employee Relations Report,* No. 227, January 15, 1968, pp. F-1 to F-21.

workers are out, we can take the train, ride a bus, or drive that new Chevy.

Indeed, both parties to collective bargaining are keenly sensitive to the restraints of the market place. Unions are not interested in forcing employers out of business, or even driving substantial numbers of the employer's customers into the arms of non-union competitors. Employers know that a long strike might drive customers away forever.

What are the cost considerations in teacher-school board bargaining? What kinds of economic calculations do the parties make as they prepare their bargaining strategies? There is this similarity: teachers do take the risk of being heavy cost bearers. If the strike is long and the concession won very small, they have miscalculated badly.

But what about the board? Aside from the adjustment of resources that tough bargaining sometimes imposes (curtailment of some actual or projected services to provide funds for higher salaries) the impact of the strike on the board seems to be essentially political and psychological. Boards have no profits to consider and certainly no loss of markets to worry about. Rather than concern itself about how best to run an enterprise to get a money, a board's primary concern is how it can get the necessary money to run the enterprise. What a board fears is dysfunction, the temporary breakdown of the system. The chief purpose of the public sector strike is to create this dysfunction.

Another important difference between public employee strikes and private sector stoppages is that the immediate and direct cost bearers are the consumers of the public service. Unlike situations in the private sector, alternative services are not usually available in public enterprises, and consumers must therefore just do without. The problem takes on an added poignancy when we consider that in four recent public employee strikes in New York City (welfare, transit, sanitation, and public education) the heaviest cost bearers were the poor. The well-to-do send their children to private schools, burn their garbage in fancy incinerators, stay home from work (without loss of income) if transportation is difficult to secure, and, of course, none of them are on relief.

The public interest is difficult to define and all but impossible to locate. But we nevertheless assume that it is always there lurking in the shadows, ready to assert itself at the propitious moment. The crisis brought about by frequent disruptions in public service makes us wonder if that moment has not arrived. If it has, what public interest standard should we apply? There are many, but foremost, I think, is the belief that there are certain limits as to the amount of concerted pressure a democratic political structure can tolerate. As Kurt Hanslowe has observed:

> At some point the risk arises of a dangerous dilution of governmental authority by its being squeezed to death by conflicting power blocks. If that point is reached, foreign policy is made by defense industry, agricultural policy by farmers, and public personnel policy by employee organizations, and *not* by government representing the wishes of an electorate consisting of individual voters. If that point is reached, an orderly system of individual liberty under lawful rule would seem to be the victim. For surely it is difficult to conceive of a social order without a governmental repository of authority, which is authoritative for the very reason that it is representative and democratic.[5]

Yet it is argued that if we open the door wide enough to admit public employee bargaining, how can we close it to the strike? If we take the position that bilateral determination of teachers' employment conditions is sound public policy, how can we deny to one of the parties its most important source of persuasion? This seems to leave the whip hand where it has always been—with the school board.

The statutes providing for public employee bargaining have declared the strike illegal and some have provided "alternative" methods of dispute settlement: mediation, fact-finding, advisory arbitration. Now we seem to be moving toward compulsory arbitration. The difficulty with the first category of settlement devices is that they are not really substitutes for the strike since they still leave final authority with the employer; the trouble with compulsory arbitration is that rather than being a substitute for the strike, it will probably replace bargaining itself. Moreover, what if the arbitration award is turned down and the employees strike anyway, believing that such action will induce the arbitrator to sweeten the ante? Public employees have shown an increasing tendency to ignore injunctions against striking; what is it about an arbitration award that would make them any more law abiding?

---

[5] Kurt L. Hanslowe, *The Emerging Law of Labor Relations in Public Employment* (Ithaca: New York State School of Industrial and Labor Relations, Cornell University, 1967), p. 114.

And is it true that the public interest is always damaged by public employee strikes? Might there not be occasions when short-term disadvantages to the consumer result in long-term advantages? If among the settlement terms of a welfare strike, for example, it is provided that the case loads shall be smaller than previously, could it not be argued that the welfare recipient is the chief benefactor? Or take the case of a teachers strike that results in a salary scale reducing turnover, in smaller classes, in more teacher aides and fewer onerous non-instructional chores, in more protection from administrative whim or favoritism. Are not the students the chief beneficiaries? They may have born the initial cost, but have they not also reaped certain rewards?

Why then not make teacher strikes legal? Certainly it would eliminate the sham bargaining that goes on in so many school districts. But more important, it would cease to make law breaking appear virtuous in the eyes of school children. For when teachers do strike in violation of law, win substantial benefits thereby, and then suffer no penalties, they provide a lesson in *realpolitik* for their students that will not soon be forgotten. Legalizing the strike would at least get rid of that problem. For surely we are going to have more strikes, whether we legalize them or not.

I realize that this analysis sounds uncomfortably close to the "You might as well relax and enjoy it" school of social philosophy, and let me say that I do not necessarily subscribe to it. But neither do I know what the alternatives are.

Indeed, as I said at the beginning, I don't pretend to have the answers to any of the questions I pose. No doubt private sector experiences have a certain relevancy for the management of our affairs in public education. Just how relevant these experiences are is an issue that will probably eventually be worked out in the real world of pressure politics and naked economic power. I have very serious doubts that the words of sweet reason so characteristic of the utterances of college professors will prevail. Perhaps the best we can do is point out to teachers, administrators, and school board members as forcefully as we can that they are not the only ones involved in this problem. We all have a stake in it.

Resolving Impasses in Negotiations

Kenneth McLennan and Michael H. Moskow

In private employment, the strike or threat of a strike resolves impasses in negotiations by putting increasing pressure to settle on both parties. In most cases, competition in the product market and the elasticity of demand for the product limit the size of wage settlements through the employment effect.

A strike in public employment does not have the same effect as in the private sector because government agencies feel no economic pressure when they are shut down by a strike. Of course, they probably are subjected to considerable political pressure, depending on the effect of the work stoppage on the public. In these cases public opinion or political pressure may exert some downward pressures on wages.

Based on the differences between the public and private sector, some question exists whether the strike is a viable tool in the public sector. Public policy presently opposes the use of the strike in the public sector probably because of the essentiality of so many government services. No state legislature has granted the right to strike to public employees. With only one or two exceptions, every judge issuing a decision on this topic has maintained that public employees have no right to strike in the absence of permissive legislation.

Despite the well established legal structure concerning the strike among teachers and other government employees, the recent increase in the interruption of public services has prompted several proposals for dealing with disputes in education and other areas of public employment.

Relative Political Power

Governor Rockefeller's committee on Public Employee Relations in New York (the Taylor Committee) rejects the strike as a means of resolving impasses in public employment. The strike in public

Dr. McLennan and Dr. Moskow are Professors of Economics, Temple University, Philadelphia, Pennsylvania.

employment "introduces an alien force in the legislative process"[1] and interferes with the proper functioning of representative government.

The Taylor Committee recommended mediation, fact-finding, and voluntary arbitration as means of resolving impasses in pulbic employment negotiations. If either party rejects the award of a neutral tribunal, the dispute is to be submitted to the appropriate state or local legislative body which holds a "show cause hearing" "...prior to final legislative action on the budget or other enactment."[2] Thus, the final step in the impasse procedure is the legislative body which usually bases its decisions on relative political power.

> It is ultimately the legislature and the political process which has to balance the interests of public employees with the rest of the community, to relate the compensation of public employees to the tax rate, and to appraise the extent and quality of public services and the efficiency of their performance to the aspirations of public employees. The methods of persuasion and political activity, rather than the strike, comport with our institutions and traditions as means to resolve such conflicts of interest.[3]

The Taylor Committee favored use of the term "collective negotiations" instead of "collective bargaining" "... to signify the participation of public employees in the determination of at least some of their conditions of employment on an occupational or functional basis." It emphasized that joint determination of working conditions by unions and management as practiced in the private sector "cannot be transferred generally to the public employment sector."[4]

The Taylor Committee favored a statutory prohibition against strikes in public employment. If a strike took place, the agency administering the statute would determine if the employee organization had called the strike. In assessing penalties, the agency would determine "whether these were such acts of extreme provocation on the part of the public employer as to detract from

---

[1] George W. Taylor, *et al.*, *Governor's Committee on Public Employee Relations,* Final Report 1967, p. 15.

[2] *Ibid.,* p. 8.

[3] *Ibid.,* p. 39.

[4] *Ibid.,* p. 11.

the fault of the employee organization in permitting the strike to take place." Presumably penalties would be levied if the employing agency was found to have provoked the strike.

Mediation—Fact-Finding

Almost all of the state statutes regulating collective bargaining in public employment prohibit the strike, but none, except for New York State, provide for impasses to be referred to the legislative body. The impasse procedures in the other statutes end with mediation and fact-finding. In addition, the study committees in Illinois, Michigan, and New Jersey appointed to recommend or review public employee legislation all favored mediation and fact-finding as the terminal point of the impasse procedure.

The essential nature of most government service is probably the main rationale for public policy based on the mediation concept.[5] The proponents of mediation and fact-finding claim that these procedures will minimize strikes in public employment. An increase in strikes by public employees may occur temporarily when negotiations statutes with mediation and fact-finding first take effect, but this is only because of the parties' lack of sophistication in labor relations. Once the parties gain experience, very few strikes will occur in public employment.

Binding Arbitration

Binding arbitration is another procedure for resolving impasses in negotiations. Under binding arbitration, a neutral person or committee listens to each party's point of view and then issues a binding decision for settlement. The Rhode Island statute, which is the only public employee statute providing for binding arbitration, limits the scope of arbitration to "all matters not involving the expenditure of money."

Binding arbitration can be either compulsory or voluntary. If established by statute, it is compulsory; if agreed to in advance by the parties, it is voluntary.

5 Hildebrand, *op. cit.*, pp. 137-140.

Unlimited Right to Strike

Several commentators have suggested that only public employees whose work endangered the public's health and safety, such as policemen and fire fighters, should be denied the right to strike.[6] Those groups denied this right would have to submit disputes to compulsory arbitration.

The advocates of this proposal argue that the strike is a necessary ingredient to collective bargaining. The employees must have some power to reject management's proposals. This will induce meaningful bargaining and subsequently an agreement. Without the right to strike to back up their demands, public employees are merely able to make suggestions and recommendations which the employer will be free to reject without fear of reprisal. The strike or threat of a strike thus resolves impasses in public employee negotiations in the same way it operates in private employment.

Modified Right to Strike

This impasse procedure combines advisory arbitration with a limited right to strike. The procedure was first suggested by Donald H. Wollett and later supported and expanded by Robert E. Doherty and Walter E. Oberer.[7]

Doherty and Oberer strongly oppose teacher strikes for many of the reasons mentioned above:

> The strike is a pressure from which the public should be free. Any pressure on the public to this end should be a *political* pressure rather than an *economic* pressure. The former allows for the free play of the political forces and techniques of a free society. The latter smacks of a kind of extortion or blackmail.[8]

---

[6] Theodore W. Kheel, "Report to Speaker Anthony T. Travia on the Taylor Case," February 21, 1968. Many others have favored this approach including Myron Lieberman, "Teacher Strikes: An Analysis of the Issues," *Harvard Educational Review*, XXCI (Winter, 1956), pp. 39-70; and Jack Stieber, "A New Approach to Strikes in Public Employment," *MSU Business Topics* (October, 1967), pp. 67-71.

[7] Robert D. Doherty and Walter E. Oberer, *Teachers, School Boards and Collective Bargaining: A Changing of the Guard* (Ithaca, New York: New York State School of Industrial and Labor Relations, Cornell University, 1967).

[8] *Ibid.*, p. 105.

Whether the pressure is political or economic is not the crucial issue. In any dispute, in the private as well as the public sector, both types of pressure will frequently be applied simultaneously. The argument against the unlimited right to strike in education should not be based on whether the pressure is economic or political but on the proposition that the individual consumer or interest groups may have difficulty in imposing a cost on the parties to the settlement. The absence of such a consumer response may mean an eventual settlement which involves an excessively high wage package.

If this proposition is valid there will be an automatic restraint on the size of the settlement as in the private sector. The results of the case study described earlier indicated that on several issues interest groups were able to impose a political cost on the parties. Whether they also provide a restraint on the size of the settlement is a question for further research.

Nevertheless, the advantage of the modified right to strike proposed is the recognition of the possibility that a board of education may reject an award of a fact-finder or arbitrator. Under such circumstances, the teachers are given the legal right to strike. Presumably this would minimize strikes and provide some assurance to the teacher organization that bargaining will be meaningful.

Analysis of Dispute Settlement Proposals

Public policy on teacher negotiations is in a critical stage of re-evaluation. The future direction will depend on the merits of the proposals currently being suggested. An analysis of these proposals is useful in assessing their future role in the industrial relations system.

The basic feature of collective bargaining in the private sector is the presence of joint decision-making in the negotiating process. It seems clear that future dispute settlement policy in education will attempt to transfer this concept of participation from private sector bargaining.

Most dispute settlement proposals favor some participation by employee organizations in decisions affecting employee wages and working conditions, but there is disagreement on the extent of this participation. Theodore Kheel is the leading advocate of the same type of joint determination found in private employment collective bargaining with the strike or threat of strike used by the employees in order to enforce demands. The Taylor Committee favors a modified form of joint determination without the right to strike and with the final decision being made by the legislative body. Doherty and Oberer would agree with the Taylor Committee except that they would give further assurance of joint determination to the employee organization.

Joint determination is clearly a necessary ingredient of collective bargaining, but Kheel is incorrect to assume that the absolute right to say "no" or the right to strike is necessary in order to have joint determination. The right to strike is not necessary to joint determination if both parties are able to impose a cost on each other. It would be more accurate to say that the employer has no incentive to bargain in good faith if he suffers no cost for failing to do so. In public employment, the employee organization can impose some costs on the employer without actually calling a strike. For example, slowdown, "work to rule," picketing, disseminating unfavorable publicity, or impugning the integrity of the administrators of the employing agency have all been used to induce public employers to bargain.[9] The appointment of neutrals to make non-binding recommendations on settlement terms also gives the employees a right to say "no" to the employer's original proposals and to obtain review by a neutral tribunal. The employee organization's bargaining power is enhanced further if it can impose a cost of disagreement on the employer if he rejects the recommendations of the neutral.

Although many of the above pressure tactics have been used by employee organizations, the most effective way of imposing a cost after the employer rejects an award is probably the strike which becomes a stronger demonstration to publicize unfair actions.

From a public policy point of view, it is essential to avoid shutdowns of public schools due to strikes as much as possible. Relying on the strike or the threat of a strike to resolve impasses conflicts with this goal of public policy. On the other hand, prohibiting strikes denies public employees one of their most effective means of ensuring joint determination.

Some institutional modification must be found in order to balance the public policy goals of continued operation of schools and of increased participation of employees in the determination of their working conditions. The advantage of the Doherty-Oberer modified right to strike proposal over the Taylor Committee approach is that it places greater pressure on the employing agency to bargain with its

---

[9] For an analysis of alternative means of bargaining power used by teacher organizations see: Michael H. Moskow, *Teachers and Unions* (Philadelphia: Industrial Research Unit, University of Pennsylvania, 1966), pp. 194-210.

employees and to accept the awards of neutrals. The threat of the strike and its accompanying interruption of service will also encourage interest groups to apply pressure on the employer. Presumably the proposal envisages much greater use of fact-finding and advisory arbitration and hopefully will minimize strikes in public employment. The employee organization legally cannot reject the award of the neutral tribunal, but no-strike laws, of course, do not always eliminate strikes. The award, however, can be used as an effective "face-saver" for the organization so that little incentive will exist for the organization to call an illegal strike.

A disadvantage of the Doherty-Oberer proposal is that the negotiating parties may present extreme positions to the fact-finder on the assumption that his decision will frequently attempt to "split the difference" separating the parties. Should this pattern develop it is unlikely any serious bargaining will occur.

A further possibility is that school boards may show little resistance to fact-finder awards since the award can be used to support budgetary requests from the legislative body. If this occurs there is little pressure on the parties to limit wage increases; the fact-finder becomes the substitute for market forces.

The Taylor Committee proposal of deciding impasses by relative political power tends to give greater bargaining power to numerically larger unions. The union with more potential voters will wield greater political power with the legislative body. This, of course, is the way most governmental decisions are made in a democratic country, so that criticism of the proposal on these grounds is really a general criticism of representative government. It is also similar to the Taft-Hartley Act 80 day injunction procedure in private employment whereby after fact-finding, the President may submit an unresolved dispute to Congress. The success of this proposal depends on the vast majority of disputes being settled independently by the parties.

Applying the Taylor Committee proposal for final resolution of unresolved disputes to public education poses some unique problems. The committee recommends that in the event of the rejection of a fact-finding recommendation, the legislative body or committee hold a form of "show cause hearing" at which the parties review their positions with respect to the recommendations of the fact-finding board. The appropriate budgetary allotment or other regulations are then to be enacted by the legislative body.[10]

---

[10] Taylor, *op. cit.*, p. 39.

It is not clear what "legislative body or committee" would be the final step in the impasse procedure for local school districts. Most school districts in the United States are fiscally independent, and they can set their own tax rates within state legislated minimums. A minority of school districts, mostly in large cities, are fiscally dependent and must obtain approval of their budgets from a local legislative body such as a city council or town council. In the fiscally independent districts, however, the board of education is the local legislative body possessing a high degree of autonomy. Presumably, the city council would serve as legislative body for fiscally dependent districts, but it is not clear who would perform this function in fiscally independent districts. The authors doubt whether the Taylor Committee intended the board of education (which is also the employer) to serve as the final step in the impasse procedure. They also doubt whether the Taylor Committee envisioned submitting disputes in local school districts to the state legislature.

Giving public employees the right to strike as Kheel suggests will give greater bargaining power to a different group of unions. His suggestion favors unions with members performing services that the public can least do without. Groups of public employees who can most inconvenience the public by withdrawing their services will have the most bargaining power.

Nevertheless, there is evidence of increasing pressure from teacher organizations to obtain the right to strike. They claim that the cost of any ensuing strikes will not be a hardship on the public since the industry is not in the essential category. The argument against this pressure is not based on the essentiality of the industry but on the fact the consumer of the service has little opportunity to impose a cost on the parties by switching to another source of supply should he not like the newly negotiated terms under which the service will be provided.

In response to the extension of the right of bargaining to teachers, community interest groups and citizens have attempted to exert most influence on educational policy decisions. Giving teachers the legal right to strike probably would increase community participation even more.

Contract Administration and Grievance Procedures

John E. Massey

When I was teaching school, there were no such terms as "professional negotiations" or "collective negotiations." In the years since I left the teaching profession the term "collective bargaining" has been, you might say, my daily companion.

There is significance in the fact that some teachers are searching for their own special term for what, historically, has been called "collective bargaining." Collective bargaining, today, is a well-defined process. Wherever we find it in operation, we recognize it—because it has certain distinguishing characteristics. But collective bargaining is also a democratic process. So each individual collective bargaining agreement will have characteristics of its own. For, to be successful, each agreement must meet the unique needs and objectives of the two very special parties who create it.

We need to keep this fact in mind. Certainly I think TVA experience in contract administration and grievance procedures can be helpful to you. Just as certainly, I think it would be a mistake to imply that every *specific* of our way of doing things can be guaranteed to serve you as well as it has us.

Let me give you some "handles" by which you can compare your own situation with that in TVA. This should help you to select, from what I have to say, those ideas which are relevant to you.

Let's eliminate one possible source of confusion at the outset. Many of the articles and books on the current movement of teachers toward or into collective bargaining mention President Kennedy's Executive Order 10988 which gave the Federal Government as a whole its first formal program for employee-management cooperation. TVA's collective bargaining agreements preceded the order by many years and were not affected by it. So our agreements have much more in common with the collective bargaining contracts in private industry than they have with the agreements now existing in the Federal service as a whole.

John E. Massey, "Contract Administration and Grievance Procedures," in Gerald Ubben, ed., *Collective Negotiation in Education,* Report of the Superintendents' Conference, University of Tennessee, 1967. Reprinted with permission. Mr. Massey is the Director of Personnel, Tennessee Valley Authority.

The TVA Act of 1933 created an autonomous Government corporation. Its three-man Board of Directors was given the authority "without regard to the provisions of Civil Service laws" to appoint and remove employees, fix their pay, and define their duties. Notwithstanding this broad authority granted the Board, TVA is subject to certain Federal laws, regulations, and Executive orders which affect the areas open to collective bargaining. So the position of the TVA Board, with respect to its authority to bargain with its employees, might be described as somewhat similar to that of many local school boards.

The TVA Board delegated to the Director of Personnel the responsibility for representing TVA management in negotiations with employee organizations. I carry out this responsibility with the advice of management representatives. Negotiated matters of major policy significance, including pay rates, must be approved by the General Manager and the TVA Board, and, as negotiator I keep in close contact with the General Manager and the Board.

I gather that practice and recommended practice vary widely in the matter of whose responsibility this should be in a public school system. In their book, *Collective Negotiation for Teachers,* Lieberman and Moskow state that some large school districts have fulltime, permanent personnel or a consultant to do the negotiating; and these people usually get their instructions from the superintendent. In such systems, evidently, there usually is also an administrative team which is made up of associate or assistant superintendents, principals, and others who provide information for the negotiators. In medium-sized systems, the assistant superintendent—often the one in charge of personnel—is the negotiator or this task falls to a school board committee or the entire board. In small systems, negotiations may be directly with the board rather than with the superintendent.[1]

I want to point up some advantages we see in our placement of this responsibility for negotiating. The provision that *one* TVA official represents management in negotiations assures that management will present to the unions a united front. Conversely, the immediately available advice of top management representatives assures that the positions taken by the Director of Personnel in negotiations represent management consensus and that the experience of line and operating managers as well as personnel people are

---

[1] Myron Lieberman and Michael H. Moskow, *Collective Negotiation for Teachers, An Approach to School Administration* (Chicago: Rand McNally and Company, 1966).

reflected in that consensus. These top managers also bring to negotiations some of their own staff personnel. I would guess that these aides function in TVA in a manner similar to the administrative team which Lieberman and Moskow mention as providing information for the negotiators in large urban school systems. The presence of all these people at negotiations means that we have management personnel throughout the agency who are familiar—not only with the provisions agreed to—but with the *intent* of those provisions at the time they were adopted. This can be a tremendous advantage when it comes to administering agreement provisions.

There is another idea I want to stress at this point. As Director of Personnel it is part of my job to be accessible to employees and their representatives and to discuss a wide variety of matters with them. But there is no ambiguity about where I stand. I am strictly a management representative.

Now to another matter. When the TVA employee signs his employment contract, he signifies that he has read and understands the Public Law 330 printed on the back of that contract. This law provides that no person may hold a Federal job who participates in a strike, or asserts the right to strike, against the Government or who belongs to an employee organization that he knows asserts the right to strike against the Government. TVA management has been most conscious through the years that this law deprives TVA employees of the unions' traditional ultimate weapon. Consequently, management has striven for flexibility in its attitude toward employee proposals and has tried to avoid that automatically negative stance which stifles meaningful employee-management relationships. I have no doubt that our union representatives would join me in affirming that realistic collective bargaining is possible where recourse to the strike is absent. In this respect, our experience may hold reassurance for school board member, superintendent, and teacher alike. I can offer further reassurance. This flexibility has been returned in kind by the unions. There have been times when we have had to go to unions with some very sensitive issues where their understanding support was essential. We found that support.

I have hinted at the length of TVA's collective bargaining experience. Let me be more specific. In 1935—two years after TVA's creation—the Board of Directors issued its Employee Relationship Policy. This policy stated that employees had the right to organize and to choose their own representatives to bargain collectively. It also dealt with recognition of bargaining units, settlement of disputes, determination of rates of pay, and many other matters. Even prior to issuance of this policy statement, TVA had dealt with individual AFL craft unions and those unions, as members of the Tennessee Valley Trades and Labor Council, entered into a written agreement with TVA in 1940.

More relevant to you is the fact that, by 1941, TVA had recognized the first union representing part of our white-collar workers or, as we call them, "salary policy" employees. Again there were negotiations with individual unions and with the Salary Policy Employee Panel. In 1950, a formal written agreement was made with the Panel. The Panel today includes the representatives of five unions. Each of these unions has exclusive recognition to represent its bargaining unit. We believe that exclusive recognition is indispensable to the development of fully responsible union leadership. We still deal with an individual union on matters which affect only that union, but our agreement is with the Panel, and we negotiate only with the Panel on TVA-wide matters such as salaries, fringe benefits, promotion, etc. Out latest tabulation shows that almost 85 percent of the positions represented by the Panel unions are filled by union members.

Under both our agreements certain preferences are given to union members, but I haven't time to go into this in detail. Union membership is not a requirement for employment by TVA.

There has been a great deal of discussion about whether or not supervisory personnel should be represented by teachers' organizations. This is an important matter and deserves the attention it is receiving. And it can be a difficult matter. From the beginning our white-collar agreement covered employees only up to a certain grade level. Employees above that level were and are considered to be management people who may not be represented by the unions. But it has taken some years to evolve our current provisions for those people who are in grade levels represented by the unions, but whose duties are such that their participation in and representation by the unions would create conflicts of interest. Today certain whole classes of employees, such as personnel officers, are excluded from representation. Additionally, individual positions in represented classes are excluded on a job-by-job basis. For example, some administrative officers have personnel responsibilities and are excluded; other administrative officers without such duties are represented. These arrangements recognize the shared belief of management and unions in TVA that no individual can be on both sides at once; indeed, that no individual should be placed in such an intolerable position.

My reading suggests two other areas I cannot pass up without comment. Many educators are concerned about what may happen, where collective bargaining emerges, to those concerns traditionally held in common by all the people employed in public education. It is pointed out that the classroom teacher, the principal, the administrator, the superintendent, and the school board member must work as a team to effectively improve the quality of public education. And there is fear that placing these people on one or the other side of the bargaining table will make it impossible for them to continue to work together creatively to fulfill the public purpose for which every school system exists. I suggest that comparable misgivings have beset every public agency standing on the threshold of collective bargaining. The TVA Board's policy statement of 1935 contained ample proof that it, too, had had to wrestle with such doubts. There was the statement that the full cooperation of management and employees was essential to getting TVA's job done. And that job, like the function of your school system, is to serve the people who live in this Tennessee Valley area. The Board said it believed that formal union-management relationships provided the best way to get this management-employee cooperation. But it also stated that TVA was an agency of the sovereign Government of the United States and made clear that mutual recognition of this fundamental nature of TVA was basic to employee-management relationships. These facts and ideas are now a part of our written agreement.

But the Board took another step and it is this step which may have special meaning for educators. It recognized that there were matters in which TVA and its employee organizations had a strong common stake but which were not appropriate for negotiation. To get at this area, the policy statement provided a device which we call our cooperative program. Throughout TVA, conferences meet regularly at which representatives of management and employees work together to improve the efficiency and effectiveness of TVA's service to the people of this Valley. Among the problems tackled are means to get better communication within TVA, to have employees better informed about TVA's varied programs, to establish safer and healthier working conditions, to find better ways to do the work at hand. The important point about this program is that it provides a channel for management and employees to work as a team to reach those common objectives to which both are devoted. I do not suggest that this program has not had its own problems—one of which has been that of defining which areas must be left to the negotiating table and which are suitable for joint endeavor. Yet in May of 1967 William E. Simkin, Director of the Federal Mediation and Conciliation Service, stated that the achievements of this program illustrated the possibilities inherent to "an effective dialogue, an effective mechanism, by which labor and management can get together and talk constructively and act constructively when there is no deadline, and the crisis atmosphere is absent." The basic functions of this program are described in our salary policy agreement.

Thus far I have attempted to describe the general framework within which collective bargaining operates in TVA and to point out how that framework, in several ways, is similar to that which might be found in a local school system. Before getting into the details of contract administration and grievance procedures, it might be helpful to think about school systems. Let me say first, though, that I realize there are conflicting views about the role the superintendent should play in collective bargaining. It is not my intention to take sides in this controversy. I'm simply talking about a situation in which the superintendent would play a role somewhat similar to my own in TVA. To assure my neutrality in the competition between the American Federation of Teachers and the National Education Association, I will use the term "organization" rather than either "union" or "association" when referring to teachers' groups. I will use "union" only when referring to TVA employee organizations.

As I see it, the critical first step, once the agreement is signed, is for the school board and the superintendent to recognize that the Rubicon has been crossed. School management and the organization have entered into an agreement; the parties have a joint responsibility to apply the provisions of that agreement. The good faith of school management from the board to the vice-principal is now on the block. The board and the superintendent must make clear to all supervisory personnel that nonorganization or anti-organization bias has no place in the school system; that school management has entered into relations with the organization and expects supervisors to make it work. I would like to quote from an article in the August 1966 issue of "The American School Board Journal:"

Uncritical acceptance of collective bargaining as joint decision-making, rather than the means of defining the rights and benefits of employees, is fraught with danger. If school boards will approach the bargaining table with realities in mind, conflicts with teachers, within and apart from the bargaining relationship, may be reduced or at least confined.[2]

The task of changing attitudes is always a formidable one, but the change, obviously, must start at the top. Lip service or grudging consent are not enough. Perhaps school management, at this point, can take comfort in the thought that the organization will also have some attitudes to change. It will have dissident members who will still want to see if they can't get further with a little personal "politicking." And school management will have to be very strict in promptly referring such people back to their organization. Contract administration will fall apart if management makes side deals with individuals or small groups, or if it takes action behind the organization's back. It is well to remember that such tactics can be used by the organization, too, if management sets the precedent.

While both management and the organization are responsible for administration of the agreement, it is basically management which administers it. The organization raises questions when it feels management makes errors or willfully violates the provisions.

The most important level of contract administration is the day-to-day interpretation by first-line supervisors, which would be the principals or vice-principals and department heads in a school system. The principal can do this vital job well only if he is made fully aware of the commitment of the board and superintendent to the joint relationship. He must also know what is expected of him in doing this job and what is in the contract. Finally, he needs to know where to get help if he needs it.

The principal will probably have to look to the superintendent or the superintendent's staff for this advice. It will be the job of the superintendent or members of his staff to assure that the contract provisions are not stretched beyond their intent; to recognize when issues are raised which (1) require internal discussion to find an answer, or (2) need to be discussed with the organization. (To avoid repetition, please assume that any time I mention the superintendent in this discussion that I'm also referring to members of his staff who may act as advisors, too.)

[2] George W. Combe, Jr., "How to Minimize Teachers vs. Boards Conflicts Over Collective Bargaining," *The American School Board Journal* (August, 1966), p.53.

Above all, the superintendent must establish good relations with the top organization representatives so that frank dialogue between the two is always possible. The kind of relationship at this level will set the tone for the relationship between the principal and the organization representatives in the individual school, where—as I've stated—administration of the agreement meets its most important tests.

Quite frankly, there are problems ahead for the school system which has just entered a contract relationship with its teachers. And many of these problems will begin at the lower levels of the system. When they arise, the superintendent and the top organization representatives must be able to work together to resolve them. And good relations develop when both sides, at every level of the system, accept their respective obligations under the agreement and respect the rights of each other under that agreement.

It will probably fall to the superintendent to train the principals so that they know the scope of the contract; understand the functions of the organization representatives; and know who speaks for management at various levels in the school system. In this training it should be stressed that the "good guys" in management do not give away what management has not given away in negotiations. It should be clear that supervisory people learn to read *what is* in the agreement, not what they think *should be* in it. Supervisory training is a continuing job so the first sessions should concentrate on the most important provisions and on those which require changes in past practices or those which are stated in not too specific terms.

A word here about the wording of the agreement. Ideally the parties should seek to set down the general rules by which they agree to abide and to avoid spelling out exactly how each rule will be put into force. This is especially important at the beginning of the relationship. In the first place the parties cannot anticipate all the situations to which a rule will need to be applied. And secondly, words are a two-edged sword susceptible to many interpretations. The more specific the wording—the more words there are—the more need there will be for interpretation. Finally, both parties need room to maneuver, to accommodate each other's problems in the day-to-day administration of agreement provisions. Agreement wording which is too specific will tie the hands of both sides. As time passes, both sides will feel compelled to seek more specific contract wording, but by then specifics will be based upon actual experience rather than what, at the beginning of the relationship, each party *thought* that experience would be.

The superintendent, on the basis of his review of the contract and the questions raised about some provisions, will have the continuing task of making management interpretations which must be made available to all supervisors. This central interpretation of provisions which may not be clear or which may need to be applied to peculiar situations might be described as the second level of contract administration.

There should be specific procedures in writing to spell out the number of organization representatives in the school system and how they will be designated. Procedures are also needed on how matters not resolved at the principal-teacher level are referred to higher levels for resolution. The third level of contract administration is the grievance procedure which I will tackle at more length in a moment.

The final level is arbitration. In TVA's agreement with the Salary Policy Employee Panel, arbitration may occur under two separate sets of circumstances. It is the final step in our grievance procedure. It also may come about when TVA and the Panel fail to reach agreement on changes in negotiated agreement provisions. In the latter case either party may call for a jointly selected mediator who attempts to bring the parties together. If mediation fails, either party, with the assistance of the mediator, may ask the other party to voluntarily submit the controversy to arbitration. If arbitration is agreed to, the jointly selected arbitrator's decision is final and binding on both sides. From 1950, when the agreement was signed, through last year neither mediation nor arbitration was required to resolve an impasse in negotiations. We do not have a case at this time which is to be mediated.

Before getting into grievance procedures, I would conclude my overall discussion of contract administration by repeating a few ideas. It is imperative that management, from top to bottom, establish relations with organization representatives which will give those representatives confidence in and respect for school management. Management should deal with these representatives above board; should not withhold or twist facts; and should admit errors when they are made.

A grievance procedure will work best when both school management and the teacher's organization accept the idea that there is nothing wrong with grievances. They are a means to formally raise questions on interpretation of the agreement. Neither side should be concerned primarily with winning the point raised in the grievance. Rather they should try to find the right answer. If the grievance procedures provide for arbitration as a final step, that's good. But neither side should use arbitration too much. Management and the organization representatives should try to settle their problems within the family if they can.

Because you are most likely to be concerned with a negotiated grievance procedure, I will restrict my remarks to that type of procedure. I will just note in passing that, while TVA is not under Civil Service laws, a few Federal laws and regulations allow some TVA employees the choice of appealing certain kinds of personnel actions either through our negotiated procedures or to the United States Civil Service Commission.

The grievance procedure is a basic element in the collective bargaining contract. It provides the means by which differences of opinion about the proper application of negotiated procedures in specific instances may be worked out. It is the means by which individual misunderstandings can be cleared up before they turn into burning issues involving large groups of employees. In some instances the grievance procedure is a means of settling individual complaints about matters not mentioned in the collective bargaining agreement. This might be called "negotiating in miniature." In fact, there is some negotiation in miniature in all grievances under a collective bargaining contract.

What are the steps in an effective grievance procedure? The first step, it seems to me, is discussion with the immediate supervisor—probably the principal. Most grievances can and should be settled at this point.

In TVA the second step is appeal to the division director. A division is a major subdivision of TVA, and a division director reports to the General Manager. If there were an intermediate supervisor between the principal and the superintendent, he would be the point of appeal at this second step; in a school system perhaps the superintendent would be the man. At this step in TVA a hearing is usually held, and a verbatim record is made and submitted to both employee and management representatives for approval as to accuracy. All facts about the grievance are supposed to be presented at the hearing, and the record thus established is the basis of decision at this and any subsequent steps. Ordinarily the division director is not present at the hearing. An officer named by the director conducts the hearing. The director makes his decision from the record.

In a negotiated grievance procedure, it seems to me that the management person who is responsible for negotiating the collective bargaining agreement should make the final grievance decision within an agency or a school system. If the superintendent has that responsibility, his would be the final decision, and this would occur at the second step described above. However, if the school board does the negotiating, then there would be a third step, with the school board making the final decision as, in TVA, the Director of Personnel makes that decision. Whoever makes the final decision can and should in arriving at a decision, take into consideration the impact of that decision on all the elements of the relationship between management and the employee organization.

In TVA we also have provision whereby the union or the Director of Personnel may request a conference before a final decision is rendered. The conference is attended by the top representative of the union involved, one or more representatives of the Panel, the division director, and the Director of Personnel. The principal value of this conference is that it may clarify for both union and management the extent to which and the manner in which the overall relationship is involved in a particular grievance.

Grievances should be settled promptly. If not settled promptly, the feeling of dissatisfaction may grow; and it may be spread to employees not directly involved. Most grievance procedures set time limits for each step. The time limits in TVA's agreement with the Salary Policy Employee Panel are set out in the agreement. These limits are less numerous than those in our agreement covering our craft employees. Where there are no time limits, the salary policy agreement provides that "employees, unions, and representatives of management are nevertheless expected to act promptly." It is important that sufficient time be allowed for the employee and his representative to think through the case. Time for thinking may lead to a decision not to file a grievance or at least it may lead to a grievance presentation in which the problem is clearly defined. Too many time limits or time limits so specific as to require almost immediate action may discourage employees and their representatives from taking thoughtful approach to a grievance action.

What about arbitration in grievance procedures? We have it in TVA and the arbitrator's decision is binding. We call this process "referring a case to an impartial referee." The impartial referee usually makes his decision on the basis of the record developed within TVA. He can call for a hearing if he wishes clarification of the record.

The individual employee may not have a case referred to a referee. At this stage a grievance is not an individual matter, but a matter affecting the relationship between TVA and the union. Both parties have put considerable effort into getting all the facts about the case so as to reach a solution acceptable to both parties. If they cannot agree, they need a final resolution of the matter so they can go on to other matters. The referee provides this resolution.

Should a grievance procedure exclude certain types of complaints? Clearly, a grievance procedure should not be used for the purpose of changing an established standard or procedure or a provision of the negotiated agreement. Such changes should be made through negotiation. Aside from this, under the TVA grievance procedure an employee may file a grievance:

1. If he believes he has been treated unfairly, or
2. If he disagrees with his supervisor as to the application of a policy to him as an employee.

We believe that in a grievance under a negotiated procedure the employee organization has a stake in the matter and is entitled to be present even when the grieving employee is not a union member or does not want the organization to represent him. The union, in TVA, is present as representative of all employees in the bargaining unit who may be affected by the terms of settlement of a grievance.

Ideally the supervisor—or principal—looks upon a grievance, particularly a grievance supported by the employee organization, as an attempt to bring to his attention a condition which may impair the employee-management team effort. He will consider it worth his time to listen. He will hear what is said. He will ask questions to learn as much as he possibly can about the condition. Of course, these attitudes will not develop if other management people, from the top down, do not support the whole organization-management relationship. His attitude will also be affected by the attitudes and conduct of the employee organization representatives. Some of these desirable supervisory attitudes are discussed, along with other matters, in a small booklet we have prepared as a guide for our management people in handling grievances under our white-collar agreement.

You may suspect by now that I believe in collective bargaining. And you know that collective bargaining has long been a way of life for TVA. "Why?" you ask. "What possible advantages do you find in it?"

For one, negotiating, administering agreements, and working with grievance procedures helps develop able supervisors. It is training that is sometimes disconcerting—but it is effective. In large systems, dealing with the complaints of numerous individual employees can be a time-consuming task. Where you have a written agreement which spells out exactly what the individual may expect in many areas of concern to him, you can expect that the organization representative will get many of the visitors who used to come to you. And, if he is able, many complaints will stop with him. He may point to the agreement and say, "Look here. What you want would violate the agreement."

There is another plus which affects the large and small system alike. A teacher comes in and says, "I represent all the teachers at Blank School, and we just don't like such and such." How do you *know* he represents all the teachers at Blank School? And, if you agree to go along with his request but require, as a condition, that the teachers will agree to do something also, how do you *know* they will meet that condition? When you deal, under an agreement, with the official representative of an organization which has exclusive recognition to represent a particular group of teachers, you will no longer have such uncertainties. With a formal agreement the organization assumes responsibility along with management to enforce the agreement. With time you will find you have gained, perhaps, an able adversary but an adversary who has agreed to play by certain established rules. More likely you will find you have gained a partner. When problems arise—whether covered by the agreement or not—management can sit down with the organization, lay the facts on the table, and hammer out a solution. I should stress that this does not come about immediately upon the signing of an agreement—it comes from good faith and mutual trust developed through many and sometimes difficult encounters. But when a joint solution to a problem is found, management is not alone in explaining why a certain thing will be done a certain way in the future. And, as I suggested in my remarks about our cooperative program, the years bring more and more areas to light in which mutual interest makes cooperative effort the only sensible means of doing business.

But underlying all I've just said is something more elemental. The employee who has an officially recognized representative whose job is to look out for his interests is a more secure employee. Where he has a representative to present his ideas for improvements in how to do the work or for changes in many other areas—as in our cooperative program—he is a more committed employee. He has helped to build the house in which he lives. Parenthetically, if the plumbing is bad, he must accept some of the blame. This employee is likely to have a greater sense of his own worth and dignity. In short, because his voice is *officially* recognized, he believes he is trusted and he can, in turn, trust.

Recent studies made by the behavioral scientists at least suggest, at this time, that such an employee is also more creative, more effective.

Perhaps no other group to which I could speak would be more prepared to share with me and many others a conviction that every human being possesses a basic impulse to strive for that which is excellent. You may or may not agree with me that collective bargaining is one alternative to authoritarianism and paternalism. And some of the best, if indirect, criticism I've ever read about those two "isms" is said to have been the product of an ancient Chinese philosopher, Laotzu:

> If I keep from meddling with people,
>   they take care of themselves,
> If I keep from commanding people,
>   they behave themselves,
> If I keep from preaching at people,
>   they improve themselves,
> If I keep from imposing on people,
>   they become themselves.

Labor Relations Negotiators on Bargaining: Factories vs. the Schools

Robert E. Doherty

During the academic year 1967–1968, hundreds of New York State school boards and teacher organizations negotiated their first collective bargaining agreements under the state's new Taylor Act, a law mandating local boards and other public employers to deal collectively with their employees if the employees so request. In many school districts, particularly in the smaller ones, a committee of board members, rather than members of the administrative staff, constituted the bargaining team. In a handful of districts, school boards had among their members individuals with considerable experience in private sector labor relations. In the latter case the chances are that the labor relations expert would be selected to head up the board's negotiating team.

Dr. Doherty is Professor of Industrial and Labor Relations, New York State School of Industrial and Labor Relations, Cornell University, Ithaca, New York.

For a researcher who has been puzzling over the similarities and dissimilarities of private-sector and public-school negotiations almost since the time public employee bargaining began in earnest, this happy circumstance of finding labor relations specialists who had now struggled in both arenas seemed to provide an excellent opportunity to find out just what these similarities and differences are. All one had to do was to identify those labor relations practitioners who served as chairmen of board negotiating committees and persuade them to submit to interviews. The observations presented below are based on a dozen such interviews. (Actually, I had identified almost twice that number, but the laws of logistics and diminishing returns suggested that I confine my study to a smaller sample).

Of course, twelve interviews do not a scientific survey make. And to continue for a moment playing the role of the caveator, I should point out, even at the risk of severely weakening the force of what will be said later, that all the board members visited represented small suburban, rural, and central districts, the largest having fewer than 200 teachers. Moreover, the teachers in each of the districts were represented by National Education Association affiliates. Had the districts been urban, and had the teachers been represented by affiliates of the American Federation of Teachers, I might have elicited somewhat different responses to my questions.

It is also important to know that, as far as the practitioners are concerned, about half had confined their activities to the negotiation of supplemental plant agreements, the important issues of wages and fringe benefits having been previously settled in company-wide, regional, or industry-wide agreements. This is an important consideration to keep in mind, not only because supplemental agreements usually cover items of limited economic consequence, but because under this arrangement the local labor relations manager often has little to do with developing manpower policy, nor does he usually know at first hand what implications the company's manpower policy might have for the health or long-range plans of the firm. Probably a negotiator for a school district would have to be keenly sensitive to this relationship. Another point worth considering is that the experience of the practitioners interviewed was limited to dealings with production and maintenance workers. This is important to know, if only to help us guard against making hasty generalizations about bargaining relationships in the private sector being pretty much the same. There may indeed be almost as many "differences" in negotiating an agreement, say, with a clothing workers' local on the one hand and a building tradesmen's local on the other as there is between the bargaining problems of "typical" production workers and teachers. In the same vein, it is at least conceivable that a director of labor relations in a large electronics company whose specialty is dealing with a union of professional engineers would feel more comfortable negotiating with a group of public-school teachers than he would bargaining with production workers in his own firm.

So our observations are based on something less than an adequate sample or a rigorous, time-tested methodology. And with that bit of caution in mind, let us proceed to find out what it is in the collective bargaining agreement between teachers and board members that strikes the experienced practitioner as being similar or dissimilar to what he is accustomed to in the private sector.

Board members thought that not all the apparent dissimilarities could be attributed to the differences in institutional arrangements between public schools and private industry. The teachers were beginners, and the nature of their demands, their posture, the way they went about their business generally, had as much to do with the novelty of the situation as it did with the uniqueness of the industry. For the most part, teachers' demands were not well thought out, nor was there much of an attempt to establish priorities or prepare trade-offs. It seemed not to occur to them, so ran the complaint, the bargaining called for an element of *quid pro quo;* many teacher leaders tended to look upon anything less than total acceptance of their demands as total defeat. Not a few practitioners began to long for that hardheaded business agent who could talk turkey to the members as well as represent them.

One of the most pronounced similiarities, the practitioners believed, was employer-employee disagreement over the appropriate scope or subject matter of collective bargaining. As in the private sector, employers and employees were often wide apart on their views as to what issues actually constituted conditions of work and were therefore bargainable. In their dealings with teachers, board members tended to follow the same principle that guided them in their negotiations with private-sector unions—subject matter should be confined to issues that can be clearly identified as manpower policy. On other policy issues, management must retain sole authority to make decisions. They noticed, however, that teachers were even less persuaded by the management-prerogative argument than were their company employees. Teachers had a way of seeing virtually all board decisions as having some bearing on employment conditions. Everything from the length of faculty meetings and the size of classes to student discipline and the selection of administrators, was grist for the teachers' mill. Teachers often argued, moreover, as trade unionists usually did not, that they had more competence to make judgments on these (and other) matters than did the board itself. Several board members admitted that it was sometimes difficult to draw a line separating those topics that were purely manpower matters from those that were plainly educational issues. Nor did they always feel comfortable proclaiming certain issues non-negotiable. It was sometimes difficult to defend the position that the board alone had the competence and the authority to make certain decisions in the face of some rather cogent arguments to the contrary. Yet for the most part they persisted. The leanness of the collective agreements they negotiated indicates that they also prevailed.

To a handful of board members, developments in the private sector offered a source of hope that the scope of bargaining in the schools would in time become less of a contentious issue. A few foresaw procedures similar to those under the National Labor Relations Act being someday incorporated in the Taylor Act. Under the NLRA, the National Labor Realtions Board and/or the courts rule on the bargaining appropriateness of certain contested issues. Unfortunate as many of the NLRB and court decisions have been from the employers' point of view, board members seemed to welcome the possibility of administrative or court decisions on these matters.

Some of those interviewed thought it was also quite likely that, in spite of the vehemence with which they clung to the position that there should be virtually no limits to what is negotiable, teacher organizations would come round to concentrating their demands on economic issues. A great many trade unions had also gone through the "codetermination" stage and had learned in the process that the further their demands ranged from traditional trade union objectives, the more divisiveness was created among the membership. Teacher organizations are no less politicized than private-sector unions, and the membership of teacher organizations are by no means of one mind about what constitutes a good curriculum or a sound student discipline policy. Nor do teacher leaders, any more than trade unionists, want to face the political consequences of having helped frame a policy that turned out badly.

The practitioners interviewed also noted some rather striking parallels (and differences) in the rationale private-sector unions and teacher organizations used to buttress their respective demands. "In both cases," one practitioner observed, "they seem to spend about as much time looking over the shoulder at what has happened, or is likely to happen, elsewhere as they do at the issues before them."

Neither teacher leaders nor business agents, evidently, can very well afford to settle for less than workers in comparable, or sometimes not so comparable, industries have settled for. Another stiking similarity was the way both teachers and blue-collar workers use the dramatic upward trend of the Consumer Price Index over the last few years to justify their demands for substantial wage increase.

But here the similarities seem to end. Teachers had a way of basing a large part of their case on how entirely consistent their demands were with the welfare of education and school children. ("Teachers want what children need.") Higher salaries and greater benefits would aid in the recruitment of better teachers, utilization of teacher aides and the reduction of clerical tasks would allow for more time and energy to be devoted to teaching, joint formulation of curriculum would improve the educational program and bolster morale, and so on. It is rare, one practitioner observed, for a machine tender or a maintenance worker to argue that higher wages would ease the burden of the company recruiter, or that five minutes additional wash-up time would somehow enhance the market value of the product.

What seemed to be the most striking, and from the practitioner's point of view, the most troubling difference between unions and teacher associations was that teachers almost always felt obliged to invoke such abstract concepts as justice, equity, and fairness to bolster their economic arguments. Trade unionists long ago abandoned the living-wage argument; they now tend to concentrate their attention on the realities of the market place and relative bargaining muscle. Accustomed to looking at the bargaining table as a place to press for increased efficiency while they weighed the cost of settlement against the cost of a work stoppage, most practitioners felt somewhat uncomfortable debating over the contents of salary schedules and a fringe-benefit package as if these were profound "moral" issues. As they saw it, justice was satisfied when the law provided for collective bargaining, equity was in the process, not in the settlement, and there was no "higher law" other than the one dictated by the market place.

But when it came to developing their own bargaining strategy, these labor relations experts were frequently found wanting in standards on which to base their demands and counterproposals. One thing was apparent, and that was that experience in the private sector did not always serve as an adequate guide. To summarize the views of those interviewed, the major problem of translating private-sector strategy into a public-school setting stemmed from the fact that one of the enterprises finds its *raison d'etre* in the profit motive and the other does not. Put another way, a private employer worries about how he can best organize and operate an enterprise to secure money; a school board worries about how it can best go about securing enough money to operate the enterprise. Private employers often fret over price competition in the product market; school boards know their market will always be there.

As these practitioners see it, the manager's task is, among other things, to develop a manpower policy that will yield the highest possible return on a given investment. This usually involves an efficient work-flow, a rational accommodation to skill differentials, and a competitive wage scale, often well above the federal minimum wage since productive workers don't usually flock to low-paying jobs. If the employer deals with a union he must, of course, be prepared to back off from this "ideal" arrangement. But he will not lose sight of the overwhelming importance of an effective manpower policy and its relationship to the market price of the service or commodity he offers. It is rare that he will back off so far as to jeopardize his competitive position. In a sense, and to a degree, he has an ally in the union, for unless it miscalculates badly, the union will not press its demands to a point that would result in a serious decline in production or in profits. This could also mean a decline in job opportunities and, horror of horrors, fewer dues-paying members.

One might argue with this analysis. The competitive model described is a little too tidy, and certainly it does not describe *all* private-sector bargaining relationships. It does happen to be the way most of those interviewed viewed the matter. And accurate or not, it was jarring to several of these practitioners to discover that so much of what they thought was basic to employee relations was irrelevant to the school situation; to realize, for example, that, unlike private companies, inefficiently run school systems do not go out of business, teacher associations are not threatened by unorganized or low-pay districts, and fear of unemployment, the spectre hanging over so many of their company employees, had no relevance for teachers.

It was equally unnerving to learn that virtually none of the criteria used to measure productivity in industry applied to schools; even more unsettling to discover that teacher organizations felt they had no vested interest in the efficient allocation of resources. One practitioner who had spent a number of years both in industry and the schools explained the problem this way: Unlike school management, companies can often rely on the employee organization to share their concern over notoriously troublesome or inefficient employees since a worker who gets into fights, wastes materials, and damages equipment not only threatens the job earnings but jobs as well. In education no single teacher threatens the job security of another. An incompetent third-grade teacher may make life difficult for the fourth-grade teacher who must try to teach the children she passes on, but she has no effect on causing the source of children (and employment) to dry up. In short, those restraints of the market place, which in the private sector highlight the importance of productivity and tend to force employers and employees to act responsibly toward each other, are virtually absent in public education.

If there are no market forces at work to act as a damper on teacher demands, what does? No question prompted a greater variety of responses from the practitioners than this one. It would be impossible to categorize them all, but there seemed to be roughly three overlapping interpretations. A few practitioners were persuaded that the teacher organization's expectations were governed solely by neighboring settlements, and since most school boards were willing to meet area settlements anyway, this made negotiations relatively easy. Others felt that the teacher organization was restrained by the timidity of its leaders, many of whom hadn't quite gotten used to the idea that under the law their employers were no more than their equals. In two or three instances teacher organization leaders were so timid or inept that their demands fell short of what the board was prepared to offer.

Probably the most significant restraint was the fear of adverse public opinion. About half of those interviewed thought that the teacher leaders in their community were anything but timid or would hardly be satisfied with a settlement that merely matched agreements in nearby districts. But, it was thought, teachers felt uneasy about how local citizens would respond to a tough stance at the bargaining table. In eleven of the twelve districts in which interviews were conducted, the voters had veto rights over the school budget, a right taxpayers in other districts are beginning to exercise with increasing frequency. And even though it is possible under the New York State Education Law's "austerity" provision for non-city districts to pay whatever teacher salaries it has agreed to, even if the voters turn down the budget, teacher leaders seemed reluctant to press the issue that far. For, under an austerity budget, salary improvements might have to be subsidized by cuts in "non-essential" programs and services. Teachers are aware that what appears to them to be a non-essential service could be regarded as a critical need by the community. Few teachers seemed willing in this early stage to press their demands to the point that would bring them into public disfavor. Public opinion, at least in these small rural districts, is still a factor to be reckoned with.

Thus did the labor relations experts regard the Achilles' heel of the opposition. That they assessed these restraints accurately is best evidenced by the settlements they were able to achieve. It would be hard for a taxpayer in any of the twelve districts surveyed to argue that the school board had dipped much more deeply into the public coffer than was necessary.

The moving force for producing agreement in labor relations in the private sector is the strike, or threat thereof. Under the Taylor Act public employee strikes are illegal. And while the act had been violated in a handful of cases prior to the interviews, none of the board members interviewed had been faced with a strike threat during negotiations. Indeed, in only two cases had it been necessary for the parties to resort to mediation. Moreover, only two practitioners (not from the same two districts) believed that the teacher organization leaders in their school districts could get their membership to go out, and that would have to be under extremely provocative conditions. Board members may have underestimated the determination of their teachers, but that's not the point. The point is that negotiations were carried on in an atmosphere much less beset by pressures than usually exists in industry. The question then is: Did the school boards make substantially fewer concessions under these circumstances than they would if the strike threat were ever present? Or, put a little stronger, is it true, as most trade unionists who represent public employees allege, that there can be no meaningful bargaining if there is no right to strike?

As we shall see, there was no general agreement on this question. But before we explore the practitioners' views on the consequences of strike prohibition for their particular bargaining strategies, we should first get some understanding of the *purpose* of the strike. To most of those interviewed, the function of the strike in both categories is to create dysfunction, to force (or threaten to force) a temporary breakdown of the system, the employees anticipating that the employer will be so concerned about keeping the enterprise going that he will grant the necessary concessions.

The difference between the strike in industry and in the schools stems from the differing reasons for fearing this dysfunction. A private employer faced with a strike threat will attempt to weigh the cost of the strike against the cost of settling at or near the union's terms. Can the increased costs incurred by meeting the union demands be recouped by price increases, or productivity savings, or a combination of both? Will his willingness to take a strike bring the union's demands significantly closer to the company's last offer? Is there a stockpile sufficient to meet customer demands over the short haul? If it is a long strike, how many customers will go to other suppliers never to return?

A school board faced with a threatened strike will (perhaps one should say "ought to") make somewhat different calculations. For, even though the dispute almost always involves money—teachers rarely demand the same deal as before—a board cannot rely on economic calculations alone for guidance. To illustrate, local tax revenues do not cease merely because the school plant is not in operation. It is possible for striking teachers, who obviously don't get paid while they are out, to partially subsidize their own pay increases, at least for the current fiscal year. If the schools are somehow kept open on a make-shift basis, and the state's contribution is continued (in New York the state's contribution averages about 50 percent of total operating costs, based on average daily attendance), the teachers might wholly subsidize their wage increase, depending, of course, on the length of the strike and the amount of the increase.

Thus it was believed that the issue was only partly economic, that probably the most important calculations were political. The *ability* of the district's taxpayers to come up with more revenue was one thing; their *willingness* to do so was another. The difficulty school boards face is that the former, which is an economic consideration and relatively easy to figure, is less important to their overall calculations than the latter, which is fraught with political complications.

Translating these political restraints into the more easily understood language of market restraints was an intellectual exercise none of these practitioners felt prepared for. Some of the issues raised by the threat of a teacher strike seemed not to be translatable at all. Is the accountability a board member owes his constituents at all comparable to the responsibility a corporation executive has for his stockholders? What is the industrial counterpart of the school children? Are they the product, the market, what? One thing seemed certain in the eyes of these practitioners, and that was that children, much more than board members, stand to be the real cost bearers in the event of stoppage. Board members could gain as well as lose political capital, depending on how things worked out. Children could not only lose valuable school time, but stand to bear the cost of a strike-forced reallocation of resources, such as the abandonment of important (though non-mandated) educational services in order to subsidize a pay raise.

To return to the original question: Does the strike prohibition make a mockery of public employee bargaining? If one might generalize from the responses of the practitioners interviewed, the answer is—not entirely. In the first place, the hovering presence of fact-finding induced several school boards to make concessions. The Taylor Law provides that, in the event the parties are at impasse and the budget submission date is fast approaching, a fact-finder shall be appointed to investigate the dispute and make public recommendations for settlement. Although boards are not bound by the fact-finder's recommendations, most of them would prefer not to take that route. Fact-finders, it is feared, will not always see the issues clearly; a few have made recommendations that are almost identical with the teachers' demands. Better to give half a loaf at the bargaining table than risk having a neutral publicize the "fact" that you really ought to give up three-quarters.

Another reason for believing that the strike prohibition does not entirely subvert collective bargaining is that the bargaining process itself has a way of forcing concessions. In the pre-Taylor Act era school boards did not usually feel obliged to give reasons for turning down teachers' requests. Now they had to. And there is something about having to justify one's position that makes one slightly more vulnerable to counterarguments. More than one practitioner reported that he felt constrained to recommend that the board abandon its stand on a particular issue only because the teachers had been able to muster sufficient facts and supporting logic to make the board's position untenable. In other words, teachers do have muscle, even without the right to strike, not as much as they would were the strike legalized, but muscle none-the-less.

Is there a lesson to be learned from this somewhat adumbrative survey? If there is, it would seem to be that there are enough dissimilarities between private-sector and teacher bargaining to give pause to those sitting on labor relations boards which have jurisdiction over employee relations in schools. Most of those charged with the responsibility of administering public employee bargaining disputes, or those who act as neutrals in public employee bargaining disputes for that matter, have had virtually all their experience in the private sector. Some of these individuals are too quick to analogize from their industrial experience, where one can usually depend on market forces eventually to set things right. If one thing has been made clear during these interviews, it is that in public employee bargaining there is no comparable market mechanism that can be relied upon to serve as a restraint.

There is another lesson coming from this survey, and one somewhat contradictory to the conclusion reached immediately above. Board negotiators who have not had experience in private-sector negotiations have something to learn from those who have. The pressure to maintain efficiency makes it imperative that industry negotiators take the initiative in deciding what sort of manpower policy is in the best interests of the firm. They know that there will be times in their dealings with the union when a retreat is necessary. But because they have planned carefully, the retreat is rarely turned into a rout. If school negotiators can learn how important it is to develop a manpower policy that makes sense in terms of an efficient and orderly operation of their enterprise, they will stand a much better change of having a manpower policy that makes sense when negotiations are completed.

Section B

The Analysts: Collective Negotiations and Organization Theory

In a critical look at the causes of militancy, Wildman pays particular attention to the basic questions involved in the redistribution of control between management and teachers and the changing form of teacher control. Corwin views militancy within a bureaucratic context. Based to a large extent on a comprehensive study of teacher militancy, Corwin's article first focuses on the particular problems encountered now that administrators can no longer maintain centralized control over education practices. Corwin then points up a number of basic considerations inherent in negotiations which are not often explicitly recognized, such as the power of minorities.

Kimbrough and Williams are concerned with the power of teacher militants from a pluralistic viewpoint. They focus on the interaction of "teacher power" with the numerous other power groups in the community. The principal, often regarded as the forgotten man in the negotiations process, is the concern of Cunningham. Looking at the principalship in its broader organizational context, and with regard to the bases of the principal's leadership and authority, Cunningham outlines the problems and difficulties of the principalship as it undergoes a major redefinition of function. In the concluding article, Goodwin and Thompson briefly review the general "causes" given for teacher militancy, outline the concept of countervailing power, and show how this broader theory can be useful in explaining the rise of teacher militancy more effectively than the more particularistic explanations.

What's Negotiable?

Concessions and compromises are often the facts of life in the power relationship, but bargaining must not mean abdicating responsibility.

Wesley A. Wildman

Is it crucial to distinguish between subjects which are bargainable and those which are not in a collective negotiation relationship in a school district?[1]

It can be persuasively argued that the distinction between negotiable and non-negotiable subject matter is quite important once a school board and teacher organization have entered into a formal collective bargaining relationship. Collective bargaining is a power relationship and a process of power accommodation, the essence of which is compromise and concession-making on matters over which there is conflict between the teacher organization and the board. It is true that the requirement to bargain, even under the labor laws applicable to private industry, does not carry a corollary requirement to abdicate responsibility, to capitulate on any given demand, or even to reach an agreement. I would stress, though, that while concessions and compromises are not demanded by the legal concept of good faith bargaining in either public or private employment, it is a practical fact that in the context of the power relationship that marks true collective bargaining, matters discussed for the purpose of mutual decision-making are often compromised when they become subjects of dispute between the board and the teacher organization.

Thus, with regard to "policy" matters over which a board of education may wish to maintain completely unilateral control, a "first line of defense," as it were, may be the insistence by the board

Reprinted with permission from the *American School Board Journal,* November, 1967. The National School Boards Association. All rights reserved. Wesley Wildman, "What's Negotiable?" *American School Board Journal,* CLV, (November, 1967), 7-10. Dr. Wildman is director of labor management projects at the Industrial Relations Center, University of Chicago.

[1] Some subjects, of course (tenure rules and regulations, for example) which are legislatively determined will not be bargained at the school district level. The discussion in this article does not relate to such "automatically" excluded issues.

that such subjects are simply not appropriate for discussion and attempted co-determination at the collective bargaining table. Moreover, it can be argued that refusing to allow a subject considered by the board to be "policy" into negotiations will lessen the risk that a dispute over such a subject will lead to a bargaining impasse and will avoid the possibility of having a fact-finding board or an arbitrator effectively deprive the board of decision-making power over the issue.

On the other hand, the argument may be made that because a distinction between "policy" and "working conditions" is difficult to make in the schools, and given the fact that teachers as professionals are interested in and presumably knowledgeable about all aspects of the educational enterprise, boards should avoid a "bad image" and the bitterness among teachers which might result from declaring a "policy" matter taboo for discussion and negotiations, and should agree to at least exchange views in bargaining sessions on any issue the teacher organization wishes to raise. Advocates of this position may also argue that when "policy" issues arise in negotiations on which the board wishes to maintain unilateral control, the board should support rationally, through argument, the need and justification for unilateral control on the issue at hand, and should "bargain hard" to protect its position.

My judgment is that the latter argument gives too little weight to the political, vested-interest dynamics of the collective bargaining process, and reflects an over-optimistic appraisal of the extent to which reason rather than power controls the outcome of bargaining in school districts. Also, a healthy skepticism is in order concerning the identification of self-interest with the public interest by any employee organization, in schools or out. Thus, I tend to conclude that boards engaging in bargaining may be well advised, in some cases at least, to take the position that there is a realm of policy over which the board is charged by the public to exercise continuing unilateral discretion, and that such matters should not be subjected to the give and take of the bargaining arena.

Views on What Is Negotiable

The two major organizations representing teachers in the U. S. leave little doubt as to where they stand on the question of legitimate subject matter for negotiations in the schools. The proclaimed goal of many NEA affiliates is negotiation over "all matters which affect the quality of the educational program," while the AFT feels it wholly appropriate for its locals to bargain over "anything that affects the working life of the teacher." A team of prominent labor attorneys who serve as counsel to the NEA state the case for a broad definition of bargainable subject matter in these terms:

> *Statutes governing . . . negotiations (in the private sector) restrict the scope of mandatory bargaining to "wages, hours and other terms and conditions of employment." However, such a definition applied to teacher negotiations makes mischief. Teachers will continue to assert their claim of special competence to participate in decision-making over educational programs and services . . . It is socially desirable for teachers to participate in decision-making in respect to educational program and services. Their special knowledge and competence as educational practitioners should, when blended with the "lay" perspective of the school board, produce better policy decisions . . . The best way to accommodate the basic difference between teacher negotiations and other types of negotiations is to avoid prior restraints on the scope of bargaining by treating teachers separately and adopting (a) broad definition (of bargainable subject matter).* [2]

However, other voices are being heard on the issue, some from rather unexpected quarters. Myron Lieberman, for many years a staunch proponent of collective bargaining in education and long identified with the teacher-union movement has written, "One would hardly expect or desire that curriculum, methodology, or educational services be subjected to the pressures that inevitably characterize negotiations over conditions of employment." [3] And recently he has stated, "If teachers want to be equal partners in formulating educational policy, then they should give up any right to teacher tenure if they are going to make educational policy on the same level

---

[2] Government Employee Relations Report, "NEA Attorneys Urge that New Jersey Commission Recognize Differences between Public and Private Sectors," a statement by Frederick R. Livingston and Donald H. Wollett, (Washington, D.C.: The Bureau of National Affairs, Inc., May 1, 1967), No. 190, GERR E-1.

[3] Myron Lieberman and Michael H. Moskow, *Collective Negotiations for Teachers: An Approach to School Administration,* (Chicago: Rand McNally & Company, 1966), p. 244.

as the school board, because in a democratic society we ought to have the right to change our policy makers."[4]

What Is Being Bargained?

But let us deal now in specifics: in what ways have teacher bargaining agreements begun to move beyond salaries and narrowly defined "working conditions" issues into broader areas traditionally the unilateral preserve of boards and school administrations? Increasingly, contracts are providing for teacher organization representation in curricular, textbook, and educational policy decision-making generally by affording to organization representatives the right to confer on such matters with board and administrative personnel during the term of the contract away from the collective bargaining table. For instance, the New Haven, Conn., contract provides the right to teachers to "meet and consult" on textbook selection, and for the purpose of developing recommendations to the board "in the field of educational programs." Also, teachers in the New York City system have long enjoyed the right to "meet and consult" every month with the superintendent on matters of educational policy and develement which are beyond the scope of the subject matter dealt with in the agreement between the parties.

Elsewhere, contracts bargained with the teacher organization have provided for the establishment of "Educational Policy Committees" (often with classroom teachers in the majority) which are charged with issuing reports and recommendations to teachers, the board, and the community on matters concerning the educational policy of the school district. At least one district is experimenting, by contract provision, with teacher organization representation on all board of education policy committees.

Besides providing a process through which teachers may have a voice in deciding professional and policy matters which may not be appropriate for the negotiating table, some recent teacher contracts have specific clauses 1) giving teachers the right to challenge administration judgment on teaching methods, 2) providing guidelines for the achievement of pupil and teacher integration in the school

---

[4] Myron Lieberman, "Teacher Negotiations," *School Boards: A Creative Force*, Proceedings of the 1967 Convention of the National School Boards Association (Evanston, Illinois: National School Boards Association, 1967), p. 76.

district, 3) assuring teachers a voice in the promotional policies of the district, 4) granting the classroom teacher more control over grading policy, 5) providing for the election of department heads by teachers, 6) providing for peer evaluation of teachers in the event of disagreement over the principal's rating of a teacher, and 7) providing protection to the teachers' organization in the event of instructional automation.

"Policy" Matters and "Working Conditions"

There is no question but that it is exceedingly difficult to distinguish between "educational policy" and "salaries and working conditions" where teacher bargaining is concerned. For instance, it is generally accepted that the salary schedule and teacher benefits are "bargainable" if anything is. However, if raising teacher salaries in a district as a result of bargaining forces a budget re-allocation of sums set aside for textbooks, hiring of additional professional personnel, building maintenance, or even new school construction, a decision on school district "policy" is clearly involved and may, indeed, be discussed as such although all that is ostensibly under consideration is the salary schedule. Or, take, for example, the problem of teacher transfers. Transfer rules and procedures have long been considered, in both private and public employment, as falling clearly within any reasonable definition of "working conditions." Yet, in our major cities, where schools in lower socio-economic areas have a grossly disproportionate share of the system's inexperienced teachers who are minimally qualified in terms of training and advanced degrees, the problem of fairly and equitably balancing teaching staffs, and thus curtailing the sacred right of transfer by seniority, has become for large city boards a "policy" issue of great significance. Examples of this kind pointing up the difficulty of distinguishing between "policy" and "working conditions" can be cited endlessly.

The most recent dramatic instance of a "policy" versus "working conditions" confrontation occurred in bargaining this fall between the New York City Board of Education and the United Federation of Teachers. A key teacher demand in New York was for the extension to more inner-city schools of the expensive "saturation services" More Effective Schools program. The board, which has judged that the additional outlay for the MES program has not been justified by the results and that the extra sums could better be spent on alternative compensatory educational activities, argued that the issue was clearly an educational matter not appropriate for resolution through collective bargaining. Similarly, another major obstacle to settlement was the UFT demand that teachers be given broad authority to expel from classrooms students judged by the teachers to constitute intractable disciplinary problems. The board countered with the argument that significant educational "policy" decisions were involved in this problem which could not be delegated and that the issue was not appropriate for compromise in negotiations.

The Laws and the Courts

The "bargainable subject matter" problem in private sector negotiations is highly complex and designation of an issue as "bargainable" or "nonbargainable" under our federal labor law is fraught with significance for both management and the union. However, the technicalities and refinements of private sector bargaining are not much in evidence as yet in collective negotiations in education.

Eleven state laws enacted to date on school negotiations have dealt with the question of negotiable or bargaining subject matter in a variety of ways. The relatively comprehensive and detailed laws covering all public employees (teachers included) in states such as Wisconsin, Michigan, Massachusetts, and New York employ variants of the private sector definition of "wages (salaries), hours, and other conditions of employment." Several of the more rudimentary "teachers only" or "professional negotiations" statutes provide for "conferring" or negotiating on a much broader range of subjects. In the state of Washington, for example, matters to be discussed in negotiations include "proposed school policies relating, but not limited to curriculum, textbook selection, in-service training, student teaching programs, personnel, hiring and assignment practices, leaves of absence, salaries and salary schedules and non-instructional duties." Similarly, in California, issues on which the board is required to "meet and confer" include "matters relating to the definition of educational objectives, determination of the content of courses and curricula, selection of textbooks, and other aspects of the instructional program to the extent that such matters are within the discretion of the public school employer or governing board under the law." On the other hand, one of the narrowest definitions of bargainable subject matter to be found in any law in the country appears in the new, relatively simple "teacher only" Minnesota statute which calls for boards to attempt to reach agreement with teacher organizations only on "conditions of professional service" defined as "economic aspects relating to terms of employment ... but not educational policies of the district."

The courts are just now beginning to issue decisions interpreting the scope-of-bargaining language in school negotiations statutes. For example, the Wisconsin Supreme Court has just ruled, in a decision which is hardly any surprise, that the school calendar is a negotiable subject-matter under the Wisconsin act "to the extent that it affects wages, hours, and conditions of employment." More interestingly, a lower court in Michigan has recently ruled that a board of education in that state was not empowered under the Michigan negotiations act to relinquish, by contract with the teacher organizations, its continuing discretion over the use of federal funds and participation in federal programs. This case is now on appeal.

What Can Boards Do?

Boards must recognize the perhaps unpalatable fact that the internal politics of any union engaged in collective bargaining demands that the employee organization continuously expand the scope of issues on which it attempts to take action. Moreover, it seems clear that the lack of definitive legislative and judicial guidelines and precedents on bargainable subject matter in education will make it that much more difficult for boards to resist the rapid proliferation of issues which will become fair game for the power plays and stresses and strains of collective negotiations.

In the midst of this uncertainty, or if you will, confusion and chaos, what can boards and school administrations faced with collective bargaining do?

For boards embarking on collective bargaining the negotiable subject-matter issue is, or course, only one part of the problem presented by the need to plan and implement a consistent and workable approach and strategy for the entire negotiating relationship with the teacher organization. In my judgment, it is impossible to promulgate rules-of-thumb in the abstract which will provide useful, specific guidance to this or that board of education having to decide how to handle *its* unique bargaining problems (including the issue of "what's negotiable") in *its* district with *its* teacher organization. My best advice is that those responsible for the board (or administration) strategy and tactics in collective negotiations read widely in the field and take advantage of available training opportunities so that they may be constantly aware of experiences and best practices elsewhere in school districts throughout the country. Hopefully, with such a background and at least a modicum of skill and ability developed and matured on the negotiating "firing line" over time, board and school administration officials will be able to represent and defend the appropriate interests of the community in any bargaining which may affect control over the educational enterprise. On occasion, of course, it may be prudent and necessary for a school administration to seek expert consultation and assistance from outside the district.

The Anatomy of Militant Professionalization

Ronald G. Corwin

I first want to simply call your attention to several of the now familiar forces within our society, and some within the schools themselves, which have contributed to the militant professionalism of teachers. And then I would like to identify some qualifying principles which often have been overlooked in the heat of the controversy about this perplexing development. Needless to say, much of what I will say will be speculative, and some of it merely obvious. The question is whether we can *agree* on what is "obvious" and what is speculative.

I would maintain that at least one point is clear, however: teacher militance is not a down-trodden group's reaction to despair; rather, it reflects the hope of an increasingly important segment of the society. This hope rides a wave of recent institutional changes.

Institutional Developments

National Relevance of Education

First, there is the now familiar "revolution" in technology which has thrust institutions of formal education into unprecedented positions of national relevance. However, this revelance has been extracted at a price, for it has meant that the limited resources of schools have been strained as they have assumed increasing

Dr. Corwin is Professor of Sociology, The Ohio State University, Columbus, Ohio.

responsibilities for a growing number of the society's needs—and most recently this has included responsibility for alleviating its human welfare problems. The full implicatons of this transformation of schools into welfare agencies have been barely recognized.

At first these new functions (or new definitions of old function, if you will) seemed only to require that teachers be trained in better and novel ways. But we are now recognizing that new concepts of administration, and of school organization itself, will have to be devised.

In fact, there is a sense in which the recent problems have resulted from the failure of educational structure to become adjusted to the diversity of demands being placed on schools, and with the trend toward specialization among teachers in particular.

Affluence

These new responsibilities are being assumed in an affluent society, which many people take as evidence that we have the way, if not the will, to pay for the requested reforms. Expensive modifications demanded by teachers make sense only within the context of a revolution in expectations which has fed upon our national wealth. Of course in practice, part of the problem is that the ability of local communities to compete for national resources varies, while the demands of teachers benefiting from national networks of communication, are more uniform. The Vietnam War also has drastically altered expected resource allocations. And in practice too, teachers have been forced to compete for resources with even better organized local employees, such as nurses, policemen, and transit workers.

Involvement in Politics

This competition for vast amounts of resources inevitably has thrust educators squarely into the political arena. In particular, teachers seem to have adopted some of the tools of protest which have worked for the civil rights movement and are so well adapted to this age of existentialism with its doctrine of personal commitment and decisive action. This is a generation, after all, which blames much of its plight on a self-conscious sense of alienation and loss of control, and it is asserted that this alienation springs from failures of existing organizations; to such people, collective action can be an attractive recourse.

Changes in School Systems

These developments on the national level are paralleled by pressures on schools to develop new points of departure.

The Climate of Innovation

Under recent criticisms, schools have become enveloped in a climate of innovation. They are in the process of reorienting themselves from routines to more problem-centered approaches to education. Of course, change is not new to schools; but innovation has been elevated to the level of a principle. Not only has the pace been stepped up, but the scope of some of the changes proposed promises to be more sweeping than usual, encompassing entire systems and regions rather than individual classrooms.

Teacher Power

In this time of change and experimentation, it is perhaps natural that teachers are becoming more powerful. For this is, by definition, a time when no particular group has a monopoly on the answers. And in practice it has become *necessary* to delegate decisions, implicitly if not officially, because administrators cannot maintain firm centralized control over a system that does not work effectively; the failures of the system cannot help but reflect on the authority of those who run them. And teachers are not likely to enthusiastically submit to the authority of the administrative system that has failed to come to grips with their occupation's problems.

Added to this general situation is the fact that in this era of job opportunity and a supply-demand ratio that is favorable to teachers, the proportion of teachers in the work force is also expanding four times faster than the general population explosion, so that the projected growth, together with the continuing trend toward concentration in metropolitan areas, will only serve to strengthen their influence.

But probably the most important bases of the teachers' sense of power is the growth of specialization within teaching. Not only has a segment of teachers made substantial gains in their education level, but there is likely to be marked increase in the specialized use of teaching techniques for distinct populations; perhaps separate career lines for teaching various classes and types of students are beginning to appear as well. All of this gives teachers leverage in knowledge and skill over the administrators, who nevertheless are still responsible for evaluating them. We may be rapidly approaching the time when it will be difficult, if not impossible, for administrators to assume the exclusive responsibility for evaluating teachers.

And if teachers have more opportunity to gain power, they also have found reasons to exercise it. There are a disproportionate number of lower class people being attracted to the profession precisely as a way of improving their social status, and they are finding that their own positions depend as much on the fortunes of their occupation as a whole as upon their individual efforts; in other words, the relative lack of opportunity for individual mobility within the occupation only encourages their efforts to achieve collective mobility.

It is important too, that at a time when teachers are beginning to develop a sense of competence by which they seek to justify greater control over some decisions, they are bearing the brunt of much of the criticism for poor quality education, particularly in the inner city schools, for which many of them feel they really are not responsible. Many of the changes being proposed are aimed at altering the *teacher's* classroom behavior, which seems to suggest that they somehow are responsible for the problems; and many of them seem to be saying that if they are to be held responsible, they have the right to exercise more control over the situation.

There are a number of crucial but unanswered questions here. For example, do reading scores reflect the quality of classroom teaching, or do they more accurately reflect the quality of administration? Perhaps they reflect the unrealistic goals and inadequate procedures of the *system* itself.

One problem that has to be faced is to the extent the *system* of organization is at fault, it is not too likely that people who benefit from the system will be willing to *change* their own roles—and often these are precisely the roles that need to be changed. This is true of teachers as well as administrators.

Erosion of Traditional Modes of Administration

The corollary of teacher power is the impending change in the roles of administrators. Their traditional jurisdictions, which already are being undermined by the growing influence of the Federal Government and of local militant groups, are being challenged by the demands of teachers as well. It is probably significant in this connection that in our study of staff conflicts in the public schools at Ohio State University, which included nearly 2,000 teachers and

28 high schools over a five-state area, the most frequent type of dispute described to us—one in every four—concerned authority problems between teachers and administrators. What seemed to be most significant about teacher militancy was that they are demanding a greater role in the decision-making process.

We now recognize that the logical distinction between "policy decision" and "administrative decisions" has never really provided an effective division of labor between administrators and school boards. And similarly, the presumed division between "administrative" and "teaching" responsibilities will be no real barrier against the encroachment of teachers on traditional administrative prerogatives.

The situation is also accentuated by age differences between teachers and administrators, who are often separated by more than a generation of experience. Probably most administrators were trained in an era when the problems of classroom teaching could be reduced (so it was thought) to the psychology of individual learners, and when the central administrative problems seemed to revolve around efficient internal mangement; the current generation of teachers, by contrast, has been reared in a sociological era characterized by rapid social change and group conflict, and during which administration has become largely a matter of managing an increasingly complex balance of forces from both outside and inside the schools.

But in final analysis, the professional status which teachers are demanding is in many crucial respects incompatible with traditional principles of administration—principles originally fashioned in a unified, small-town America, premised on teacher compliance, and justified by the legal fact and fiction that administrators are, and can be responsible for literally every facet of what is sometimes referred to as "their" system. Centralized authority and system-wide uniformity are difficult to reconcile with decentralized decision-making, which is the central component of professionalism. If classroom teachers are to professionalize, therefore, they must gain more control, perhaps the primary control over key matters.

Limited evidence that professionalization is a militant process also comes out of the Ohio State study where we found that the incidence of most types of conflict in a school (with one important exception to be noted) increased with the faculty's average level of what we took to be indicators of their professionalism.[1] But what is

[1] Professional orientation was determined from the extent of teachers' agreement with 16 statements regarding their beliefs about their relationship to students, to their profession and to their colleagues, as well as the degree to which they emphasize knowledge as a basis of competence, and the level of decision-making authority they considered to be appropriate for themselves.

perhaps even more important, this association was most prominent in the more bureaucratized schools (compared to the least bureaucratic). In other words, it is in precisely the most highly organized schools that support for professional concepts seems most likely to produce conflict.

In summary, then, I have merely tried to outline the situation from my own perspective. I would now like to elaborate by adding a series of qualifications, which often don't get into the discussion, at least not explicitly.

Some Qualifications

First, in spite of all the discussion about teacher militancy, probably only a minority of teachers are militant, and an even smaller minority are what might be termed militant professionals. However, it is equally apparent that, given the growing concentration of the population, small proportions can be numerically large enough to be important. The numerical minority of militant professionals identified in most of the schools in our study was far from being a minority socially speaking. They were not marginal people, but on the contrary, they constituted a core leadership group having the backing of the majority of teachers. Compared to their colleagues, they were better educated and more respected, better integrated into their peer groups, and had more support from their peers. Also, although it is often thought that the youngest, least "mature" teachers are the ring leaders; in our sample it was the middle-aged, well-established men who most frequently actually became involved in conflict (even though it is true that the youngest teachers expressed the most belligerent *attitudes*). This seems to indicate that opposition to professionalization, in effect, means opposing the most influential segment of teachers.

In this connection, our evidence also suggests that there are no clear answers to the great debate over the relative degree of militancy of the AFT and the NEA. The AFT officers in our sample were more professionally oriented and expressed more militant attitudes in some respects, in comparison to the officers of the NEA: and they became involved in more disputes over authority. But overall, the NEA officers had become involved in more of almost every other type of conflict. (It should be noted here, however, that this sample was from the middle west and did not necessarily include the most militant chapters of the AFT.) What is more important than this debate is the fact that there were a group of informal leaders in the sample, who had not been officers in either organization, who were by far more militant than either group of official leaders. In other words, while militancy is the posture of only a minority of teachers, it is an important and perhaps largely unidentified minority.

The second point that is sometimes confused in these discussions concerns the question of whether teaching is in fact a "profession" (in some ultimate sense of that term). This question now seems less important than the fact that a large proportion of teachers *believe* that they are entitled to more authority than they now have; for example, 70 per cent of the sample believed that they should have "the ultimate authority over major educational decisions."

Perhaps they gain some sense of having influence by participating in militant causes. It is in this connection that one finding from our study finds its real significance: We found that both the job satisfaction of individual teachers and the morale of school faculties *increased* with rates of conflict among the faculty. One interpretation is that engaging in conflict provides people with a sense of meaningful participation and influence that is not provided in the system itself.

However, as a third qualification, I would hasten to add that it would be a mistake to assume that millitancy comes about as a reaction to any presumed *loss* of control on the part of teachers. It is sometimes assumed that they have lost influence as schools have become less personal and more bureaucratized. Perhaps there are elements of this, but our data suggests that teachers in the larger, more hierarchical schools actually have more decision-making authority over the classrooms than teachers in less bureaucratic schools. And these are also the schools where the most conflict occurs.

The fourth point is connected to the last one, and will be of interest to those persons who hope to pacify teachers' desire for authority by giving them only minor concessions. We found that increases in the decision-making authority of teachers lead to more, rather than less, conflict in the school. Apparently a little authority does *not* "go a long way" towards pacifying them. On the contrary, expectations in this area seem to be increasing faster than achievements. Success feeds aspiration; and involvement in the decision-making process, even in a minor way, can involve teachers in a wider range of issues than they would otherwise have become involved in.

But there *is* one important qualification here; for it *is* true that some of the most *severe* conflicts in our study did occur in schools where teachers reported having more authority. In other words, opportunity to participate in decision making seems to be more conducive to disputing in general, but it may prevent grievances from accumulating and erupting to major outbreaks. The establishment of regularized communication procedures may have the same effect.

Fifth, I would qualify my earlier generalization by recognizing that professionalization obviously does not *necessarily* lead to conflict—if the environment is already compatible or if accommodations have been made. Regarding the former point, we found that professionalization was not necessarily associated with conflict in the less bureaucratic schools. And regarding the latter point, there were some signs that schools are making at least some minor adaptations to professionalization. For example, the more professionally oriented faculties in our sample reported having more decision-making authority over classroom matters.[2] Also, our data suggests that we might have found even more conflict were it not for the fact that the most professionally oriented teachers were randomly distributed among the schools, instead of being concentrated in a few; while the most employee-oriented people were concentrated in the most bureaucratic schools, which they probably find compatible.

The corollary to the previous point, of course, is that bureaucratization in *itself* does not necessarily lead to conflict either. The problem occurs when close supervision, standardization, tight rules, and centralized decision-making are applied in faculties which are attempting to increase their professional status. We did find that in the least professionally oriented faculties the rates of conflict *were* lower when they were more bureaucratized. The effectiveness of administrative practices, therefore, obviously is not inherent in the practices themselves, but depends largely on the setting to which they are applied. While this point is perhaps obvious, it seems safe to assume that most administrators probably have not systematically tailored their practices to fit the changing conceptions of their faculties.

Next, as another point of qualification, it should be recognized that professionalization does not only produce conflict within the administration but also conflict and segmentation among the teachers themselves. One primary source of tension arises between the militant teachers who are professionally motivated and the teachers who are militant for other reasons. It is essential to keep this distinction in

---

[2] However, the overall index of bureaucratication was not negatively related in any significant way to the degree of support given for professional roles, as might have been expected in bureaucratic schools which were de-bureaucratizing in any appreciable extent.

mind when interpreting the meaning of militancy. We found that while the most professionally-oriented faculties in our sample did have higher conflict rates than those which were less professional, the former did not necessarily subscribe strongly to professional principles. Among other sources of tension are the organization itself, i.e., complexity and the authority structure; general conditions within the society such as the adolescent revolt and the civil rights movement in the big cities. As others have noted, the civil rights movement in particular seems to be in a head on collision with teacher militancy. Questions can be raised about the degree of support which teacher organizations have given to desegregation plans and experimental projects leading to more community control and about what this means for professionalization.

This leads to still another qualification which, while obvious, nevertheless sometimes eludes the discussion. Militancy can take a variety of forms and degrees of intensity. While the term is most frequently used in connection with work stoppages, strikes are only the most visible sign of a much more prevalent phenomenon which is a posture of challenge to authority, which can be expressed in a variety of ways. In particular, we found that the most professionally-oriented militants in our sample were involved in very different *forms* of conflict than their less professional counterparts who also became involved in disputes. In particular, the most professionally-oriented faculty members did shy away from what we called the "major incidents"—i.e., the sustained, heated conflicts involving large numbers of persons. While this could imply that the most professionally-oriented teachers are not the ones actively leading the recent rash of strikes, our data does not warrant such a conclusion. It seems more reasonable to assume that the role which professionally-oriented teachers play in the recent strike situation will depend heavily upon the circumstances. We found that, in contrast to the general pattern, in the *most bureaucratic* schools professionalization was associated with even the frequency of major incidents.

Perhaps the lesson here is that administrators may have to put up with many forms of friction if they want to maintain professional faculties; but supporting professionally-oriented teachers may be a more effective way to control the outbreak of at least the major incidents than attempting to suppress them by imposing more bureaucratic control—which is probably a more typical reaction.

Another neglected principle is implicit in much of what has been said; namely, that the behavior of teachers can be explained better in terms of principles of social power than exclusively in terms of either idealism or economic considerations. This means, for one thing, that teachers no longer have to rely exclusively on cultivating the public's benevolence toward them. Many people believe that this is unfortunate, and perhaps is only natural to formulate the philosophical questions about whether this or that practice is "right" or "wrong," according to one's personal values, and I might add, his own personal interests. But the questions that need answers right now concern what is going to happen not only whether or not the trend is acceptable to us.

But if the immediate concern of teachers is for power, they eventually must return to the question of how to legitimate their power once it has been achieved. Perhaps at this point it is too early to expect that teachers be concerned about justifying their every move or demonstrating how teacher control may be an improvement over administrator control. But eventually teachers will have to face that question. Therefore, I would add one final qualification. Within *all* professions (and not just teaching) there is a generic tension between idealism and self-interest. Professionalization *is* motivated partly by material gain as critics frequently point out; but what is distinctive about professionalization is that it represents a shift from self-interest, or what Hofstadter calls "interest politics" toward what he calls "the politics of status." And in order to legitimate *professional* status, the occupation eventually must demonstrate its ability to protect its clients' welfare. Therefore, it is obviously to the profession's advantage to combine self-interest with idealism. Teachers, for example, maintain that they cannot do their best for students under poor working conditions and without sufficient authority, and that higher salaries are needed to attract qualified people. It is no accident that these assertions are difficult to prove or disprove and that there is no clear-cut answer to the question of the "real" motives of teachers.

But the point is that *all* professions seek to use ideals in the service of self-interest; and to combine self-interest so that it better serves the ideals. The situation is not unique to teachers. Physicians don't often strike, for example, but they restrict the number of people who can enter the profession and restrain economic competition among themselves. Teacher militancy is not so unique that the process has never happened before.

Our evidence on this point is not very convincing, but it did appear that among the militant teachers, those who were most professionally oriented were at least more concerned about the welfare of their students than their less professionally oriented, but equally militant colleagues. At the same time, it appeared that teachers were more ready than administrators to define certain children as being unable to learn.

It also should be noted in this connection that professionals obviously are not the only ones who have ideologies. There are competing contentions that are equally difficult to disprove, such as the notion that "employees must be supervised," that there is a special class of "decision makers" in schools, and that school boards' sovereignty must remain inviolatible in a democracy. In these ideological disputes, of course, each side seeks to define the public interest to suit its own purpose.

Conclusion

In conclusion, we have to recognize that generally speaking, the existence of organizational conflict simply reflects the fact that there *already* have been changes in social function which have not as yet been recognized and incorporated into the ongoing social organization. We are well beyond the point where school policy can be equated to the proclamations made by administrators; and yet that is the myth we are trying to live with. School systems have become so complex and must adapt to such a wide range of circumstances, that in fact, administrators no longer can maintain centralized control over educational practices, even though they may feel obliged to do so because of tradition and their legal responsibility. That is the administrative role conflict. This persistent effort, on the part of teachers as well as administrators, to maintain customary routines and traditional evaluation standards in a climate of failure has only served to aggravate the tension.

Alternatives, then, are needed to the industrial-military models of organization with their chain-of-command, system-wide uniformity, and universal evaluation standards. We are only beginning to learn that, in practice, "bureaucratization" has not meant more centralized control; but on the contrary, it has meant more autonomy of groups within the system. The immediate problem, then, is not how to preserve central control, but how to harness the *potential* of the autonomy. There need to be more effective ways for teachers to participate in the schools, and effective participation means more than confrontations annually or semi-annually at the negotiation table.

It may mean that teachers will evolve their own line of authority and communication within each school and school system. A dual line of administrative and professional authority found in some hospitals provide one model, though not necessarily the only one.

Also in this connection, it is possible that if teachers pursue state-wide negotiations, they may be able to eventually gain control over the certification and accreditation standards, which eventually could mean much greater control over the entire occupation. If that happens we can look for substantial changes in the authority roles of teachers.

Ultimately, these changes will mean that administrators will have to find some new roles as teachers assume at least some of their traditional functions. One possibility is that they will turn more of the internal matters over to teachers and become more concerned about managing the sociological problems inherent in schools' relationships with their communities and governments. At least it seems that the present crisis faced by the public schools has occured partly because the external sociological problems have been for so long neglected.

It may be that in order to achieve stability, the growing power of teachers will have to be recognized by including them more centrally in the decision-making process within school systems themselves. Historically in this country we have had to learn either to include the excluded or to live with strife. Until teachers create a more central place within the system for themselves, we can expect that they will continue to go around it.

An Analysis of Power Bases and Power Uses in Teacher Militancy

Ralph B. Kimbrough and James O. Williams

Educators view with mixed reaction the increased frequency in the use of such terms as negotiation, strike, sanction, and injunction. Yet, these terms follow in the wake of the use of bases of power which were not previously employed widely by teachers. The

Ralph B. Kimbrough and James W. Williams, "Analysis of Power Bases and Power Uses," *The High School Journal*, LII, (October, 1968), 3-9. Reprinted with permission. Dr. Kimbrough is Professor of Educational Administration and Chairman, Department of Educational Administration, University of Florida, and Dr. Williams is Assistant Professor of Education, Columbus College.

so-called militancy of teachers is bringing about a significant realignment of the professional establishment. The way in which teachers use their sources of power will determine how much power teachers can accumulate to improve education. Many teachers are seeking answers to some complicated questions. What are alternative bases of power which teachers have used to influence education? Can teachers anticipate accurately the political consequences of using these alternatives?

For many years knowledge of the sources of power in educational decision-making was limited. Beginning in the early 1950's much research has been invested in the objective study of community power structures.[1] A considerable body of knowledge has been accumulated about community power systems of school districts. From these data one may obtain considerable evidence regarding the bases of power in making educational policies.

Among the school districts of a state, there are various arrangements of community power. For example, in some communities the power structure is characterized by much openness with a pluralism of forces in which the people participate effectively in policy decisions. Other communities may be dominated by a singular group of power wielders and are characterized by a high degree of closedness. The power structures of some communities are characterized by a high degree of consensus on community policies, whereas regime conflicts are characteristic of other school districts. In all of these different types of school district power structures, there are variations in the leaders' sources of power.

What are the sources of power of leaders and groups within a local community power system? Answers to this question are not definitive because there are many and diverse sources of political power. A person or group has power by virtue of control over resources perceived by constituents to be important in meeting needs. Examples of power resources used to gain political power are wealth or control over wealth, friendship ties, family ties, official position, social status, leadership ability, control over votes, control over mass media, position in informal and formal groups, control over critical services, and many other things valued by people. Power is not simply

---

[1] Examples of publications follow: Robert Agger et al., The Rulers and the Ruled (New York: John Wiley and Sons, 1964); Robert Presthus, Men at the Top (New York: Oxford University Press, 1964); Floyd Hunter, Community Power Structure (Chapel Hill, University of North Carolina Press, 1953); Ralph B. Kimbrough, Political Power and Educational Decision-Making (Chicago: Rand McNally and Company, 1964).

control over such resources. One must use power resources effectively. As an example, a person who attempts to use his resources arbitrarily to obtain political advantage will certainly lose power. All studies of power provide examples of persons or groups who are "has-beens" or who have lost political power because they did not use their resources wisely. If educators do not use their resources wisely, they, too, will lose power in the political arena.

Political power is not something which educators can expect to monopolize in the average community. There are some severely poverty-stricken school districts in which the schools have by far the largest payroll among community agencies. In some of these communities the school superintendent has built a political dynasty which heavily influences policies in all government. Nevertheless, these communities are atypical.

Power in most school districts is held by leaders representative of numerous institutional sectors. Among these sectors the leaders in the economic sector are usually very powerful. Some suburban, bedroom communities would be an exception to this rule. The political type leader represents a potent influence in power structures. The influentials of a complex power structure will represent numerous different occupational pursuits. All of them control some power resources. The point of the discussion is that the power of teachers in decision-making is only one sector in the numerous centers of power interacting in the school district power structure. Consequently, educators must view the consequences of the use of their power in interaction with the power used by other leaders and groups that teachers do not control.

Thus teachers may exercise choices among a number of alternatives. In any event educators need to assess the consequences of these alternatives. This they have not done. In many instances their attempted use of power has failed to produce desired objectives. There are a number of questions: What effect does the use of sanctions have upon public opinion? Will educators increase or decrease their political power by splintering into separate organizations for teachers and administrative personnel? What are the long-term consequences of adopting traditional labor-management procedures in education? What are the long-range consequences of a local or statewide strike? School administrators and teachers have tended not to think through the consequences of alternatives. The teacher who wrote the following letter to one of the authors obviously had not foreseen the consequences of the recent statewide resignation procedure in Florida.

Dear Sir:

I would have liked to have made an appointment with you but time and circumstances just haven't been on my side lately.

Due to the happenings of the past four weeks, I did not take the final examination for your course as I am sure you have noted. I do not make a habit of making excuses but feel an explanation is owed you.

Being an officer and leader in the Filmer Classroom Teachers Association, I found myself caught squarely in the middle of a real "mess." Not always supportive of some of our methods or objectives, I was still responsible to my profession. Without going into detail as to the issues, I will say that I will never again take on a leadership role in any organization without knowing who my real enemies are and how they load their guns.

After three weeks of loss of friends, loss of pay, ($1,200—teacher—wife resigned also) strained home life and a good long look at mental weaknesses, I found myself in a position to put your course on "the bottom of the stack." Having come past the Master's level 15 hours ago and on no planned program (just taking courses that look interesting), I couldn't put the necessary energies or time into the last class or final exam preparation.

Fully expecting to be relieved of my local job or having legal action brought against me if the problem continued further, I spent the week of your final seeking employment in another public service elsewhere in the state. I had three fine opportunities but an "unknown power group" rose and ordered no hiring of resigned teachers. When not seeking other employment, I seemed to be meeting continuously at all hours with everyone from the Chamber of Commerce representatives to my own discouraged teachers. Interesting, but never again. There has to be a better way to earn a living.

I would appreciate your help in fulfilling your course requirements without leaving a "black mark" on my university record. However, if it is not possible to do so, then I'll assure you that this will just cost tuition. (A drop in the bucket lately.)

If you wish a conference, I am in a somewhat better frame of mind for such than last week and would make every effort to come in. Sorry for any inconvenience to you.

Teacher militancy should be viewed as activity in a larger societal or community system. As teacher groups within the larger system exert force in the form of strikes, sanctions, or other means, the system is convulsed with a resultant shift in other forces. As the various power groups react to teacher militant action in an effort to reproduce stability in the system, their force will likely be directed toward members of the educational profession. This may produce undesirable consequences for teachers, as was the recent case in the statewide Florida resignation movement. The source of power held by the Florida Education Association was almost exclusive control of the critical service of public education. The result of the withdrawal of this service was an almost instant reaction toward teachers by elements of the power system with an effort to restore the stability of the system.

As a system struggles to regain adaptive balance, all the forces begin to align themselves to exert pressure where it appears to be needed. In the recent Florida action, groups emerged whose sole purpose was to take a position either for or in opposition to the teacher action. Teacher groups and individuals were harassed by parent, business, professional, governmental, and church groups. Whereas some of these advocated negotiations to end the walkout, there were powerful groups whose vehemence toward teachers was solidified as the length of the walkout increased.

Teachers are perhaps more conscious of the existence of power groups and the potential power residing in teacher groups than ever before. Few would question that teacher groups across the nation are experimenting with the use of power in their quest for better working conditions and quality educational programs. It is not clear at this point with which power group teachers will choose to identify or whether there will be a national alignment of teachers with any one organization. The most likely possibilities are the National Educational Association, American Federation of Teachers, and local education associations. The power struggle is evident even within the profession.

Regardless of the power groups with which teachers could align themselves, three possible uses of their power appear evident. The initial course followed by teachers was to use persuasion techniques or mild coercion. The approach used in many states has been for state education associations to employ lobbyists to work with legislatures. In some instances this has been successful, whereas in others the opposing groups have been too closely allied with the legislatures. Indeed, in some cases members of the opposing groups have actually been members of the legislatures. The use of the persuasion technique has resulted in rather cordial relations between teacher groups and other power groups, but in some cases the gains for education have been somewhat less than satisfying.

An alternative to the mild persuasion technique is the sanction technique. This approach is somewhat more aggressive than the persuasive approach in that it is more visible to the public. When teachers apply sanctions, the consequences are different. Relations with other groups become strained and the consequences become apparent in the operations of the schools.

Probably the most consequential use of power is the revolutionary approach where teachers walk out, resign, or use some other means to withhold services. The consequence in the revolutionary approach is normally the creation of a win or lose climate. The lines are clearly drawn with the opposing forces in a controversy making certain demands. The demands by opposing power groups are usually amplified through the mass media. This inevitably introduces the possibility that someone will lose face in the settlement of issues. When teacher groups apply the revolutionary use of power, practically every home in a community is affected. For instance, when schools are closed because of a teacher walkout, many working mothers must remain at home with children. This, in turn, affects the business or employing agency who then has a work position unmanned. Economic consequences become almost immediately evident.

Each use of power by teacher groups has its own set of consequences, and these should be clearly examined before a course is chosen. Leaders should be eager to seek outside advice from competent advisors experienced in the various disciplines and fields of study. A consequence of blundering leadership in teacher organizations could be a complete loss of the power base or possible loss of membership to a competing organization.

Revolutionary action by teachers has certain economic consequences for the individuals involved in the action and for the community. Teachers who do not work are not paid during a walkout in most cases; therefore, they do not spend money which would ordinarily be placed into the local economy. The severity of the economic consequences is dependent upon the number of people involved in the action and the length of time consumed in reaching an agreement.

Revolutionary action by teachers may also have certain social consequences. Social pressure may be exerted by militant teachers upon those not in support of the action. Conversely, the public may exert social pressure upon militant teachers who have abandoned the traditional image of the benevolent teacher, dedicated to teaching even at the expense of personal sacrifice. Social pressure may also be evident among members of factions within the profession, as was evident in Florida. Considerable friction developed between those who did resign and those who did not resign. This type of pressure is especially real to the principal who has traditionally attempted to identify both with teachers and with the administration. The principal is the man in the middle who gets squeezed from both sides.

The use of revolutionary strategies within the profession is likely to cause further pluralism within education. Some specialized groups have withdrawn their affiliations with the education associations. Other groups seem destined to disassociate themselves from the parent professional groups.

Although some pluralization of forces in the profession will produce a more democratic and vigorous profession, too drastic pluralization will deplete the power base of teachers. Vicious opponents of education have for years played educational forces against each other in attempts to defeat progressive educational legislation. Furthermore, educators should beware of thoughts that they will exercise the ultimate power. In the Florida experience teachers found themselve facing overwhelming odds in the political arena. Evidence was convincing in many areas that these forces would have sacrificed quality in the public schools to defeat the resignation procedure. Consequently, if the teachers are genuinely interested in playing power politics, they will need to generate the strongest power possible within the profession and negotiate alignments with strong bases of power outside the profession. Rampant pluralization or an arbitrary use of power in disregard for other bases of power in the power structure would be self-defeating.

Several questions have been raised by the authors which may be answered in the coming years. Teacher militant action will become more frequent as teachers demand a greater share in decision-making. While the most appropriate use of power by teachers remains unclear, a number of logical generalizations may direct our thinking in the matter of teacher militancy.

First, teachers are more aware of the potential power in collective action than ever before and appear determined to develop and use such power to improve their profession.

Second, mistakes have been made in the use of power held by teacher groups. At least to date, teachers have shown only limited expertise in using power and limited understanding of the political consequences of the use of political power.

Third, any use of power implies certain consequences which may be carefully explored by educators, possibly in consultation with outside assistance.

Fourth, attempts should be made to discover ways in which power can be used by teachers and administrators for the improvement of education without harmful pluralization of the existing power bases.

Collective Negotiations and the Principalship

Luvern L. Cunningham

Students of organizations know that the descriptive value of an organizational chart is limited. The flow of power and control within a school system is often a result of informal associations rather than the product of strict definitions of formal line and staff relationships. Such charts often have limited value. They depict control, or what we might better call authority, only in legal or formal terms.

There are actually several authority structures in a school system—the formal and legal delegation of authority to an office by reason of its placement in the organization; the informal and extra-legal delegation of power and control to an individual above and beyond the formal limitations of his office; and the collegial or professional authority structure, which will be discussed later in this presentation. Officers at the top of the formal organization have more legal authority than those who follow; consider, for example, the broad discretionary powers granted a board of education or superintendent. In contrast to such formal or legal authority, there is that wondrous phenomenon where individuals such as the school

Luvern L. Cunningham, "Collective Negotiations and the Principalship," *Theory into Practice,* VII, (April, 1968), pp. 62-70. Reprinted with permission. Dr. Cunningham is Dean, College of Education, The Ohio State University, Columbus, Ohio.

custodian wield power far out of proportion to his formal office. If one has any doubts about this comment, he need only read Willard Waller's *Sociology of Teaching* or Bel Kaufman's *Up the Down Staircase*. Indeed, it is an unusual administrator or teacher who does not recognize the significance of events emanating from the basement boiler room.

From the point of view of professional negotiations, the of the board and the teachers are relatively clear. Each is a representative body given the task of protecting certain interests which it represents. The positions of persons at various other administrative levels in relation to these negotiations is by no means clear, and, as a result, there is a deep unrest and growing frustration among administrators who see negotiations going on around them, but rarely with them.

It is a rare negotiating team which includes a principal or other school officer from that area we affectionately label as "middle management," although a negotiating team may consist of the board of education and/or anyone it appoints as its bargaining agent.[1] In most cases, the board negotiates directly with the teachers, while the superintendent acts as an "advisor" for both sides; or, the superintendent is designated as the official bargaining agent for the board and is empowered to effect a contract with the staff within prearranged limits agreed upon by the board. When the superintendent is a member of the bargaining team, he frequently calls upon the business manager and the assistant superintendent in charge of personnel to serve with him.

If the voice of the principal is weak and ineffective at the board's side of the negotiating table, it has been excluded almost without exception from the other team.[2] Although some professional negotiations agreements allow for a merging of administrative and teaching personnel as a single negotiating unit vis-a-vis the board of education, a more radical cleavage between "labor" (teachers) and "management" (administrators) seems to be emerging. The precedent of big city AFT contracts, along with the growing sensitivity of the

---

[1] In addition to these interviews as a source, many of the ideas contained in this paper are drawn from "Implications of Collective Negotiations for the Role of the Principal," in *Readings on Collective Negotiations in Public Education,* Stanley M. Elam, Myron Lieberman, and Michael H. Moskow, eds. (Chicago: Rand McNally and Co., 1967), pp. 298-313.

[2] No mention is made, for example, of the role of the principal in the 1965 NEA *Guidelines for Professional Negotiation.*

NEA to charges of being a "company union," has made the position of the principal within the local teachers organization tenuous at best. Thus in many bargaining agreements, principals, department chairmen, and guidance counselors are excluded from the employees' bargaining team.[3]

Middle Management Frustrations

Regardless of how suspicious we are of analogies which link the problems of the school with the experience of private industry, there is a parallel too close to be ignored between the first and second line supervisors of industry and the principals and department chairmen in our schools. For years, industrial supervisors, who are crucial in maintaining an efficient and productive operation, have stood by helplessly as new relationships between labor and management were carved out at the bargaining table without them. Without exaggerating the analogy, we have seen a similar exclusion take place in education. About all that can be said definitively, for the present at least, is that if the principal is to be heard, he must be heard as a member of the administrative team rather than as a spokesman for the teachers.

It is very likely that the ambivalence of the superintendent's negotiations role will polarize in the direction of "agent for the board," not of "professional educator." If such is the case, his ability to protect the interests of other administrators will be seriously hampered. Teachers' organizations have already recognized this role shift and insist that their voice is the teacher's negotiating team, rather than the superintendent. Against such polarization, the principal stands out in bold relief as the "man-in-the-middle."

The spectre of two negotiating parties, neither one of which represents the principal, reaching accord by swapping such things as work rules which have been the principal's prerogative until now, is the source of increased frustration, if not panic, for the building administrator. In an article in *Phi Delta Kappan*,[4] Wildman and Perry commented that it was the school principal who stood to lose freedom when negotiations included certain areas of administrative discretion. They referred especially to bargaining on matters of class

---

[3] Robert E. Doherty, "Documents," *Industrial and Labor Relations Review,* July 1966, 19, 573-95.
[4] Wesley A. Wildman and Charles A. Perry, "Group Conflict and School Organization," *Phi Delta Kappan,* January 1966, 47, 250.

size; the extent to which seniority is to be used as a criterion for assignment to classes, promotions, and transfers; transfer policies in general; the distribution of teaching and nonteaching assignments; the collection of textbook rentals; and the length of the teaching day.

In a more recent statement, Lutz, Kleinman, and Evans are much more direct: The principal is the ". . . . one who (1) operates from a powerless base; (2) has been stripped of most of his leadership roles by the central administration; and (3) does not participate in most of the decision-making that affects his building staff." Furthermore "He is out of the mainstream of the organizational line, being neither a part of the administrative oligarchy, nor the teacher collectivity."[5]

Interviews[6] with principals in districts negotiating contracts reveal as much disillusionment and distrust with the superintendent's role as with the teachers' organization. These principals felt that the negotiating process was basically a fight for survival and that the first group to suffer from agreements reached at the negotiating table were those not directly represented there, giving examples from big-city contracts which, if implemented, would impede seriously the smooth functioning of the school. For example, one such contract article allowed individual teachers to expel troublesome students from their classes, presumably placing the principal in a position of having to place in some class that student whom no teacher wants. Principals insist that their jobs must be anointed with equal parts of authority and responsibility and that a reduction in authority necessarily created problems in the principal's efforts as he tried to fulfill his responsiblities.

Many of these principals felt that if they could be calm and resolute, those bargaining agreement articles, which they interpreted as undermining their authority, would be stricken from future contracts—the optimism implicit in this attitude may be comforting, but it hardly seems realistic. The passing of power from

---

[5] Frank W. Lutz, Lon Kleinman, and Sy Evans, *Grievances and Their Resolution* (Danville, Illinois: The Interstate Printers and Publishers, Inc., 1967).

[6] Many of the observations are based on the perceptions of a small number of principals, both elementary and secondary, as well as others involved in collective negotiations, gathered through interviews conducted about 18 months ago in Illinois, Indiana, and Michigan. Some of the comments of principals are in some cases imbedded in emotion, since they were made at the time the principals were involved in situations where militancy was pronounced. In fact, we encountered a climate of considerable disquiet and uneasiness among those principals, and I suspect that those feelings extended far beyond the extremely limited number of persons with whom we talked.

administrators to teachers, once begun, may be expected to continue until a major realignment has occurred in the organization of the schools.

Perry and Wildman concluded a survey of collective activity in education by noting that school administrators will have increasing, rather than decreasing, numbers of responsibilities vis-a-vis collective behavior and that the ultimate impact of collective activities on school systems is not known.[7] Watson pointed out recently that the coming of collective bargaining does not mean that the management function is any less significant or vital to the organization. It does, however, raise the question of who will have the crucial function of adapting the school organization to the new relationships which bargaining brings. "For the principal, this dictates asking himself how he can adjust his role in order that he may maintain effective avenues for the exercise of professional and administrative leadership."[8]

The ability of the principal to survive and flourish during and after this transition period will depend on his capacity to respond and adapt to new circumstances. Since genuine participation of the principal in teacher negotiations seems an unlikely prospect, it will be the individual building principal who has kept his fences mended in the important area of principal-staff interaction, and, thus, has won the respect of his teachers who will ultimately prevail. The administrator who has drawn his authority from the nature of his office, rather than from personal and professional sources, will not survive the change in the authority structure.

How Principals See the Outcomes

Assuming then, that teacher militancy marks a move toward a change in the authority structure of the schools and recognizing the complex issues impinging on the role of the principal, it is helpful to take a closer look at the reactions of the "men-in-the-middle" to collective teacher behavior.

During our interviews only two of the principals perceived positive outcomes from the altered principal-teacher relationships. With these two exceptions, principals stated that it would be more

---

[7] Charles A. Perry and Wesley A. Wildman, "A Survey of Collective Activity Among Public School Teachers," *Educational Administration Quarterly,* Spring 1966, 2, 133-51.

[8] Bernard C. Watson, "The Principal: Forgotten Man in Negotiations," *Administrator's Notebook,* October 1966, 15, 8.

difficult for them to supervise the instructional process in individual buildings and that the search for power among teachers was an attempt to usurp the prerogatives of the building principal, the individual legally responsible for the educational program. One respondent suggested that his discretion might be so reduced that he would spend most of his time "signing papers."

In one upper middle-class suburb, a high school principal noted increased difficulty in supervising staff during the period of intensive bargaining between the board of education and the teachers' organization. According to this principal, teachers were less inclined to accept administrative direction, the level of cooperation and the quality of teaching declined, and the staff appeared to be interested in becoming involved in the determination of building policy as distinct from district policy. Each of these developments was viewed as a threat to his authority and autonomy as high school principal, and, in his view, such restrictions on his autonomy and authority threatened the functioning of a viable educational program.

There was general agreement among administrators that the leadership of the militant teachers was coming from young, married men in secondary schools and that many of them aspired to supervisory and administrative positions in the school system. In only one district were the leaders described as "troublemakers" or "soreheads" with "an axe to grind." Ironically, this was one of the two situations where the principal did not perceive teacher militancy as threatening to his autonomy. As a matter of fact, this principal felt that many of the teachers' demands were justified and grew out of "questionable administration" within the district.

It is not difficult to understand the concern of a principal when the issues at the heart of bargaining crises were linked directly to what he perceived as his prerogatives. When more than salary was at issue, teachers' demands seemed to relate directly to teacher involvement in decisions concerning class size, the number of days in the school year, the determination of the school calendar, the assignment to extracurricular paid activities, and building grievance procedures.

In the districts visited, principals were attempting to deal with negotiations matters in a variety of ways. One had appointed a faculty committee to advise him on matters of policy and procedure, but teachers had rejected his committee and had insisted on electing their own representatives to a policy body. In another district, the principal had permitted the faculty to elect a seven-member grievance committee. Each teacher was entitled to one vote, and the principal and his assistant had one vote between them. The committee apparently operated smoothly until the local teachers' organization insisted upon the right to appoint its own grievance committee. Both committees functioned for a time, but the teachers' organization group eventually replaced the faculty elected committee. The principal involved stated that the committee appointed by the teachers' organization was very effective, and the only "radical" on the committee was "kept in check" by his teacher colleagues.

The principals' salary schedule was linked to the teachers' salary schedule in all of the districts visited. There was usually a ratio or an index arrangement for determining salaries of principals. As a result of this arrangement, teachers, when bargaining for their own salaries, were also bargaining for principals' salaries. In one of the districts, teachers had over the years consistently refused to accept the teacher salary schedule until principals were satisfied with the administrative salary schedule! Recently, however, the teachers' organization had insisted that principals bargain independently; one of the demands of the teacher group was that the two salary schedules be separate and distinct. Principals reacted to this demand by threatening to file unfair labor practices against the teachers' organization if it persisted in this demand—the demand was withdrawn.

Another significant result of the growth of teacher power was the change in the patterns of communication between teachers and principals. Because principals were not included in the bargaining process, they felt uninformed about issues being negotiated. Principals attempted to deal with this situation by probing for information from individual staff members informally. Such procedures were effective in several of the districts, and principals reported that teachers freely discussed with them their feelings, attitudes, and the pertinent issues in negotiations. Some of the principals described the teachers who discussed these matters as being "more professional" or as representing the "more conservative professional organization." Other principals stated that their teacher informants were militants, and, furthermore, that these teachers were frequently the best teachers in the system.

Personal Variations Among Principals

Our interviews led to the conclusion that, while feelings about what was happening to the role of the principal were consistent, the reactions—the ideas of what to do about it—were quite different. The differences expressed by the principals can be explained to some extent by several theoretical formulations that researchers have developed in the recent past. For example, in a study of executive succession, Carlson identified two general types of superintendents—those who were "place bound" and those who were "career bound."[9] Applying his construct of a "place bound" and "career bound" typology to principals, it may be safe to say that a "place bound" principal (one who has come up through the ranks of one particular school system and who views his authority as vested almost totally in the office he occupies) may feel considerably more threatened by teacher militancy than does the "career bound" principal (one who moves from system to system). The "career bound" person generally shows less identification with a particular school system and more identification toward what he conceives as a "professional" orientation concerning his role.

Another theoretical formulation seems particularly germane to the reactions of principals to new power alignment in the schools. Rokeach, in his book, *The Open and Closed Mind,* defines "open" and "closed" belief systems.[10] People who possess "open" belief systems are characterized as viewing authority in terms of its cognitive correctness and consistency with reliable information about the world, while those with "closed" belief systems view authority as an absolute. Principals who fall within the "open" category probably view people positively regardless of their beliefs, possess a rational conception of power and status, have a persistent "need to know" that is predominant, and feel little need to ward off threat. Principals with closed belief systems, on the other hand, probably accept or reject teachers on the basis of how congruent teachers' personal belief systems are with theirs and whether teachers have an excessive concern for power and status. Such principals would appear to have a stronger need to ward off perceived threat and, consequently, a weaker cognitive "need to know."

These are descriptions of the extremes of a continuum of belief systems; it is as unlikely that a paragon of "openness" exists as it is that the archtype of the "closed" belief system exists. Nevertheless, reasearch does indicate the presence of people with belief systems which relate to each of these extremes, and our interviews seemed to

[9] Richard C. Carlson, *Executive Succession and Organizational Change: Place-Bound and Career-Bound Superintendents of Schools* (Midwest Administration Center, University of Chicago, 1962).

[10] Milton Rokeach, *The Open and Closed Mind* (New York: Basic Books, Inc., 1960).

confirm these concepts.[11] Principals expressed a variety of reactions to teacher militancy, but they tended to reflect beliefs in a manner that indicated a propensity toward one or the other end of this continuum. For instance, one principal admitted an inability, as well as little desire, to cope with any radical shift in the control structure of education. He said, "I was appointed to run this school and just can't accept giving away my authority to teachers. I'll get out first." This principal was accustomed to being "the boss," being recognized as the educational leader, and making decisions. The thought of bargaining with teachers on matters traditionally considered to be in his domain was obviously repugnant. In this case, clear indicators of a "closed" belief system were present: authority was absolute, resided in the office, and was presently being threatened.

On the other hand, a few administrators, instead of responding to threat, believed that contracts developed by negotiation would actually expand their role and allow them to routinize many details that had previously been handled by the more time-consuming method of individual consideration. These principals felt their attention could be focused on more important concerns of educational leadership, such as community involvement in the development of educational programs and the fostering of collegial methods of attacking educational problems in the school. They possessed considerable faith in the professional integrity and general competency of teachers. When asked if they were concerned about being forced to live by written rules and procedures, they were likely to reply that "teachers will be bound by the rules, too," and that "a bargaining contract can only result in a more uniform handling of problems from which we will all benefit."

In a recent paper, Erickson described six images which principals seem to have of themselves.[12] The *first* of these is the principal as housekeeper. The housekeeper has a smooth operating building, details are cared for, the premises are neat and clean, and he takes pride in those surroundings. This type of principal would probably not be terribly upset by teacher negotiations.

The *second* in the principal as "Daddy." In this case, the principal is seen as the teachers' protector: the man who stands

---

[11] For an example of the use of these concepts in administrative research, *see* Edwin M. Bridges, "Bureaucratic Role and Socialization: The Influence of Experience on the Elementary Principal," *Educational Administration Quarterly,* Spring 1965, 1, 19-28.

[12] Donald A. Erickson, "The Principal as Administrator" (University of Chicago, 1966) Mimeographed.

between the teachers and the community, the person who runs interference for them and is counsel for the defense in those instances where the school is under attack. The "Daddy" type would be shattered by collective action because his teachers would no longer have need for his protective services.

The *third* is the image of the principal as a "super-teacher." This image, Erickson believes, marks the elementary school more vividly than it does other levels of the school organization. The super-teacher image incorporates the expectations that the principal has been a polished, experienced, effective teacher prior to entering the principalship and that once entrenched in the role can pass on all of the secrets of his success to those with whom he will associate. This image is totally incompatible with teacher militancy—the principal would be caught squarely in the middle of the clash between the legal or bureaucratic and collegial authority systems.

A *fourth* image is the principal as foreman. The foreman is the supervisor who sees that teachers follow advice he or some other responsible superiors give. The foreman's fate, like the "super-teacher's," is uncertain under conditions of collective action. He may be asked to enforce or administer policies, rules, and regulations which he has had no part in formulating. Indeed, he may disagree with them in principle, and he may run the risk of being rejected by the teachers in the process.

The *fifth,* a more recent image, is of the principal as a change agent. As a change agent, he is expected to keep his school abreast or in advance of current developments, is knowledgeable about new things occurring through all of education and trying to implement or incorporate as many new ideas into his school program as he can. The success of the change-oriented principal has hinged on his ability to manipulate his administrative environment, and in my judgment, this type of principal will be reasonably successful in accommodating to collective action situations. To have been effective in achieving innovations, the change-agent principal has already developed considerable finesse in diagnosing the significant features in his work setting; he knows those variables that either inhibit or facilitate change. He can accept collective action on the part of teachers as another fact of administrative life and incorporate that phenomenon into the leadership strategies he has developed through experience.

A *sixth,* and newly emerging image, is that of the principal as systems analyst. In this instance, he is seen as the person who can make genuine assessments of the level of performance of those who work in his building. He has developed some sophistication in understanding how organizations behave, and he has learned how to perfect feedback mechanisms to assist him with administrative decision-making. This is, of course, an advanced definition of the principal's role and few persons have so far developed the skills necessary to perform in this way. Collective action on the part of teachers would probably not threaten such a principal. As a part of his systems training, he would have acquired sufficient understanding of organizational decision behavior to incorporate teacher participation into a rational model of administrative performance.

Although Erickson's images are only observationally based conceptions, they do indicate types which all of us have seen in operation.

Impact on the Principalship

Based on the foregoing discussion, several areas of speculation or tentative conclusions seem defensible concerning the impact of teacher collective activity on the principalship:

(1) Provisions must be made for genuine, legitimate participation of principals in the collective negotiation process.

The severe feelings of being "left out" of the negotiation process is a serious matter. Undoubtedly, many factors must be taken into account in the involvement of principals: the purpose of their involvement, the nature and type of their representation on bargaining teams, the precise nature of their bargaining roles, and the issues on which their participation is germane.

I suspect that superintendents by and large, as well as boards of education, are not aware of the feelings of their "middle managers." In the heat of battle, many ordinary communication processes break down. It may also be that superintendents and boards deliberately keep principals out of bargaining because they want to avoid burdening them with the responsibilities of participation in negotiations. They may feel that keeping principals "informed" completes top management's obligations to principals in this aspect of a school district's total administrative function. Whatever the individual circumstances may be, the problem needs exploration.

On this problem, Lutz, Kleinman, and Evans commented:

> This "leadership" role, in the light of the reality of the distribution of power among the teachers, school boards, and superintendents, and the prescribed role of the principal in

the school bureaucracy, is an unrealistic one. Many teachers realize that although their building principal functions in the formal organization as the communication link in the line between themselves and the central administration, they can more readily achieve their goals via the informal communication channels maintained among teacher organization leaders, chief administrators, and board members. This is especially true in school districts where in their rush to mollify teacher militancy, superintendents maintain an "open door" and board members an open telephone line. In situations where blatant dysfunction of the formal organization exists teachers perceive of the principal as being in a position to provide only tentative decisions pending approval of the higher-ups, at best. Where such relationships exist, teachers soon find it more fruitful to by-pass the principal completely, or out of consideration for the "Good Joe" principal, engage in a mock and/or courteous interaction.[13]

(2) There will be an intensification of collective activity in education involving a large number of power groups which reflects the increase in specialization of work activity within school systems.

Garbarino predicts that in the future, administrative and managerial authority will be increasingly limited in all types of organizations. The "consent of the governed" notion will be extended to all employer-employee relations, in public as well as private sectors. "Bargaining out of decisions" will be generalized throughout and over all institutions. He argues that operation of employee relations systems will " . . . require a high degree of administrative skill and these skills will be in short supply. Successful industrial democracy, like successful political democracy, requires that both governed and governors work at their job."[14]

In education it is safe to predict that we will have strong organizations of administrators, counselors, and other specializations in addition to teacher groups which will bargain collectively.

(3) The tension that currently exists between bureaucratic and/or legalistic authority and collegial or professional authority will be sustained and increased.

[13] Lutz, Kleinman, and Evans, *op. cit.,* p. 82.
[14] Joseph W. Garbarino, "The Industrial Relations System," in *Designing Education for the Future,* Edgar L. Morphet, project director and editor, 1966.

Part Three

There is some discussion regarding whether or not schools are pure examples of bureaucratic organizations. They are probably not perfect examples; nevertheless, they possess some of the characteristics of bureaucracy. One of these is an hierarchical authority structure; another is the presence of rules and regulations to govern operations.

Collective action on the part of teachers is partially based on an emerging sense of collegial loyalty, identity, and opportunity for the exercise of power. Thus, two basic authority systems, one bureaucratic and the other collegial, must somehow coexist in the school organizations of the future. It is apparent that the two interact and that growth in collegial power may elicit certain bureaucratic responses.[15]

The school principal's response to expressions of collegial power and authority is to challenge with symbols of bureaucratic authority, in this case his own rules and regulations. Time does not permit a discussion of the tension producing rules enforcement syndrome which frequently occurs in organizational life.

(4) Preparation programs for administrative posts in education, especially the principalship and superintendency level positions, will need to include substantial work in superior-subordinate relationships in complex social organizations.

For the past two decades, we have emphasized the development of conceptual and human skills in the training programs for the principalship and the superintendency. Technical skills have been emphasized less, although still considered significant.

Research in industry, and in education, indicates that the percentage of an organization's actual productivity affected by leadership or administrative discretion is rather limited. Dubin in summarizing research on the influence of supervisory behaviors on productivity reports that the difference between "good" and "bad" supervision has little effect on the output of an organization.[16] Possibly as little as ten per cent in the variation in output of a well-supervised and poorly supervised operation in industry can be accounted for by supervision.

Dubin argues that the strength of industrial middle management resides in maintaining communication between top management and

[15] James G. Anderson, "Bureaucratic Rules: Bearers of Organizational Authority," *Educational Administration Quarterly,* Winter 1966, 2, 28.

[16] Robert Dubin, George C. Homans, Floyd C. Mann, and Delbert C. Miller, *Leadership and Productivity: Some Facts of Industrial Life* (San Francisco: Chandler Publishing Co., 1965), p. 5.

the work force—he is an essential link. Likewise, the maintenance of work force discipline and order usually devolve on his shoulders. Supervisors in industry do more than stimulate output and productivity—"Indeed, among all the functions of supervisors, the stimulation of individual output *may* be of middling or even minor importance."[17]

It may be that the limited effectiveness of contemporary supervision in education can be tied to the relative emphases on the perfection of human and conceptual skills in contrast to technical skills in administrator training programs. Woodward argues that technical skills represent an extensive underdeveloped dimension of managerial training in industrial and business enterprises.[18] The same may be true in education—one example is the technical area of the assessment of individual and organizational performance. The pressure for adopting performance budgeting in education may force us to return to a stronger emphasis on the refinement of technical skills.[19]

As collective teacher action becomes more pronounced, with the consequent increases in the extension of rules and regulations, obviously substantial attention must be given to that meaning for programs of administrator preparation. A new perspective, more technical, may emerge as we learn more about the changing distributions of power and authority in the years ahead, and this leads to the following fifth conclusion.

(5) An assessment needs to be made of which administrative skills, conceptual, human, or technical, have the highest pay-off for the school principal.

The point has been made several times that the boundaries of middle level administration are being narrowed and that the future promises even further restrictions on their discretion. Certainly conceptual skills, human relations know-how, and new technical competencies will be in demand. Considerable attention should be given to identifying the appropriate mix among the skill types in terms of what is required in the effective operation of schools.[20]

[17] *Ibid.*, p. 6.
[18] *Ibid.*, p. 11.
[19] J. Alan Thomas, "Educational Decision-Making and the School Budget," *Administrator's Notebook*, December 1963, 12, 1–4.

[20] For an advanced treatment of the school as an instrument of production and ways and means to measure its output more definitively, see J. Alan Thomas, *The Productive School* (New York: John Wiley and Sons, Inc.) (in press).

Teachers, through the assumption of new responsibilities commensurate with their new-found collegial authority, must become increasingly more responsible for educational innovation and improved organization performance. They will be expected by the public to respond directly to the critics of the schools rather than through administrative spokesmen. Few "Daddy" type principals will be around to act as counsels for the defense. A principal, therefore, will need human skills, but these may not make or break him as a principal. His effectiveness will hinge upon possession of a rich array of new technical competencies which are just beginning to emerge.

(6) Considerable research is in order on the impact of collective action on the school organization itself, its productivity, and the relationships among those who hold occupational membership there.

The consequences of collective behavior for school systems are difficult to conceptualize for study purposes. One of the reasons that more research has not been done is the simple fact of the magnitude of the task. With or without collective action or teacher militancy, we are being pressed toward more and more definitive assessments of our productivity as an enterprise. National assessment efforts are currently under way through the Carnegie Corporation and the U.S. Office of Education. Thus, we may need to develop highly sophisticated performance criteria and assessment instruments.[21]

With the refinement of new assessment technologies and the acquisition of these skills by principals, principals will have a powerful new tool for institutional control. They will be able to provide superintendents and board members with extensive data which top educational management can bring to the bargaining table. These data will become a part of the bargaining exchange—if the data are positive in terms of reporting good productivity they provide top management with one set of strategies. On the other hand, if teacher performance has been shabby such data provide the board with quite another bargaining perspective.

Erickson, in a recent paper, poses a sobering prospect:

> I think there is widespread danger that teacher negotiations will help produce an educational backlash, particularly as far as depressed areas are concerned. Shortsighted self-

---

[21] Support for this position can be found in Anne E. Trask, "Principals, Teachers, and Supervision: Dilemmas and Solutions," *Administrator's Notebook,* December 1964, 13, 1—4.

aggrandizement (on the part of teachers) may enormously reinforce the sameness of urban schools, negate the efforts of principals and dangerously delay educational reform. Teacher organizations will then probably clash head-on with another newly militant group—the oppressed, downtrodden poor, even now battering at the ramparts of privilege. The collision of these two forces could eventually identify teacher groups as unworthy stewards and strip them of prerogatives hard won through years of effort. As another outcome the schools themselves could be shorn of responsibility for many educational functions, and new agencies could be created to accomplish tasks so shabbily performed thus far. The tendency is already apparent in Head Start, Upward Bound, Job Corps, numerous educational components of OEO Community Action Programs, and many demands for a new emphasis on private agencies and inter-institutional competition. If ill-guided, collective teacher activity may defeat its own purposes through short-sighted opportunism and help to end the ascendancy of the public schools. Under such conditions, one may even prophesy wholesale abandonment of public education by middle class parents, for our systems also need extensive rejuvenation for creative, nonconforming youngsters who now survive its regimentation, but at unknown costs.[22]

From my own recent contacts with inner city parents in a number of places, I can only echo Erickson's observations. I sense a growing hostility toward our schools and an impatience with our teachers that is serious indeed. Such parents have no tolerance for teacher failure when the life chances of boys and girls are so closely linked with success in school. I suspect that in the very near future our teachers will be confronted with court actions charging malpractice or malfeasance where parents believe pupil growth has been inhibited by poor teaching.

Given refined assessment capabilities, research can be done on the impact of teacher action on the school organization. We should be able to account for those increments or decrements in production which relate to collective activities.

(7) Another conclusion which may seem to conflict with what I have said earlier is the following: the results of teacher militancy are

[22] Donald A. Erickson, "Rebel Principals and Teacher Power" (Department of Education, University of Chicago, 1967) Mimeographed.

leading to positive educational improvements in many school districts.

In some districts teachers are achieving, almost overnight, desirable educational changes which principals have been trying to achieve for a long time. Some examples are reductions in teacher-pupil ratio, improved physical facilities, strengthened provisions for problem children, better schedules, more auxiliary personnel, released time for inservice education, and more and better materials for instruction. As professional educational leaders we dare not overlook these gains. In fact we should find ways of supporting our teachers in their search for such improvements.

(8) We need to understand, as a professional group, what collective negotiation means for recruiting new persons into the principalship.

Lortie has eloquently described the powerful socialization processes that are at work within the teaching occupation.[23] Teachers, like no other occupational group, begin occupational socialization when they enter school as pupils and continue the process through their formal education, professional training, induction, and experiences with the occupation. Administrator socialization on the other hand, may begin with the teaching experience for some, with professional training for others, but, in either case, it is in no way as shaping or determinative as teacher socialization.

The meaning of teacher collective action for the source and supply of future administrators is not known. It is, however, interesting to speculate on the question. Administrators, at all levels, may be drawn from outside of education or recruited with a minimum of classroom teaching experience; indeed, they may be drawn directly from the ranks of undergraduates. The present system of recruiting administrators from teacher ranks may prove to be dysfunctional; the socialization process for administrative responsibilities may have been inhibited by teaching experience. Obviously, this is pure conjecture and must be so labeled.

Summary

That we must provide opportunities for principals to participate in collective negotiations; that one means of participation is through the growth in power of administrator organizations as bargaining

---

[23] Dan C. Lortie, "The Balance of Control and Autonomy in Elementary School Teaching," in a forthcoming book, *The Semi-Professions,* Amitae Etzioni, editor.

groups; that there exists a growing tension between legal and collegial authority; that preparation and inservice programs for administrators should reflect these changes; that a new appraisal be made of administrative skills needed by the "middle manager"; that considerable research is needed on the impact of negotiations on the productivity of school systems; and, finally, that negotiations may lead to some very positive extremes—all of these make it clear that changes are the order of the day in the principalship. New challenges are present, and the future of the position appears to be anything but dull and uninteresting—the trauma, unsettledness, and near chaos which exist now will pale in the shadow of what lies ahead.

Teacher Militancy and Countervailing Power

Harold I. Goodwin and Gerald W. Thompson

Unless we operate on the proposition that teacher militancy is an historical accident, we must assume there are explanatory factors. That assumption is a general and obvious one. A developing literature attests to the multiplicity of reasons for militancy among teachers. It is not our purpose to argue the validity of the reasons. We suggest that most, if not all of them, can be accounted for within a general conceptual framework.

Collective negotiations is closely associated with teacher militancy. Wildman points out on page 230 that collective negotiations is a "power relationship and a process of power accommodation." Let us amend that statement to indicate an equivalent power relationship and a process of mutual power accommodation, as Wildman intends. Now we find within his statement the essential objective of teacher militancy: to obtain a status of power equivalence vis—a-vis school management, and from that status to gain specific economic and other benefits. We suggest Galbraith's concept of countervailing power as a general framework within which to view the issue of militancy in education.

Dr. Goodwin is Associate Professor of Education Administration and Research Associate, Human Resources Research Institute, West Virginia University. Mr. Thompson is a doctoral student in the Department of Education Administration, West Virginia University.

The Concept of
Countervailing Power

In 1952 economist John Kenneth Galbraith advanced the concept of countervailing power, explaining it in the following way:

> To begin with a broad and somewhat too dogmatically stated proposition, private economic power is held in check by the countervailing power of those who are subject to it. The first begets the second. The long trend toward concentration of industrial enterprises in the hands of a relatively few firms has brought into existence not only strong sellers, as economists have supposed, but also strong buyers as they have failed to see. The two develop together, not in precise step but in such a manner that there can be no doubt that the one is in response to the other.[1]

Countervailing power is a direct response by those persons subject to the power of monopolistic conditions. As one segment of the economy accumulates a disproportionate amount of control or power over the conduct of a second segment, the latter, in time, develops mechanisms to equalize that power. It is necessary to recount the foundation conditions giving substance to the concept of countervailing power so that its relevance to militancy in education is more clearly established.

A primary assumption upon which the economy rests is that no seller of goods or services should have any jurisdiction over the prices he receives for them. When this condition characterizes an economy, we find imperfect competition or monopolistic tendencies. The condition of monopoly will result in excessive profit taking on the part of the monopolistic firms. Consider the ball point pen. When first introduced on the market, it was made only by one manufacturer. Early ball point pens sold for several dollars each. Now with several manufacturers they sell for pennies. In relation to their cost of production, the early pens brought the manufacturer excessive profits.

Imperfect competition creates an imbalance between the money incomes of those who buy the majority of the economy's goods and services and the money incomes of those firms who produce the majority of the goods and services. Such conditions should result in

---

[1] John Kenneth Galbraith, *American Capitalism: The Concept of Countervailing Power* (Boston: Houghton Mifflin Company, Sentry Edition, 1956), pp. 8-9.

the workers being unable to obtain sufficient income to buy goods and services.

A second assumption is that the economy should strive to have perfect competition: no single buyer or seller of goods or services can influence price. In other words, no monopoly should exist. Galbraith observed that the existence of monopoly is rare. There are usually a number of producers of the same item. The crucial observation was that the *power of monopoly* is held by those industries where there are only a few producers of a product who can thereby exercise monopolistic power.[2] This condition is called an oligopoly. In our economy the automobile industry is an oligopoly with Chrysler, Ford, American Motors and General Motors producing all the domestic cars. Given these circumstances, the economy after World War Two should have sunk into a depression. But of course it did not, and Galbraith indicated that capitalism must be re-evaluated to take into account these new realities.

The classical economic model assumed the necessity of competition between many sellers within an industry. We have noted that this assumption does not accurately describe our economy. Instead of perfect competition, or many sellers and buyers determining price, we have imperfect competition, its form is oligopolistic and its power is monopolistic. The critical observation was that the expected competition did not appear among firms who should have been competing, but *between firms and their customers and suppliers.*[3] This insight is the essence of the notion of countervailing power and of teacher militancy.

This new form of competition, the surrogate for perfect conditions. The unions' success in establishing collective action brought forth a power equal to that of management. An equivalent condition was true of the chain stores. Because of their volume purchases accounting for a major portion of a manufacturer's production, the chain stores could demand an equal voice in the determination of prices they paid for goods. In effect, countervailing power had been achieved by the unions and by the chain stores.

For example, over a number of years the steel industry obtained the power of monopoly vis-a-vis labor. This power was challenged by the rising power of the United Steel Workers. In similar fashion, the automobile industry was challenged by the United Auto Workers, the food processing industry by the Great Atlantic and Pacific Tea

2 *Ibid.*, p. 9.
3 *Ibid.*, p. 111.

Company, and the electrical appliance industry by Montgomery Ward and Sears, Roebuck and Company. Those who achieved countervailing power were able to make demands upon those holding the power of monopoly. What was usually demanded was higher wages by the unions and a price concession by the mass buyer, the chain stores.

Countervailing Power and Militancy

What has the concept of countervailing power in the private sector to do with education in the public sector? The attainment of a position of countervailing power in education is a direct response by teachers to the power of monopoly held by school boards.

Using legal, hierarchical and traditional arguments, school management has acquired and maintained a disproportionate amount of control or power over teacher-management relations. This was not difficult to do. Teachers have not been noted for their political activism in the sense of generating and applying significant power to obtain their goals. They have tended to regard militant action as unprofessional. According to teachers, intelligent dialog between teachers and management should provide equitable economic return for services rendered. With this built-in prohibiter of power action, school management easily held the power of monopoly. But, of course, there were more fundamental reasons.

One of the assumptions of the economy is perfect competition. But as in the private sector, education does not really operate under the conditions of perfect competition. If such conditions did reflect reality, no single buyer or seller of services could influence price for services. Such conditions simply do not exist. While there are many school systems, there is very little direct competition among them for teacher services. For example, salary levels are based on state minimums and on the average of salaries in surrounding communities. There are comparatively few school districts to choose from in which the rewards are much different from the ones available where a teacher may now be employed. In effect, just as the limited number of automobile manufacturers form an oligopoly in the private sector, the lack of choice among school districts gives them the character of an oligopoly. The lack of alternative school districts means, in effect, imperfect competition for teacher services.

Teachers are the sellers of services, the utilization of their professional expertise. One assumption management has long held, with at least the implicit consent of the public, is that, like the union members in the private sector, teachers as sellers should have no meaningful voice in the determination of the price for their services. Without the necessary condition of many buyers in competition with each other, the school districts, closely resembling oligopolies, hold the power of monopoly. They have used that power to control wages, working conditions, and to prevent teachers from having a meaningful role in policy formation. In other words, school management has used the power of monopoly to prevent an equivalent power relationship and a mutual power accommodation.

The expected competition among school districts did not substantially materialize after World War Two. As in the private sector, the form of the competition changed instead. It developed between teachers and management. This condition in education is the surrogate for perfect competition in the economy and is the direct response by the teachers to the monopolistic power of school management.

Countervailing power arises in education as a result of school management being oligopolistic with the power of monopoly under conditions of imperfect competition. But this is the umbrella concept under which are arrayed a variety of particularistic factors specifically moving teachers away from the inadequate roles and techniques of the past.

Particularistic Reasons

The most frequently cited explanation of teacher militancy is low salaries. Stinnett condensed the argument thusly:

> *The first and obvious causal factor is the mounting anger of teachers with economic injustice* . . . Teachers have simply become irritated beyond the point of tolerance with the failure of the American people to demand the right of teachers to share equitably in the fruits of an affluent society.[4]

---

[4] T. M. Stinnett, *Turmoil in Teaching* (New York: The Macmillan Company, 1968), p. 34.

Such an analysis has its roots in the American trade union movement which initially became militant in order to gain increased wages. Certainly concern over income has strong *prima facie* validity as a reason for teacher militancy. But teachers were regarded as a low income group long before the militant sixties. It takes the added concept of the affluent society to support the salary issue.

The extent to which the National Education Association and the American Federation of Teachers maintain an organizational rivalry is often cited as a militancy cause.[5] When the two organizations compete for members, it is reasoned, each organization is under pressure to produce more benefits for its members or those it seeks to enroll. Such competition concludes in a dynamic situation whereby the Association and the Federation attempt to out-perform each other and nurture militant action.

The rapid growth of the educational bureaucracy seems to foster militancy conditions. By this line of reasoning, as school system size increases schools assume a mass production approach to education. Teacher-administrator relations tend to become impersonal, procedures for determining conditions of employment break down, and teachers find it difficult to identify with the system.[6] Thus it is reasoned that the lack of identity can be overcome only by organizing, and through organization to combat the power of the bureaucracy.

There is also a problem with teacher and societal expectations. According to this interpretation, teachers developed rising expectations in the face of the post-Sputnik attention to and demands made upon public education. Teachers reasoned that their educational and personal goals would be fulfilled as a consequence of this increased attention. They also reasoned, correctly, that government at the local level, state, and federal levels would increase the amount of financial support for education. Unfortunately, the rising expectations were dashed on the rocks of reality: the extra monies were insufficient to solve the educational problems of the 1960's.[7] It is said that teachers became alienated from response inadequacy by society and began to agitate for redress. They adopted the methods

[5] John Scanlon, "Strikes, Sanctions, and the Schools," *Saturday Review*, XLVI, (October 19, 1963), 52.

[6] James Cass and Max Burnbaum, "What Makes Teachers Militant?" *Saturday Review*, LI, (January 20, 1968), 56.

[7] *Ibid.*, pp. 54-56.

of the activist civil rights groups. The parallel is that both groups reasoned that breaking the law is justifiable if a higher moral principle is served. The teachers learned that if the cause is perceived by the larger community to be just, civil disobedience is an approved tactic.[8]

Teacher militancy may be a function of the fact that teachers have always held an equivocal position in our society and that society has always been ambivalent toward them.[9] With several groups and agencies performing the teaching task, it is difficult to observe any kind of uniqueness in the role of the classroom teacher. Furthermore, and most damaging, it has not been established that there is a direct correspondence between high salaries and "good teaching" or high pupil achievement.[10] So society views the teacher in an ambivalent way, and this has helped alienate him from the school where he teaches and the community which he serves.

This explication of commonly attributed reasons for teacher militancy is not exhaustive, but it serves an illustrative purpose: by and large it is impossible to isolate pure reasons for militancy. We must be satisfied with the mixed and consequently overlapping reasons. But given this condition it is still possible to view the more particularistic notions within a larger setting.

Each of the reasons expressed above, and many that are omitted, are tied to the concept of countervailing power. Each in its own way represents an attempt to break down the existing power relationships between school management and teachers.

Salaries are comparatively low because the school management operates within conditions of imperfect competition. This gives them, as an oligopoly without significant competition, the power of monopoly—the power to fix wages, working conditions and policy involvement practices. We are in an affluent society, and teachers no longer accept the notion that they should be paid rather poorly. They know that the "power structure" will not of its own volition offer the conditions teachers feel they must have. Their recourse has been to organize as militants and seek to counter the power of school management. They, the teachers, will provide the competition missing from a lack of school districts competitively seeking their services.

The competition between the two teacher organizations is a further test of the power of monopoly. School boards have long dealt

---

8 *Ibid.*, p. 55.
9 *Ibid.*
10 *Ibid.*, pp. 55-56.

with both the Association and the Federation, or either separately. Until recently that interaction was fairly unproductive. Now, however, as the two teacher powers struggle against each other for memberships, they must confront the school management. That confrontation thrusts at the very foundations of the power of monopoly in education—the right to control wages, working conditions and policy. In order to attract members, each organization must challenge the present level of teacher participation in management affairs and thus produce additional benefits for members. This form of challenge is an effective surrogate for the fact that there is little natural competition among school districts for the teachers as sellers in the economy. As with the salary reason, organizational combat gives a base for the development of countervailing power under economic conditions of imperfect competition.

This line of attack could continue with other common reasons for militancy. But the salient point has been made. The commonly mentioned reasons for militancy are too particularistic. They do not focus on the larger phenomenon Galbraith put forth—that the power of school management is held in check by the countervailing power of those subject to it. It is simply not enough to seek higher wages. That is a constant teacher "want." What must be recognized is that the singular reasons involved in militancy are born because of imperfect competition, oligopolistic tendencies of school management, and the power of monopoly held by management. The singular reasons are expressions of the assumption of competition by the teachers, the end goal being the acquisition of a power balance which will continue to give them a significant voice in all future major educational decisions within their legitimate concerns.

The Power Mechanism

Given the power differential between teachers and school management and the commonly attributed reasons for militancy, there remained the requirement of a power device to bring about the expression of countervailing power. The key word in the illustrations of the United Steel Workers and the United Automobile Workers is *united.* In the private sector it was quickly realized that only through expression of collective power would contervailing power be meaningful. The other major factor was the willingness to express that power.

Teachers needed a mechanism to put validity to their demands and thus to operationalize countervailing power. That mechanism was collective bargaining with its power tool, the strike. Teachers have long been a collectivity. They have had their professional association and a union for many years. They had a power tool in the Association—professional sanctions. But the collectivity was not really united around a cause and their power tool was ineffective. Under such conditions they were no match for the power of the school management. Only when the teachers, as militant collectivists, were willing to adopt the private sector union tactic of the strike to enforce its demands did they modify the monopolistic power of schools boards. When this was done successfully, teachers emerged with a state of countervailing power.

We would argue, then, that teachers will emerge from their position of subservience to the power of monopoly held by school management. As teachers continue their militant ways they will form the competition missing from imperfect competition conditions among school districts. In their struggle they will find that they have obtained a state of countervailing power vis-a-vis school management.

Section C

Negotiations in Higher Education

There is currently a fairly strong trend toward unionization of the faculties of the nation's colleges and universities. Heim analyzes the position and the potential strengths and weaknesses of union affiliation, expresses a general dislike for the trend, and suggests as an alternative increased collegial-administrative interaction on problems of major interest to the faculties. Marmion also turns his attention on the problem of unions in higher education. His analysis centers around current organizational weaknesses in leadership, the problems of educational finance, and faculty participation in the setting of university policy. Marmion has a negative attitude towards unionizing higher education, indicating that basic reforms in the community of scholars should bring faculties into the decision-making structure. In a response to Marmion, Davis offers a point-by-point analysis of the arguments raised, particularly as he sees Marmion's "misunderstanding" of the role and accomplishment of the AAUP. Davis suggests less reliance upon organized power and more attention to collegial problem solving. Kugler represents the American Federation of Teachers position on unionizing higher education. He points out what he calls sedulously disseminated myths by the AAUP, interprets the position of the Federation, and discusses a long series of distinctive features of alleged Federation benefits. In the concluding article in this section, Frankie and Howe reject the notion of collective bargaining at the community college level on the basic assumption that, as a simple power mechanism, collective bargaining has no positive outcomes not available through current campus mechanisms.

Unions and Higher Education

Harry A. Marmion

A growing restiveness among public school teachers in certain urban areas and the rise of unionism among them in some of the nation's largest cities is by now familiar news in educational circles. The summer's discontent of 1967 stretched into the autumn in such places as New York City, Chicago, and Detroit, where strikes closed schools. In late September of 1967, a spokesman for the union movement in California said, "Collective bargaining by teachers and boards is no longer coming. It is here. . . . The question which now faces the Board of Trustees is whether it will come peacefully or with travail." Although there is nothing particularly notable about this statement *per se*, the fact that it was made by a professor in his dual role as President of the American Federation of Teachers College Council and referred to the state colleges of California and not to public schools should cause it to elicit the concern of college and university officials.

Too many college administrators and trustees think the issue is confined to the elementary and secondary levels, but the problem is theirs as well. A new labor organization affiliated with the AFL-CIO, the Council on Scientific, Professional and Cultural Employees (SPACE), was founded in Washington in March 1967, and plans to push the organization of white-collar professionals who, together with public employees and service industries' employees, are now the largest portion of a labor force heretofore considered unorganizable.[1] The prominent trade unionist, Mr. Gus Tyler, writes that "professional associations" in the teaching professions are already unions in all but name, although educational associations cling desperately to cliches of the past when defining terms in the delicate area of collective bargaining. At the 1967 annual meeting of the AAUP in Cleveland, however, a vocal minority of union-oriented delegates were present. It is easy to overestimate the strength of a movement when a minority makes its voice heard out of proportion

Harry A. Marmion, "Unions and Higher Education," *The Educational Record*, XLIX, (Winter, 1968), 41-48. Reprinted with permission. Dr. Marmion is Staff Associate of the ACE's Commission on Federal Relations.
[1] Gus Tyler, "Fresh Breezes in the Labor Movement," *New Republic*, May 20, 1967 (156), 13-15.

to its size, but the voice was there, and it came through loud and clear. The Association, after skirmishes with the union group on several issues, voted to refer to a special committee for consideration a resolution supporting the right of faculty to organize to protect group interests, or to join existing unions for such purposes, which would include the right to strike.

The history of teacher unionism follows the general development of unions in America. In 1897, the first teachers' union was formed in Chicago; in 1916, the American Federation of Teachers (AFT) was organized and the previously unaffiliated local groups became part of a national organization; in 1919, the AFT received a national charter from the American Federation of Labor. During the depression, teacher union membership grew from 7,000 in 1930 to 32,000 in 1939. This growth was exactly the opposite to the trends in general union membership at this time. In the post-World War II period of teacher militancy, union membership increased from 37,000 members at the end of the war to approximately 140,000 at the present time. The unions now comprise primarily teachers located in urban areas, with over 40,000 members in New York City.

The expansion of teacher unionism into higher education has developed very rapidly, for until the 1960's there was little known activity in this realm. In 1966, the AFT initiated an organizational change that clearly indicated the significance which the national union attaches to the recruiting of college faculty members. A separate college division having its own staff and separate college locals was formed. Until then, a college faculty member interested in joining a teachers' union had been forced by the organizational structure to join a local whose membership was composed of teachers from the kindergarten to the college level. There are now at least 70 separate college locals in the country, most of them in New York, California, Illinois, and Michigan.

Of the more than 300,000 college faculty members, approximately 10,000 now belong to unions. The AAUP has a membership of about 85,000. More than two-thirds of the total faculty population have yet to make a choice. It seems safe to assume that some will join either organization, while others will not, preferring to give their sole loyalty to a particular discipline.

Signs of Movement

The forecast of collective bargaining by teachers in the state colleges in California before the end of the academic year is not unwarranted. Early in June 1967, the 18 state colleges in California narrowly turned down (by 274 votes out of 5,756 votes cast) a question regarding the selection of an exclusive bargaining agent for the state college system. A majority of faculty voting at four of the six largest institutions in the state college system in California favored the proposal. The unionists will probably proceed in California on an institution-by-institution basis, rather than attempt to force a statewide referendum—unsuccessfully tried last summer. In October 1966, the Board of Trustees of the California State Colleges passed a resolution rejecting the concept of collective bargaining as it applies to faculty within the California system. In Illinois, the Chicago Junior Colleges Union, after a three-day strike, secured a collective bargaining agreement that, in their words, is "probably the most comprehensive union contract for college teachers in the nation." Similar examples occurred in New York and other places. Although the list is not long, it does indicate a rising trend.

Increased group action by the nation's teachers has various causes. In the public schools, issues revolve around salary schedules, fringe benefits, and work conditions. At the college level, economic security is a major factor. The real unrest, however, lies in the following areas: first, the inability of any one faculty organization to assert significant leadership; second, the status and degree of future financial support for both public and private higher education; third, the question of institutional policy making. In public institutions there is concern over the increasing layers of external control—by state-wide systems, master plans, chancellor policies, interstate compacts, and other similar arrangements and relationships. These general issues are compounded by the growth of educational institutions, the increased numbers of students, and the rapid creation of new institutions, particularly junior colleges. Increased student militancy adds a further element of uneasiness.

Specific Stances

With respect to academic freedom, *the union* strenuously opposes all loyalty and disclaimer oaths for faculty and students. It makes no distinction between secular and denominational colleges in dealing with issues concerning freedom to teach, engage in research, and publish in accordance with individual professional conscience. This position differs from that of the AAUP which allows certain limitations on academic freedom, particularly with regard to the teaching of controversial subjects by church-related institutions. The AAUP feels that as long as these limitations are clearly spelled out, it is within the province of a church-related institution to impose special restrictions on its faculty.

On academic tenure, the union holds that tenure status be conferred upon any full-time staff member not more than three years after initial appointment. In general, the AAUP position provides for a maximum of seven years before tenure is granted. The union is also concerned about the mechanics of the tenure procedure to a far greater degree than is the AAUP. It wants the institution to establish written evaluations of performance that would be available to the faculty member concerned; to submit written reasons for non-reappointment, and to provide the opportunity for a written answer from the faculty member concerned. The AAUP, on the other hand, leaves the formalities of the tenure process to the particular institution, within a framework of acceptable practices.

Among other provisions, the union wants to do away with the rank of instructor. Faculty salaries should start at $10,000 a year and be increased by annual increments to $30,000. It is against the use of merit systems of payment, based on criteria developed by the individual institution—publications, research, grants, etc. Under the union proposal, salary schedules would be made public, and no salary privately negotiated between a faculty member and the administration. All promotions should be tied to salary increases. Once a faculty member reaches the top salary range of one academic rank, he is promoted to the next rank and to the new salary schedule during the next academic year. The union also supports sabbaticals every eighth year with full pay.

The AAUP, which pioneered the report on "The Economic Status of the Profession," supports the goal of President Eisenhower's Committee on Education Beyond the High School, which in 1957 called for the doubling of faculty salaries in the next decade. The AAUP has never, however, specified minimum or maximum salary levels, and it has never called for the abolition of the rank of instructor. It is a fact, though, that the rank of instructor is diminishing within the teaching profession because many of the duties of that position have, in some institutions, been taken over by graduate teaching assistants and part-time faculty. Finally, the AAUP position on promotions and salary increments is the traditional one accepted by most institutions and faculty members throughout the country—that of letting the institutions set up their own rules. The AAUP does not advocate automatic promotions but it believes that promotion should be granted only after deliberation by departmental chairmen, departmental colleagues, and appropriate administrators. In turn, merit increments should be granted according to whatever criteria have been established by the institution in consultation with the faculty.

Working Conditions

The union has a great deal to say about the formal and informal working conditions that should prevail in colleges and universities. It advocates undergraduate teaching loads not exceeding nine hours per week, and teaching loads of six hours per week for graduate faculty. It seeks uniform personnel policies, records of which are kept in writing and made available to the faculty member in question. It also advocates the election of departmental chairmen for definite terms by members of departments, and it favors regulating many other specific details concerning working conditions, such as adequate secretarial help, parking facilities, and the like. On some of these matters, the AAUP takes no position, preferring not to interfere in the internal operations of colleges and universities.

The unionists say they do not desire a closed shop, or a union shop, respecting instead the individual rights of faculty members regarding membership. Once a collective bargaining representative is selected and agreed to by the institution, however, the position of the individual faculty member becomes meaningless because others will bargain for him. The unionist position is that faculty salaries and other conditions of employment—such as tenure and working conditions—should be attained through the collective bargaining process, leading to a written contract. It contends there is no other process that will enable them to redress the imbalance between the individual employed professional and the administration or governing body of an institution. It further states that the right to strike is a part of any collective bargaining agreement, although it should not be exercised except under the most extreme of circumstances. What are considered by the union to be extreme circumstances are not spelled out. The AAUP position on this matter is well known. Not a union, it fundamentally rejects the employer-employee relationship upon which the concept of trade unionism rests.

In a recent interview, Dr. Israel Kugler, President of Local 1460 of the United Federation of College Teachers in New York City, and an official of the new college union organization formed by the AFT, made several distinctions concerning the union position. On the question of salary adjustments or what are commonly called "merit increases," he indicated that some faculty members may get more than across-the-board increases. He cited as examples theatrical unions, newspaper unions, and television unions, in which certain "stars" receive more money than the rank-and-file members of the union. He felt a two-track system might be in order—one track of annual increments, the other above that level for merit. Kugler also admitted that the three-year tenure proposal of the teacher union may be extreme. He felt, however, that the weight of the argument was in favor of the three-year period because tenure is very intimately tied to the concept of academic freedom. To keep a faculty member in an insecure position, sometimes exceeding seven years, is a serious limitation on his right to speak out and be heard on controversial issues. Dr. Kugler was also quick to distinguish between conditions of work and the overall policy of the university. He argued strongly that the union was trying to determine work conditions, and did not seek to control the internal operations of an institution. This last point would most assuredly be debated by college administrators and trustees.

The union position is clear. The primary thrust is for increased salaries, better working conditions, the abolition of traditional methods of promotion, tenure, individual salary negotiations, and for salary increments based on a merit formula. If it is hard to visualize the triumph of unionism, it is well to remember that few foresaw, as recently as five years ago the present degree of militancy on the part of public school teachers and college students.

A Flexible Approach

Union organizers face difficulties. Currently, the strength of the union is in a few large metropolitan areas that have unique problems. Also, the past history of the union reveals little indication of any real understanding of the problems facing faculty in institutions of higher education. There is no indication that faculty members in general favor the union approach. The formation of a separate college division within the teachers' union indicates a recognition of this problem. But this move also indicates by its attempt to counteract weaknesses that the union has the organizational flexibility to facilitate change.

Much has been recently written on which segments of higher education are most susceptible to union encroachment. The June

1967 issue of *College Management* published the results of a questionnaire concerning college faculty unions. Over 90 percent of administrators questioned, in all segments of higher education, see unions on the horizon. The most exhaustive study of the subject thus far was done by a task force of the American Association of Higher Education.[2] The results confirm a widely-held belief about which segments of higher education will first be affected. Based on visitations to 34 institutions in all parts of the country, the task force concluded that junior colleges and former teachers colleges will be the most fertile institutions for union activity.

The analysis that follows must include generalizations. There will, of course, be exceptions to any general rule; so it should be made clear that not all institutions within any one segment will be affected.

Institutional Tensions

One can probably accurately predict that junior colleges will be the first significant battleground between unions and educators. The battle, in fact, has already begun in some states. All eight junior colleges in the Chicago system went on strike in December 1966. Many junior college faculty members are former public school teachers who have had experience with the bureaucratic control of school administrators and school boards, and some have also had experience with unions. The rapid growth of the junior college movement and the diversity of educational offerings within the junior colleges have thrust this movement squarely into higher education. Further, as the number of junior colleges has increased throughout the nation, systems of control have changed from local boards to district or statewide bases, thus weakening the on-campus or local community control of these institutions. This external authority, coupled with the junior college faculty's desire for the traditional academic status of college faculty, creates tension, unrest, and—in some cases—militant action.

The evolution of former normal schools to teachers colleges and now to multi-purpose institutions that provide educational opportunities in both teacher preparation and the liberal arts, has also created tensions which may give rise to increased faculty militancy and to possible union activity. The tensions come in part as a result

---

[2] *Faculty Participation in Academic Governance* (Washington: American Association for Higher Education, 1967), p. 67.

of faculty divisions within the institutions. The new faculty, primarily schooled in subject matter disciplines, are hired to develop and enlarge the liberal arts curriculum, and at many institutions, this expansion comes at the expense of teacher preparation programs. Because the traditions of these institutions are still rooted in teacher education, the number of non-education majors is often small at first and may never reach a large proportion of student enrollment. Thus, newer faculty may have fewer contact hours and may teach fewer students. This uneven state of affairs is worsened by the fact that the older faculty are more apt to accept rigid administrative control. The newer faculty—in most cases, younger men and women—are self-consciously aware of faculty prerogative in matters of normal academic concern.

Finally, one may suspect (although the suspicion is not widely shared by others studying this issue) that certain church-related institutions that previously have been tightly controlled will face similar problems. St. John's University is an example of a situation in which union activity thrived as a result of administrative intransigence. Laymen teaching in church-related schools usually have only the option to leave if they feel the institution is curtailing their academic freedom or if they are otherwise unsatisfied. The role of the layman in Catholic institutions, however, is changing. One vehicle in facilitating this process of change could be a resort to faculty unions.

An element common to all three of these segments of higher education—the junior colleges, the transitional normal schools, and the church-related colleges—is the lack of a deeply rooted system for faculty participation in decision making concerning the educational functions of the institution. Most junior colleges, newest members of the higher education community, have not been in existence long enough to develop patterns of shared responsibility for decision making. The emerging multi-purpose institutions have problems similar to those of the junior colleges. In the past, they have been basically administered without significant faculty participation. Now there is the added problem of the cleavage between old and new elements on the faculty. Historically, most church-related colleges have not needed to be concerned about faculty participation in administration because of the reticence of faculty members to become involved in educational decision making. In many places, however, this situation no longer holds and more and more lay faculty members desire full participation in the educational enterprise.

The Contestants

The one professional organization traditionally recognized as performing a national role in matters of educational concern has been the AAUP. This is not to say that on every campus the AAUP chapter speaks for the faculty, but to acknowledge that it is an organization to be reckoned with on at least some general matters of interest to faculties. The college faculty drive of the AFT is directly challenging the 85,000-member AAUP. It is challenging it not only for individual faculty membership, but more importantly, because the union is seeking to become the established voice of the faculty in dealing with administrators and boards of trustees on matters of educational policy as well as on salary negotiation.

In a contest with the union, the AAUP faces problems. In the late 1950's, "an objective observer would say that the AAUP was Committee A"[3] —the Academic Freedom and Tenure Committee. Although it has a wide range of committees working in various areas, the Association is still best known for its efforts in the areas of academic freedom and tenure. The censure of institutions not conforming to the standards set by the Association as judged by an investigatory committee has been in general an effective deterrent to arbitrary action by administrators. The unionists say the AAUP functions in a highly centralized manner. They are also critical of the organizational structure of the Association.[4] They cite as an example the recent action at the AAUP national meeting, which, through Committee A, reversed a decision by the local chapter at the University of Arizona, requesting by formal vote that the censure status of the institution be continued.[5] The AAUP feels that the action to remove censure was taken only after extended deliberation and after significant improvements had occurred at the University of Arizona.

"Community of Scholars"

A decade ago, the Association instituted the self-grading salary survey, which has been a highlight of its activity and a widely

---

[3] Walter P. Metzger, "The Origins of the Association," *AAUP Bulletin,* June 1965, 51, 236.

[4] Israel Kugler, "The AAUP at the Crossroads," *Changing Education,* Spring 1966, 1, 34-43.

[5] "Report of Committee A, 1965-66, The University of Arizona," *AAUP Bulletin,* June 1966, 52, 125.

heralded enterprise in the academic profession. Regarding administrative relationships, the Association has taken the traditional position set forth by retiring General Secretary William Fidler in his address to the National Convention in Cleveland in 1967. He stated that the historic role of the AAUP, as a professional organization was one that views the institution as a "community of scholars" in which all faculty members participate in decision making in a democratic fashion.

"The community of scholars" approach was carried forward by the recently issued tripartite statement on the "Governance of Colleges and Universities." Formulated over a two-year period through the cooperation of the American Association of University Professors, the American Council on Education, and the Association of Governing Boards, this statement was formally endorsed by the AAUP National Convention in Cleveland in April 1967. Both the ACE and AGB commended the document to their memberships as a significant step towards the clarification of the respective roles of the various components of the educational enterprise, spelling out (in necessarily general language) the shared responsibility for institutional control by a community of scholars, administrators, and trustees. Sharing of responsibility is advocated as an alternative to the adversary relationship that would prevail if the faculty segment of the academic community resorted to unionism.

A difficulty with the statement, aside from its generality, is that it has no real status or authority. There is also a question as to whether the document can accomplish its intended purposes, "to foster constructive, joint thought and action, both within the institutional structure and in protection of its integrity against improper intrusions"—while relegating the status of students to a cursory acknowledgement at the end of the statement. Representatives of the three organizations responsible for the tripartite statement are considering a further statement pertaining to an expanded student role in governance. There is no indication that this statement will be forthcoming in the immediate future. All the while, this question looms ever larger as the strident tones of student activism increase on campus after campus throughout the nation.

Where the Action Is

A few feel that the AAUP has the further problem of suffering from a diffusion of objectives resulting in confusion between the economic goals of the college teaching profession as exemplified by salary ratings and its more altruistic professional objective as exemplified by Committee A on Academic Freedom and Tenure.[6] The AAUP may need to decide whether to continue on the high road of professionalism or to go where "the action is," where the numbers are, and where many feel the future of higher education lies. If the Association continues to emphasize professionalism, it may become an association of established tenured faculty at generally prestigious institutions. If it chooses the latter approach, it will tend to become less professional and probably more militant, but it should survive as a viable institution. Its survival may include active participation on the part of the rapidly increasing junior college faculty. In the May 1965 issue of the *Bulletin*, there is evidence of the Association's wrestling with the problem of future membership. A minority recommendation argues against admitting junior college faculty into membership, the theory being that the AAUP was founded on a long-standing tradition of membership from institutions empowered to confer baccalaureate degrees.[7] It is obvious that if the AAUP seriously considered this recommendation regarding membership, the AFT would surely move into the breach and actively solicit junior college faculty membership. There are signs, however, that the opposite is true. In 1967, the AAUP elected a junior college member to its National Council. There is a former junior college faculty member on the professional staff of the Association in Washington, and at present, about 200 chapters of the AAUP are at junior colleges, containing a total of five to six thousand active members. This figure represents about 20 percent of the total chapters within the Association and about 6 percent of its membership.

It should be noted that in June of 1967, the National Education Association formally recognized a new professional organization to serve junior college faculties. This new body, called the National Faculty Association of Community and Junior Colleges, was developed in concert by NEA and the American Association for Higher Education. The acknowledged intention of this new organization is to give attention to the professional needs of the community college segment of American higher education.

Most of those studying the question of college faculty unionism are convinced that some type of effective faculty association will emerge on college campuses in the near future. Many also feel that some existing "professional associations" in education and in other

---

[6] George Strauss, "The AAUP as a Professional Occupational Association," *Industrial Relations*, October 1965, 1, pp. 125-40.

[7] *AAUP Bulletin*, May 1965, 51, 202-04.

fields are essentially unions in all but name. The proposed solutions are really already truisms. What is needed to prevent polarization into formal bargaining situations on a variety of issues is effective communication, both formal and informal, between faculty and administrations. The most viable means of formal communication will be some type of faculty body, democratically selected, and representing, as much as possible, the total faculty. Where such a formal group exists, it is identified by a variety of titles, e.g., faculty senate, faculty council, academic council, academic senate, or university council. It would seem that the administration should be represented on such a body by election and/or through *ad hoc* membership in a limited form. Duties, responsibilities, and policy-making functions of this formal body should be carefully spelled out. Obviously, policy should encompass only academic issues clearly within the competence of faculty to decide. The body should not become involved with details or focus on day-to-day administrative problems more readily handled by other mechanisms.

The committee system utilized throughout higher education also has a role to play in effective communications, although many in education wince when the subject of committees is discussed. Proliferation of committee work can be time-consuming and cumbersome, but it does allow interested faculty to become involved in the operation of an institution.

There are certain faculty organizations outside the formal institutional structure such as the AAUP and various other faculty associations that also provide important modes of communication. College and university administrators should take every opportunity to convey information to the various organizations present on the campus. It probably will be true that no single organization will truly represent the faculty, but the president and the administration should use all available means of communication to bring these organizations to the point at which they have the information needed to make independent judgments on matters of importance to the institution.

Informal communication is more difficult to describe. In general, it indicates an institutional atmosphere in which faculty members have access to information pertaining to the educational process. It means that administrative decisions are made after consultation with those likely to be vitally affected by the decisions. It calls for an atmosphere of mutual respect between faculty and administration. Problems of communication must be solved in a decentralized manner on an institution by institution basis. What works on one campus may not work on another. If for example, the local chapter of the

AAUP does reflect the faculty constituency within one institution then it will be an important group with which the administration should work. A state-wide faculty association may not, however, provide the proper forum for meaningful communication because it is too far removed from the individual campus where the problems exist.

Senates and Bargaining

An institution with a strong faculty senate, democratically elected and functioning as a meaningful partner in the educational enterprise, will have no need for collective bargaining. Conversely, an institution that has no faculty senate or a weak faculty senate dominated by administrators, is an institution ripe for more militant action by the faculty. In the future, such militancy will probably include unions. It will not be enough for institutions to reiterate the fact that unions and collective bargaining mechanisms traditionally have no place in the college teaching profession. Viable alternatives must be provided. Effective lines of communication must be available to enable a community of scholars to share in educational decision making. If reform is not forthcoming, the results will be increased arms-length dealing through the mechanism of collective bargaining. It could happen. If you don't believe it, watch California!

Unions and Higher Education: Another View

Bertram H. Davis

I do not know how well the American Federation of Teachers will like the hobgoblin role which Dr. Harry A. Marmon conceives for it, and I confess some surprise that a staff member of an organization which co-authored the 1966 *Statement on Government of Colleges*

Bertram Davis, "Unions and Higher Education: Another View," *The Educational Record*, XLIX, (Spring, 1968), 139-144. Reprinted with permission. Dr. Davis is an executive officer in the American Association of University Professors.

and Universities would view the problems of institutional government in terms of a clinical remedy rather than a philosophical commitment.[1] Amend your systems of institutional government, Dr. Marmion has warned administrations, or the union's cry for collective bargaining will become increasingly shrill; in short, the union will get you if you don't watch out. But effective institutional government, including a prominent and often a pre-eminent role for the faculty, is by no means a sedative either for the union or for the faculty as a whole. Its fundamental justification is simply that a college or university cannot expect to fulfill its mission adequately without it. The crucial decision which administrations must face is not, therefore, whether they will hold off the union, but whether they will make full use of the professional experience and expertise available to them in their faculties. To decide otherwise is to condemn their institutions to mediocrity or worse.

It is, of course, easy to frighten some persons with the spectre of unionism, and, for this reason, Dr. Marmion's article may have some of its intended effect. The difficulty of such an approach, however, is that, lacking a philosophic basis for its actions, an institution that thinks it has blunted the threat of unionism may quickly slip back into its old ways again. It may be well to remember that there are more depressing alternatives than faculty unionization. Indeed, given a choice soley between administrative tryanny—that kind of administration which, as Fritz Machlup indicated, keeps the faculty not on its toes but on its knees—and the collective bargaining naively trumpeted by the union as an academic panacea, a faculty member not totally insensitive to his environment would probably have little hesitation in going the union way.

Dr. Marmion is worried, however, for he has looked about him and concluded that the major faculty organization which joins him in his commitment to shared authority is plodding along "the high road of professionalism" rather than going "where the action is," and that its efforts in institutional government derive their thrust from a statement which is general and has no status or authority. The union, on the other hand, seems to go where the action is, and its position is perfectly clear.

Dr. Marmion's authority on the union seems to have been the President of the United Federation of College Teachers, whom he has interviewed and whose manifestoes he has pondered. One of his

---

[1] Harry A. Marmion, "Unions and Higher Education," *Educational Record*, Winter, 1968, 49, 41-48.

authorities on the AAUP seems also to have been the President of the United Federation of College Teachers. This method of balancing one organization against another apparently does not strike Dr. Marmion as being in any way unfair, and we thus have what purports to be an objective analysis of some of the dangers confronted by our colleges and universities because of the weakness of one organization and the vaulting strength of another.

It is, of course, useful to let the union speak for itself, and in this respect, Dr. Marmion has been quite generous. The collective bargaining agreement secured by the Chicago Junior Colleges Union is "in their words...'probably the most comprehensive union contract for college teachers in the nation.' " The union's program, which Dr. Marmion has had in part from a union spokesman, includes a probationary period of "not more than three years" (although up to seven years would apparently be tolerated), salaries between $10,000 and $30,000, automatic promotions and salary increments (although apparently a "star" system would also be permitted), the election of department chairman, teaching loads not exceeding nine hours per week for undergraduate teaching or six hours for graduate teaching, elimination of the instructor's rank, and, of course, attainment of the union's objectives through the collective bargaining process. With respect to academic freedom, Dr. Marmion notes that the union "strenuously opposes" all loyalty and disclaimer oaths and makes no distinction between secular and denominational colleges.

State of the AAUP

As for the AAUP, the "unionists" say that it functions in a highly centralized manner, and they are critical of its organizational structure. A few people feel (Dr. Marmion cites only one) that it suffers from "a diffusion of objectives resulting in confusion between the economic goals of the profession . . . and its more altruistic professional objective. . . ." Although it has supported the objective of doubling faculty salaries in a decade, it has never specified minimum or maximum salary levels or recommended elimination of the instructor's rank. It has permitted church-related institutions to place certain limitations upon academic freedom, but its censure actions have "been in general an effective deterrent to arbitrary action by administrations" of both secular and denominational institutions. Its position on salary increases and promotions is the traditional one which permits the institutions to establish their own rules.

It is no wonder that, having drawn these lines, Dr. Marmion should conclude that "in a contest with the union, the AAUP faces problems." An objective observer, of course, might have given the sentence a somewhat different cast: "In a contest with the AAUP, the union faces problems." For Dr. Marmion has both overlooked the AAUP's accomplishments and obscured its positions. The union strenuously opposes loyalty and disclaimer oaths, he asserts; but he does not mention that the AAUP led the successful fight against the disclaimer affidavit requirement of the National Defense Education Act; that it supported the successful litigation in *Baggett v. Bullett* and *Keyishian v. Board of Regents;* that more than any other organization, with the exception of the American Civil Liberties Union, it has been responsible for the steady toppling of the disclaimers which legislatures in their unwisdom have perpetrated. He notes that the AAUP has established no maximum or minimum for academic salaries; but he fails to note that, for nearly a decade, the AAUP has promulgated scales for maxima and minima ranging from AA to F; that its compensation survey was the first to bring compensations into the open and thus permit an informed competition among institutions; and that institution after institution has publicly announced its decision to move its salaries upward along the AAUP scales. He has almost no appreciation of the AAUP's program in academic freedom and tenure, which—far from merely acting as a deterrent to arbitrary action—has brought a high degree of order into the probationary period, has inculcated respect for fair dismissal procedures, and has elevated academic freedom to a byword to which even those who perceive it dimly feel compelled to pay lip service. He displays no awareness of the AAUP's successful mediative efforts at countless institutions.

Where Is the Action?

Still, he says, the AAUP "may need to decide whether to continue on the high road of professionalism or to go where 'the action is'. . . ." It is a catchy thought, and one can hardly be surprised to find it quoted bodily in the *Chronicle of Higher Education's* summary of Dr. Marmion's article. What Dr. Marmion means by it is, unfortunately, not entirely clear, but he has predicted survival for the AAUP "as a viable institution" if it renounces its professional ways and goes where "the action is."

If I read Dr. Marmion's article correctly, just about all the action must be in California, New York, Illinois, and Michigan, where, as he tells us, the union's strength is concentrated. I had not myself been under the impression that higher education in the other 46 states was utterly comatose, and I find it difficult to believe that in concerning itself directly with very serious problems at Texas Technological College, the University of Mississippi, Lorain County Community College, Lowell Technological Institute, Princeton Theological Seminary, the University of Arkansas, Allen University, and Benedict College—to mention only a few—the AAUP was not going where the action was. Because I do not recall a union response to any of these situations—or several hundred others in which the AAUP has exerted its influence—perhaps the AAUP has merely been deluded in thinking that they required the attention of a professional association.

The truth is, of course, that the delusion consists in thinking that the "high road of professionalism" and the road where "the action is" (is it a low road?) are separate and distinct. Indeed, perhaps the most remarkable accomplishment of the AAUP is that it has been able to travel these roads together—that while it has maintained a professional view of professional life, it has constantly applied its principles and its experience to the situation at hand. This was true in 1915, when the AAUP's founders turned their attention to 11 urgent complaints that academic freedom had been violated, and, having completed their investigations, promulgated the first *Declaration of Principles on Academic Freedom and Tenure*. It is true today when, on the basis of principles evolved through long experience, the AAUP is assisting in the improvement of institutional practice, and in the resolution of difficulties of many kinds, on campuses in every state of the union. No one with a steady perspective should have the slightest difficulty deciding which organization has consistently gone where the action is.

Institutional Government

A major key to institutional success, as Dr. Marmion recognizes, is institutional government, although, as I have already suggested, it is regrettable that he has so unmistakably equated success with holding off the union's onslaught ("Unions Gaining, Reform Needed, Colleges Told," writes the *Chronicle of Higher Education* in summarizing Dr. Marmion's article, as though reform were not needed for other reasons). In this vital area, says Dr. Marmion, the AAUP is seriously handicapped, for—although it properly supports the principle of shared authority—the *Statement of Government of Colleges and Universities* is not only general but it has no status or authority.[2] One will be forgiven a mild blush for Dr. Marmion on reading that the statement has no status or authority, for one would have thought that the imprint of his own organization, the American Council on Education, if not of the AAUP and the Association of Governing Boards, would have given the statement at least some slight status or authority. One would have thought also that the printing of the statement by the *Chronicle of Higher Education*, the *AHE Newsletter*, and other publications, plus the quick demand for tens of thousands of reprints, might have suggested to Dr. Marmion that the statement has rather more status—and perhaps authority—than he at first imagined. But no matter, for perhaps the heart of the difficulty is that the statement is general, whereas the union's position in all matters seems to be perfectly clear and understood—merely bargain collectively and we will have probationary periods not exceeding three years (or perhaps seven?), salaries from $10,000 to $30,000, and automatic salary increments and promotions (or perhaps a "star" system?).

Let it be said that Dr. Marmion has a point. The statement *is* general. It was intended to be and ought to be, like all statements applicable in a wide variety of situations. It was not written as a set of institutional by-laws or regulations and the institution that adopts it will have to turn very quickly to the work of adapting it to its daily life. When it does so, it will discover that the statement is a very remarkable document, with implications for institutional reform which go beyond anything other organizations have proposed.

Government by Community

One might cite in this connection a sentence in the statement the full import of which may not be immediately apparent. The president, says the statement, "should have the confidence of the board and the faculty." This principle, of course, supports another provision of the same paragraph, specifically that the "selection of a

---

[2] A further difficulty, says Dr. Marmion, is that the statement relegates "the status of students to a cursory acknowledgement at the end. . . ." Perhaps so; this effort of the three associations, however, is the first serious attempt by faculty and administrative organizations to evolve a policy role for students in institutional government. Attention should be called also to the *Joint Statement on Rights and Freedoms of Students*, which prescribes an active role for students in certain institutional affairs.

chief administrative officer should follow upon cooperative search by the governing board and faculty"—a provision of key importance to an institution's health, and here usefully set down for the first time in the words of administrative, board, and faculty representatives. The implication of the sentence first cited, however, is not merely that the president should have the confidence of the board and faculty at the time of his appointment, but that he should retain their confidence throughout his tenure of office. This is an implication of considerable importance. Boards of trustees have had a tendency to act hastily, sometimes against the will of their faculties, when they have lost confidence in their presidents. They have acted with rather less haste when there has been a similar loss of confidence by the faculty; indeed, some presidents have remained in office for years, perhaps even decades, with almost no visible faculty support. Among other things, the establishment of adequate communications among board, administration, and faculty, as provided in the statement, would allow such conflicts to be brought to the conference table, where they could be reviewed by all concerned. If such communications provide no guarantee of faculty-board agreement, they do at least offer both a check to precipitate action and the prospect of mutual understanding.

Numerous other sections of the *Statement on Government of Colleges and Universities* might be cited, for the statement is worthy of careful study: the role of the board, for example, as an institution's champion and as a bulwark against ignorance or ill will—a role which boards have all too often disregarded; the implied preference for the election of department chairmen, mentioned here specifically because Dr. Marmion neglected to balance the AAUP's view against the union's; the useful restraints upon the exercise of arbitrary authority when there is a conflict between faculty and administration.

Collective Bargaining

One other provision, however, calls for more extended comment, because its spirit infuses the entire statement. The president's "leadership role is supported by delegated authority from the board and faculty." In strictly legal terms, all institutional authority may be in the hands of the board; but it has been commonly assumed that the board delegates authority to the president, and the president in turn may delegate certain parts of it to the faculty. The statement rejects that view of academic life. The faculty's authority, it is clear, rests not upon presidential understanding or largesse, but upon the faculty's right, as the institution's foremost professional body, to exercise the preeminent authority in all matters directly related to the institution's professional work. The president, in short, is not the faculty's master. He is as much the faculty's administrator as he is the board's, and the institution which accords him any other role has failed to appreciate the principles on which a successful academic community must be built.

I have expressed the view that, if the only other choice is administrative tyranny, faculty members will probably not hesitate to cast their votes for collective bargaining. The choice, however is seldom that simple, and the fact is that demands for collective bargaining have been arising on some campuses that, whatever their defects, few would describe as administrative tyrannies. I should make clear that collective bargaining as used in this connection means negotiation through an external agent which is the faculty's exclusive representative, for faculties have long bargained collectively for themselves—and with considerable success.

The reasons for these demands are numerous and complex. Dr. Marmion has called attention to the rapid growth of institutions and the establishment of statewide systems under central control, developments which have encouraged faculties to match the impersonal authority of increasingly remote administrations with an impersonal power of their own. The power of budget officials—at times wantonly exercised—to undo academic decisions with the stroke of a pen is a constant danger. The steady rise in the relative number of probationary faculty members has contributed to campus malaise and to a quest for security through collective action. The economic gains of public school teachers at the bargaining table have not gone unnoticed by their counterparts in the colleges and universities. We live, moreover, in a time of social upheaval when those who believe they have caught sight of the goal are amassing their ultimate effort, like runners who save their great burst of speed for the end of the race. On the campuses, strong-armed administrative reactions have stimulated the faculty militance they were intended to suppress. The union establishment would probably agree that, in higher education, their movement was provided its most effective leverage by the St. John's University administration.

In such an atmosphere, it is not surprising that some faculty members have clutched at the seductive strength of an exclusive bargaining agreement. For collective bargaining, as its devotees see it, holds out the prospect of matching administrative power with equivalent faculty power, and of resolving through the threat of sanctions all the problems which have been at the root of faculty dissatisfaction. The move to collective bargaining has, of course, been given a major assist, both practical and psychological, by the recent laws permitting public employees to bargain with their employers through exclusive agents, for the laws are modeled upon the arrangements prevailing in industry and do not so much as acknowledge the fact that colleges and universities have developed very different arrangements for faculty representation. In one state, faculty members on first reading the law were of the opinion that they were *required* to designate an exclusive agent.

Reliance and Power

Even if power were the key to faculty success, one would have to take issue with those who insist that the faculty can achieve that power only by placing exclusive reliance on an external bargaining agent. The truth is that there are few, if any, reasonable goals that a faculty cannot accomplish for itself if its members are persistent and imaginative, and if it draws when necessary upon the experience of the professional associations. The union, of course, may argue that its strike policy provides it with a power no faculty or faculty senate possesses, but this argument has been nullified by recent experience in Michigan, where one of the strikes last autumn was urged by a junior college faculty senate. Nor did an external agent have to prompt the Catholic University faculty when, in an action almost spontaneous, it forcefully demonstrated its revulsion with an administrative outrage.

The difficulty with this inordinate emphasis on power is that it obscures and obstructs the proper goal of college and university faculties. Faculty members have rightfully complained when boards or administrators have treated them as employees, and it would be ironic if they were now themselves to perpetuate the employer-employee concept through an industrial style of collective bargaining. For there is no question that if faculty members rely as a steady tactic upon the use of sanctions—that, if with the threat of a strike in the background, they pursue the brinkmanship policy of the unions—boards and administrators will look to the sources of their own power, and institutions may have lost the opportunity for that cooperative effort which is indispensable to their welfare. If collective bargaining techniques are to be employed, they should be directed, as the AAUP has stated, toward the establishment of those forms of institutional government that will permit faculty members to fulfill their role as institutional officers with primary responsibility for the institution's professional life. The organization which encourages them to seek anything less is selling both them and their institutions short.

The Union Speaks for Itself

Israel Kugler

The exchange of articles (*Educational Record,* Winter, Spring 1968) on unionism between Dr. Harry Marmion of the American Council on Education and Dr. Bertram Davis of the AAUP is charming and somewhat informative. It suffers, however, from the obvious limitation of discussing college teacher unionism as a major theme without the participation of a spokesman for the union's position. I would hope this contribution will provide the necessary balance.

In its history, which is co-terminous with that of the AAUP, the American Federation of Teachers (AFL-CIO) has always had college professors enrolled in its ranks. John Dewey and his coworkers, George Counts and John Childs, based their membership on the belief that teachers, primarily those in the public schools, needed a union to advance their economic interests. They conceived these interests to be part of the life of a professional. For them, professionalism did not mean abject genteel poverty.

During the great depression, many AFT college locals were formed, in large measure, as vehicles for social protest against the widespread poverty and unemployment. In this membership, which included such august institutions as Harvard, Yale, Princeton and Columbia, we find Albert Einstein, Hubert Humphrey, Paul Douglas, Mike Mansfield, and Eugene McCarthy. Indeed, two college professors have been AFT presidents.

Israel Kugler, "The Union Speaks for Itself," *The Educational Record,* XLIX, (Fall, 1968), 414-418. Reprinted with permission. Dr. Kugler is President of the United Federation of College Teachers, Local 1460, American Federation of Teachers.

The mushroom growth in more recent times of the AFT on college and university campuses is based on the relevance of collective ✓ bargaining and unionism to the current state of affairs in higher education. Well over 15,000 faculty members on over 100 campuses now belong to the AFT. Burgeoning enrollments, inadequate facilities, burdensome workloads, relatively poor compensation—all are too prevalent. The historic conceptions of the AAUP leadership simply do not coincide with current reality[1]

College and university professors have seen their public school colleagues make substantial gains in bringing about workload reductions, in improving compensation, and in sharing educational decision making through collective bargaining. The influx of younger professors into college and university faculties has not been accompanied by the impedimenta of irrelevant myths hiding the real state of affairs in higher education. A task force appointed by the Association for Higher Education (NEA), which made a careful study, states:

> In fact, the case studies indicate that the greatest discontent and most visible tendencies toward unionization are found at the junior college level. . . .Similar developments have taken place in the new or emerging four year colleges and universities. . . . In this context the conventional forms of faculty representation often are shallowly rooted or non-existent.[2]

Hierarchical Authority

We could look back with nostalgia to the *universitas* which was the essence of the governance that accompanied the birth of the first universities in the High Middle Ages in Europe. There, teaching faculty through their guilds ran the institutions and, in some instances, shared responsibility with guilds of students. This is not the situation that exists today, particularly in America. Here, colleges and universities have engrafted upon them a corporate, hierarchical, ✓administrative order. It is through this order of descending authority—the Board of Trustees (and in the case of public institutions, the legislature must be added), the President, the Chancellor, the Dean—that the power of the purse is wielded and, in

---

[1] Israel Kugler, "AAUP and AFT—Which Way for the Professors?" A reprint and revision from *Changing Education* (Washington: American Federation of Teachers).

[2] *Faculty Participation in Academic Governance* (Washington: American Association for Higher Education, 1967), p. 10.

the final analysis, the workload, tenure, promotions, and salaries determined.[3] Faculty authority has even been eroded in the traditional areas of professional concern—enrollment policies, scholastic standards, curriculum, and student activities.

A parliamentary model in which the working faculty engaged in teaching and research would select all administrators and have them responsible to the faculty for the carrying out of faculty policy is a desirable ideal, but a utopian one.

Facing reality, we must recognize that professors are not officers of an institution on appointment, but professional employees. By banding together in a union and seeking collective bargaining status, the imbalance of power can be redressed and the untrammelled authority of the administrator-trustee combine effectively checked. A truly shared authority is the result.

There is nothing antithetical to professionalism in this concept. Indeed, it serves to enhance professionalism. It provides the employed practitioner with some control over the conditions under which he practices the profession. This certainly has been the case in other professions—music, theater, engineering, public health, etc. One has but to compare conditions before and after the onset of unionism in these professional fields to verify the manner in which unionism has enhanced professionalism.

Often those who oppose unionism on campuses proclaim that unions are "outside" agencies alien to a college or university. This is a myth based upon a confusion of terms. If you identify "inside" with an intramural organization of faculty members, advisory in nature, and subject to the authority of the trustees the chief administrator—such as a faculty senate—this distinction may be correct. A union is "outside" this velvet trap in the sense that it is not beholden to an administration.[4] It is "inside" in the sense that its members are faculty who are engaged in teaching and research.

[3] The Education Editor of the *New York Times* quotes Yale Professor Yaroslav Pelikan as stating: "... at most universities the president is a member of both the trustees and of the faculty, but ... his principal role now is executive secretary of the board rather than as first professor of the faculty. In such crises as those at Berkeley or Columbia, the managerial mentality of such presidents cannot make clear to students, professors and neighbors the destructive nature of the university community. The president hides behind his vice-presidents, who hide behind the deans, etc., in an infinite progression." May 5, 1968, p. E3.

[4] The union is not opposed to faculty senates. On the contrary, we wish them to be invested with *complete* authority in the areas of curriculum, scholastic standards, student activities with proper student involvement. Since there cannot be a unitary union line in these matters, we conceive of powerful senates as complements of unions. The union will resist all efforts to reduce senates to the role of puppets.

No Monopoly of Wisdom

Still another myth sedulously disseminated by the AAUP leadership and administrators is that collective bargaining and unions presume an adversary relationship between the administration and working faculty which is destructive of the cooperative fabric—the warp and woof of a college or university. The union does not conceive of the administration as an enemy. In today's bureaucratized institutions, the administrative function of securing funds for equipment, supplies, buildings, staff, etc., is a necessary one. It doesn't follow that because of this important function, administrators have a monopoly of wisdom. The administrator often claims it, however, as the result of the unique panoramic view that he alone has from the heights of his exalted office. Collective bargaining is a process of give and take, in which divergent perceptions and interests are accommodated and transformed into a viable working relationship in the form of a binding written agreement.

✓ A key element of this contractual agreement between the practicing professional staff and the administration is the grievance procedure where final authority for unresolved differences resides in an impartial outside authority. This effectively removes from the staff the fear of administrative reprisals because of creative dissent. It serves to establish a genuine peer relationship so essential for a vital and progressive institution.

It is regrettable that much of the central AAUP's time is spent in combatting collective bargaining and urging college and university boards to resist bargaining and substitute the concept of faculty senates. One of the outlandish assertions in this connection is that collective bargaining implies the selection of an "exclusive" bargaining agent which would destroy academic freedom.

The AFT college and university program makes it quite clear that certain practices associated with unions in the industrial field are not desirable in academe. We do not advocate a "closed" or "union" shop. Faculty members under collective bargaining would *not* be compelled to belong to a union. Membership in the academic community is a function of the decision of the members of a department consonant with fair play and due process. The word "exclusive" is another way of defining a representative democratic choice. A secret ballot permits faculty to have an opportunity to vote for an organization or, if philosophically opposed to collective bargaining, to vote for "no organization." If a majority of votes are cast for the union, it becomes the duty of the faculty representative to negotiate a collective bargaining agreement on the terms and conditions of employment. Provision is made for decertification by a petition calling for new elections. We fail to see how this violates academic freedom.

The specter of strikes has often been raised to frighten faculty away from unions. Even the AAUP now asserts that, as a last resort, strikes are sometimes necessary.[5] A strike is a withdrawal of services. Certainly the firing of 32 colleagues without charges or hearings at St. John's University warranted a strike. Similarly, the faculty and students struck at Catholic University in support of dismissed Father Curran. Strikes have also been conducted in situations where administrations refused to hold elections or negotiate in good faith.

Right Reduces Incidence

The right to strike, paradoxically enough, reduces the incidence of strikes. Colleges and universities, although invested with the public interest, are not vital to the health and safety of the community. Together with all unions, we do not desire strikes or call them lightly without the greatest deliberation by the membership. They are costly in human and material resources. Only in a free society do we have free unions. Free unions imply the right to withhold services as a protest against grave unprofessional conditions. Most contracts, including our own, have been negotiated without strikes. The lost time is less than one percent of working time, less than time lost by illness and coffee breaks.

The American Federation of Teachers has some distinctive features worthy of note:

1. It is a federation of *autonomous* local unions free from domination by a central office, bound together by mutual aid, and recognizing the strong community support engendered by being part of the organized labor movement.

2. In the AFT, locals are fully integrated. The AFT was *amicus curiae* in the historic 1954 Supreme Court case. It expelled all

---

[5] This position, adopted at the AAUP annual meeting in April, 1968, stands out in contrast to a previous position of the AAUP leadership in connection with the strike against St. John's University conducted by the United Federation of College Teachers, the New York City affiliate of the AFT. This position held that strikes were inappropriate at academic institutions.

southern affiliates that had refused to have an integrated membership. It has been in the forefront of every struggle for civil rights.

3. The AFT has a public review board acting as an ombudsman, with authority to protect union members against any arbitrary act by its officialdom.

4. On-campus activism distinguishes the AFT from the usual role of the AAUP in dealing with grievances. An average of two and a half years is too long to wait before academic crimes are publicized on a censure list. We long ago decided to defend the probationary faculty members so vulnerable to arbitrary administrative acts.

5. We believe that colleges should epitomize the open society. And so we insist on *published* salary schedules. We are appalled at the practice of making secret individual deals for the favored few. We are against secret dossiers on faculty members. And we insist that personnel files and written evaluation reports be available to the faculty member for inspection with the right to file comment.

6. We encourage faculty members to remain at an institution and engage in its reform rather than to become academic entrepreneurs who hop to other institutions that are ready to pirate them away with the lure of *individual* betterment.

7. We are opposed to the trend toward increased use of the mass lecture (often magnified by closed-circuit TV) and the exploitation of graduate assistants as economy measures. These mark the deterioration of education toward alienation and depersonalization and away from the dialogue and transactional process between student and teacher.

8. We advocate a professional salary schedule ranging from $10,000 to $30,000 to be attained in a reasonable number of steps by *all* tenured faculty in regular annual increments with changes in title after reaching maximum in rank. Especially distinguished merit, as recognized by departmental faculty, should be rewarded by more rapid advancement through promotion.

9. We advocate a maximum workload of 9 semester hours for undergraduate teaching, 6 hours for graduate teaching, a limitation of 100 students per semester for undergraduate teaching (less in English composition, speech, etc.), adequate secretarial service, research facilities, and office space.

10. We believe in the most comprehensive concept of academic freedom for both faculty and students. Indeed, we conceive this to be such a fundamental working condition that its violation should result in the loss of accreditation. It encompasses opposition to loyalty oaths; the rights of students to hear controversial speakers, to

organize as they please, to have a free student press, and to have a meaningful and responsible voice in all affairs that affect them; the rights of the non-tenured probationer to fair evaluation and full academic participation; the rights of faculty as citizens under our Bill of Rights—with no distinction between secular and church-related institutions. We therefore endorse the position on Academic Freedom adopted by the American Civil Liberties Union.

Proposed Merger

As some form of higher education available to our youth becomes part of the American ideal, colleges and universities will increasingly face grave crises in staffing, if education is to maintain a high level of quality. It is therefore deplorable to find unnecessary divisions in the ranks of faculties in institutions of higher education. On several occasions, the American Federation of Teachers has proposed merger to the AAUP based upon a common program and democratic procedure. Twice the AAUP Annual Meetings have sidestepped the issue by offering "substitute" motions to "cooperate" with all organizations. In 1968, a clear cut vote took place on the issue of organic union. One third of the AAUP delegates felt it to be desirable.

We still believe it to be in the best interests of the profession. The AAUP's cultural inertia in adhering to outmoded concepts and organizational forms will doom it to continued impotence. When choices will then have to be made, college and university faculty will take the "high road of professionalism"—by belonging to the AFT and pressing for collective bargaining.

Faculty members will be compelled to overcome anxiety about status and their identity crisis when they face unionism. Many will transcend the psychological barrier of identifying unionism and collective bargaining with blue-collar workers (often a status enjoyed by their own parents), and will recognize it as a natural institutional instrument ideally suited for collective effort—a *collective* effort which paradoxically frees the *individual* professional from stultifying fear and conformity.

Faculty Power in the Community College

Richard J. Frankie and Ray A. Howe

At no time has the study of power and authority been of more vital importance to the academic community, and to every thoughtful man, than it is at present. Accounts of sit-in demonstrations, riots, and general civil disobedience on college campuses appear with regularity in the daily press—and, in recent months, accounts of faculty walkouts and strikes.

In reviewing and analyzing the causes of current faculty unrest, Weber said that "faculty dissatisfaction is clearly a child of growth and affluence."[1]

> The paradox of affluence and unrest may be explained by several factors. The improvement in the status and well-being of the college professor probably has been accompanied by a more rapid rise in his expectations. This phenomenon is well known in underdeveloped professions as well. In many institutions, the notion of professionalism is a polite fiction. With the rise in status and the expansion of opportunities, many faculty members now demand the full prerogatives of professionalism. This means that professors, like members of other professions, seek direct participation in the formulation of the policies and rules that govern their performance.[2]

Richard J. Frankie and Ray A. Howe, "Faculty Power in the Community College," *Theory into Practice*, VII, (April, 1968), 83-88. Reprinted with permission. Dr. Frankie is Assistant Professor of Higher Education, College of Education, The Ohio State University, Columbus, Ohio, and Dr. Howe is Executive Dean, Henry Ford Community College, Dearborn, Michigan.

[1] Arnold R. Weber, Graduate School of Business, University of Chicago, speaking at a Plenary Session on March 6, 1967, at the 22nd National Conference on Higher Education, Chicago, Illinois. (Weber was chairman of a six-man Task Force of the American Association for Higher Education that in 1966 studied Faculty Representation and Academic Negotiations.)

[2] *Ibid.*

At no other formal level of education are faculty members' militant efforts greater than they are in the two-year college, where their pressures to participate more directly have forced changes in its nature and administration.

Where they (two year colleges) formerly gave almost exclusive emphasis to vocational courses, many junior colleges have modified their "mission" to become part of a system of academic higher education. Where it was under the administration of the local Board of Education governing secondary education, the junior college may now be a part of a separate district or state-wide system. This change in function and administration has meant that junior college faculty members often are no longer satisfied with the passive role of a "teacher" in a highly centralized structure where control over educational policies and the conditions of employment is lodged in the hands of the president and the Board. Instead, many junior college professors now seek full academic status and rights of participation in the traditional sense.[3]

The Faculty and the College

By traditional organization, the operation of colleges and universities has been based upon the establishment of a hierarchy of authority, which has served to define points where specific decisions will be made—that is, where the best information exists and where participation is at the optimum. Basic to this approach has been the attempt to afford in the organization the opportunity to work and to make decisions as an academic team.

However, the concept of "teamwork," as viewed by social and behavioral scientists, or of peer or collegial relationships and participation differ markedly from the traditional hierarchical, bureaucratic approach. The difference may be sensed in a distinction made by Barnard between people as "objects to be manipulated" and as "subjects to be satisfied."[4]

As the junior college emerges as a partner in the field of higher education, many of its faculty members have come to feel strongly

---

[3] *Ibid.*

[4] Chester I. Barnard, *The Functions of the Executive* (Cambridge: Harvard University Press, 1938), p. 40.

that they are peers among themselves and, indeed, of the administrative officers. These perceptions of functional roles have become a major factor of conflict; the conflict has, in turn, fostered the concept of "shared authority." Directing the efforts of the faculty from the top of the hierarchy of authority has become questionable at best.

Faculty disenchantment with the traditional form of governance directs itself particularly at the organizational form of faculty participation, which in the two-year colleges, like most higher education institutions, is the traditional faculty council (or academic senate), a representative, legislative body. A definite part of the college's structure, it derives its representative status from the authority of the whole faculty. Needless to say, some faculty councils are willed much authority and others, very little. (It is to be noted that formal organization carries no guarantee of effectiveness.)

Uneasiness with this traditional internal form of faculty ✓ participation has led many college faculties throughout higher education to seek unity and strength by promoting a second form, an "external" organization—such as, for example, the American Association of University Professors (AAUP), the National Education Association (NEA), and the American Federation of Teachers (AFT). The most significant of the "external" organizations has been the local professorial unions of the AFT, which have been formed at public and private universities, but are strongest and most widespread in the junior colleges, particularly in unified K-14 districts. In general, these external organizations have in the past served as lobbyists or pressure groups and have not been active, legal participants in the formal decision-making process.

Largely as a result of the ineffectiveness of the combined internal-external structures, a third form of faculty organization has emerged, a "bargaining agency." Weber reported:

> These bargaining agencies seek to enter into a formal bargaining relationship with the administration over economic benefits and conditions of employment. The object of the negotiations is a written agreement with full legal standing. [5]

Although the bargaining agency involves direct, legal "shared authority," it differs markedly from the previous forms because the

[5] Weber, *op. cit.*

process it involves is one of direct confrontation or an adversary ✔ relationship. Implicit in this process of accommodation or ["antagonistic cooperation"]are outright tests of power among the negotiators. Hickson wrote, "Unlike most of the external associations, the bargaining agency seeks to participate directly in the decision-making process. In recent years, both unions and professional associations have acted as formal bargaining agents. This approach has made significant gains in the past year, especially in the junior colleges . . . ."[6] Interestingly, in the university setting, "collective bargaining" often is referred to as "academic negotiation." This euphemism is highly inappropriate when used to describe the recent resolution of conflicts in two-year colleges.

Confrontations of Power

While faculty members in the two-year colleges are rejecting the traditional, bureaucratic, hierarchical style in favor of a concept of distribution and sharing of authority to foster the creative potentialities of the faculty and administration, the aspiration to power, the contemplation of it, and the movement toward it, may, each or all, differ significantly from the actual exercise of it.

Power may, of course, assume variant forms, and its exercise exhibit differing functions, but, on the academic scene, the emergent manifestation has been preempted from the industrial experience. Thus, organized drives for recruitment by the NEA and the AFT are well under way, and efforts to adapt organizational policy to the emergence of collective bargaining are evident in the deliberations of the AAUP.

Two years ago, the American Federation of Teachers published a "Taxonomy of Tactics," the personal viewpoint of its then research director:

> The first principle of power tactics is randomness of action. If the opposition believes that teacher action is inevitable, it will prepare its defenses—"seek to minimize its maximum possible losses"—rather than endeavor to reach an agreement. It is best to keep the other side guessing. Never reveal the settlement position. Balance hope of avoiding reprisals with fear of reprisals.

[6] C. Addison Hickson, "Academic Negotiations," address delivered at AAHE Summer Conference, Minneapolis, Minnesota, July 3, 1967.

The second principle is sureness of action. Never threaten that which cannot be carried out. If one side backs down because it cannot do what it says it is going to do, then its next threat will be given no credence. On the other hand, one strike at a time of impasse may make a dozen future strikes unnecessary. Ironically, the reason why so many agreements are reached without a strike is that the employees are sure to strike.

The first two principles bring us to the third. Combining randomness of action—whether you are going to settle or not—with sureness of action—if you don't settle direct action will take place—deadline can be set and tension will build. Martin Luther King called this "creative tension"; people are forced to think *creatively,* perhaps for the first time in order to remove themselves from a painful situation. If there is pressure on both sides, the best reasoning occurs at this point. That is why most major agreements are reached late at night, right before dawn brings the first strikers to the gate.

Collective bargaining has a built-in deadline. The contract has an expiration date. Thus, the union invokes sureness of action by insisting "no contract, no work."

The fourth principle is mass participation.[7]

Of all states in which these action trends may be discerned, Michigan seems, momentarily at least, to be in the forefront. Here, bolstered by law which authorizes collective bargaining by faculty and, where invoked, requires collective bargaining by governing boards, a number of contracts already exist, several arrived at only after strikes of some duration. While data exists in sufficient quantity to warrant study, no basis for delineation of a prototype of such forms or functions of power may yet be available. There does seem, however, to be a legitimate opportunity to make observations and inferences about what the processes reveal to date and cautious estimates of what, if anything, they portend.

Although only one strike occurred in a Michigan community college in the fall of 1966, several others, including a second strike at one, took place in the fall of 1967. It is widely assumed that there will be more in 1968.[8]

[7] Pete Schnaufer, *The Uses of Teacher Power* (Chicago: The American Federation of Teachers, 1966), p. 9-10.

[8] *Report of the Governor's Advisory Committee on Public Employee Relations,* State of Michigan, December 21, 1967, p. 1

The incidence of strikes seems to be rising. This, if true, bespeaks several possibilities, especially if the[strike is viewed as a breakdown rather than a component of collective bargaining.)Lack of experience, sophistication, readiness to bargain in good faith, and resources may each or all be reflected. Or, there may be the undeniable appeal of the drama and emotional intensity of a strike, the fascinating combination of dread and delight. It is doubtful if even the strikers themselves can reliably articulate why they strike. But the fact that they do strike, either in defiance of the law or in an attempt to circumvent the spirit of the law, is highly significant. Justifications, real or imagined, must be present.

The bargaining process does, to date, approach the *bona fide* ✓ industrial labor-management pattern. Negotiations are tough, hard-headed confrontations on significant issues embracing a wide range of both economic and noneconomic matters. Fact-finding and mediation, through the auspices of the State Labor Mediation Board, have been extensively utilized. In various instances and for several reasons, unfair labor charges have been filed, heard, decided, and appealed. Demands and counter-demands are exchanged and positions modified considerably as a result. Even the industrial inclination for "round-the-clock" bargaining as settlement approaches seems to be coming a universal practice. Both boards of trustees and bargaining groups have employed their prerogative to reject tentative agreements recommended to them by their representatives at the table.

Problems in the Bargaining Approach

[Accepting the fact that it does exist and assuming that it may reach an even higher pitch, what are some observations of collective bargaining at the community-college level?]

The essence of the process must first be understood. Well over a decade ago a scholarly analyst attempted to provide some insight:

> The theory underlying collective bargaining is that if the parties bargain in good faith they will practically always reach an agreement. . . . Collective bargaining does not force the parties to agree. It is merely the procedure most likely to produce satisfactory agreements when employed in good faith by both parties.[9]

[9] Myron Lieberman, *Education as a Profession* (Englewood Cliffs, New Jersey: Prentice-Hall, Inc., 1966), p. 355.

However palatable this viewpoint may prove to be, it must, nonetheless, be amplified to be appreciated. There is clearly inherent in its invocation by faculty a determined effort to diminish or at least substantially alter previously existing administrative or Board of Control prerogatives, whether stated or assumed.

> Collective bargaining . . . is essentially a power relationship and a process of power accommodation. The essence of bargaining is compromise and concession-making on matters over which there is conflict between the parties involved in bargaining. The avowed theoretical purpose and practical effect of collective bargaining is to grant employee organizations an increasing control over the decision-making process of management.[10]

To the extent that this evaluation is accurate, a number of questions are generated. For example: To what degree is the administrative posture determined by a reaction to the disturbance of the total *status quo? Conversely,* how long and how well can a faculty penetration of the decision-making function be sustained? The administrative commitment to this arena is continual and essentially full time, while such commitment by the faculty will not only be part time but also peripheral to their basic function, teaching. A *substantial* commitment to decision-making by the faculty would tend to immerse them in "administrative" activities at the expense of teaching.

To a certain measure, faculty pursuit of power may emerge as a reaction against bureaucratic tendencies within administration and as a form of protest against depersonalization of faculty-administrative relationships.[11] To the extent that this is true, it would seem possible that inherent frustrations will be generated if the thrust of the faculty power apparatus is toward formalization of faculty-administrative relationships and is sustained and/or intensified. The tendency would seem to be to develop, within whatever framework embraced by the faculty to channel power, a bureaucracy of leadership all its own—thus, creating an eventual estrangement between leadership and membership as an "administration" appears within faculty ranks.

---

[10] Wesley A. Wildman and Charles Perry, "Group Conflict and School Organization," *Phi Delta Kappan,* January 1966, p. 245.

[11] James Cass and Max Bernbaum, "What Makes Teachers Militant," *Saturday Review,* January 20, 1968, p. 56.

Further, as the exercise of faculty power continues there is bound to be some internal disagreement on emphases, issues, directions, tactics, means, or ends, with a possible congealing of assent and dissent groupings. Thus, the potential for majority-minority schism would impend. Where this occurs, politics is likely to intrude with contested elections for leadership posts and create a probably overturn of leaders and/or reversal of positions. As a result, the character and direction of leadership could change significantly.

Faced with both external as well as internal rivalry, leadership would find the bargaining process not only the determinant of a contract but also the determinant of one's "political career" in faculty leadership. If such be the case, a certain wariness of compromise may occur and a degree of rigidity result which would be detrimental to the accommodation process so vital to the resolution of power confrontations.

In candor, however, a greater danger lurks for the effective conduct of the bargaining process. It will be difficult to sustain for extended periods of time the dedication of time and effort which this process demands, and the faculty may well be wary of those willing to make such a continuing commitment to an activity peripheral to their basic concern. If rotation or displacement of leadership should occur, a period of educative experience will be required for those not readily attuned to the power accommodation process. This period may well be a luxury that can be ill afforded in our fast-moving situation.

It does seem extremely probable that another aspect of educative experience will be necessary. Idealism seems to be high among the faculty. The adjustment process would entail the delineation of the distinction between the *desirable* and the *possible*. What *should* be characteristic of a protest movement of quality, and the achievement of what *can* be, the more suitable business of a power struggle, must be distinguished. It is one thing for the faculty to cry out against injustice and quite another to rectify it.

Such idealism may cause the faculty to rebel against the concept of compromise—a keystone of successful bargaining. But where compromise is regarded as synonymous with either surrender or the sacrifice of principle, it will certainly not flourish. It must be regarded as a strength rather than a weakness and as a function of, rather than a desertion of, integrity.

Beyond this, the bargaining table eschews the abstract, the theoretical, the "academic" consideration. It is a place where practical men face practical problems and attempt practical solutions in a practical manner. "What will you settle for?" and "Upon what basis can we make a deal?" are questions alien, even repugnant, to the idealist. But, to the bargainer they represent the omnipresent bases for resolution of the impasse.

The Academic Chess Game

There still exists to be considered a larger context of bargaining that must not be ignored, despite the fact that consideration of it beclouds productive outcomes—the "game" aspect. Both observers and participants are understandably prone to emphasize its seriousness. No one would deny that the advent of collective bargaining and its development have significance of great import to the particular institution and to the whole field of higher education. One analyst, at least, has noted that collective bargaining "is a type of game played under highly elaborate, if unwritten, rules and carried out under strong behavioral expectations."[12] Since a game is thought of as representing substantially a nonsense activity, this may be difficult to appreciate or even to grant credence. But, experience suggests that this is true. Certain "moves" are as applicable to bargaining as they are to chess. It is somewhat ironic that those who would never presume to question the prescribed patterns of the rook, the knight, the bishop, the king, the queen, and the pawn assume blithely the ability to transform the bargaining processes into whatever they, individually, prefer to regard them.

Embracing all of this is the need for understanding what transpires at the bargaining table. It is unquestionably the act of contest. Still, the benefit of the process would seem greater if it could be recognized that it is a conflict of roles—not of persons. "Collective bargaining is merely one manifestation of human relations. It can succeed only where there is a desire to show mutual respect and recognition of the rights and responsibilities of both parties."[13] As yet, only the most elementary efforts are discernible in the selection and preparation of faculty organizations on the one hand, and associations of administrators and boards of control, on the other.

Without deterring responsible men and women in education from the use of power, one could suggest the wisdom of the prophet

[12] Charles Perry, "School Board-Staff Negotiations," *Teachers College Journal*, December 1965, p. 106.

[13] Harold W. Storey, "Collective Bargaining Under Wisconsin Law," *Teachers College Journal*, December 1965, p. 115.

Mohammed: "He is the best of men who dislikes power." Power is a means of value, even perhaps virtue, but only tragically is it an end in itself.

Some will inevitably question the propriety and the applicability of collective bargaining to the community college as a segment of higher education. For one state, Michigan, this is a moot point. The law declares it, and distinguished opinion supports it:

> The basic premises and policy of the Michigan Public Employment Relations Act in granting "rights of unionization" to public employees seems to us to be sound and should be continued. These include rights to join unions or other types of organizations for purposes of collective bargaining free of employer restraint, the principle of exclusive representation, and the right to engage in collective bargaining with respect to terms and conditions of employment. . . .
> . . . We think that neither the Civil Service System employer (or Commission) nor the universities are sufficiently distinguishable from other public employers in terms of their relationships with their employees, or otherwise, to justify a refusal by any of them to accept and apply the policies adopted by the legislature with respect to public employers generally.[14]

There is a problem, however, that touches upon this somewhat. Should the traditional prerogatives of faculty and the current legal prerogatives of a bargaining agent not coincide or, even, in some cases, collide, how are they to be reconciled? This is a matter worthy of some concern. For example, one item in question seems to be the role of the faculty, as such, vis-a-vis the administration in an institution where bargaining prescribes wages, hours, and working conditions on a labor-management basis. Warning of a potential dilemma was made in a dissenting statement by Bierstedt and Machlup in the majority report of the Special Committee on Representation of Economic Interests of the American Association of University Professors:

> The AAUP, in short, has always maintained that the operation of a university is one of shared responsibility. Once an exception is made, no matter how extraordinary the

[14] *Report of the Governor's Advisory Committee on Public Employee Relations*, State of Michigan, February 15, 1967, pp. 4 and 7.

circumstances, the situation is radically transformed into one of antagonistic and even hostile opposition. Once this happens—even once—we become employees of an administration and of a governing board. Once this happens the administration is no longer working for us, but we are working for it.[15]

No labor organization maintains that it should determine or even be involved in the composition of management any more than it would be willing to concede any management role in delineation of its own affairs. Any faculty worth its salt would assert its right to be an effective voice in the determinations of administration. This dilemma has yet to be resolved.

Evolving from this, however, is the question of whether valid expectations of productive outcomes can be generated as the bargaining table is approached. The successful avoidance of impasse and the prevention of crises would seem dependent on this, even though neither is assured.

Conclusion

Power confrontations may be productive and even necessary; they should, however, be recognized for what they are, and, what they are not. They are not exercises in logic or reason—emotionalism is far more prevalent. Neither are they means for determining who is right. They are, rather, the means for determining who is stronger.

Power may be either a tool or a weapon, depending on its uses and outcomes. One is led to reflect on a line from Peter Bowman's novel in verse, *Beach Red:* "Battle doesn't determine who is right. Only who is left."

There is yet one more consideration. Collective bargaining, thus far, has failed to evidence a creative impulse and to demonstrate the contributory effect claimed by some of its most ardent advocates. It is concerned primarily and almost exclusively, with distributive functions—the "sharing" of the available power and resources.

Neither by initiation nor acceptance has the bargaining agent thus far offered anything to satisfy the needs of the community college and, indeed, the public reaction, often adverse, to the work stoppages may discourage both legislator and voter from the urgently needed acceleration of such support. It is this that may prove to be the real test of the viability of faculty power.

[15] Bernard Bierstedt and Fritz Machlup, "Representation of Economic Interests," *AAUP Bulletin,* Summer 1966, p. 233.

U. S. Office of Education, 269
Utah, 39, 152

Values:
  AASA reorientation, 28-29
  scale of, 101
Vietnam War, 238
Voluntary arbitration, 198

Wage package, 201
Wagner, Mayor, 136
Wagner Act of 1935, 103, 187, 188
Wallace, George, 157
Waller, Willard, 256
Walton, Richard E., 30, 58
Warner, Kenneth O., 167, 168, 172, 174, 181, 184
Washington, D. C., 24, 125, 133, 282, 292
Washington, state, 46, 235
Watson, Bernard C., 259
Watts, Gary, 131
Weber, Arnold R., 310, 312

Welfare benefits, 79
White, Leonard D., 181
White-collar professionals, 282
Whitmer, D. P., 29
Wildman, Wesley A., 229, 230, 257, 259, 272, 316
Williams, James W., 229, 248
Wisconsin, 20, 179, 185, 189, 192, 235, 236
Withdrawal of services, 40
Wolff, Kurt M., 33
Wollett, Donald H., 117, 200, 232
Working conditions, 70, 79, 91, 231, 233, 234-235, 286-287
Work stoppages, 245

Yale University, 86, 303
Yale Law School, 94
Yonkers, 136
Young, George, 29
Young, Charles R., 84, 102

Zero-sum, teacher relationship, 58